●PERSISTENCE OF DOUBLE VISION

Essays on Clint Eastwood

Persistence of Double Vision

Essays on Clint Eastwood

WILLIAM BEARD

The University of Alberta Press

Published by
The University of Alberta Press
Ring House 2
Edmonton, Alberta T6G 2E1

Copyright © The University of Alberta Press 2000
A volume in (*currents*), an interdisciplinary series. Jonathan Hart, series editor.
5 4 3 2 1

Canadian Cataloguing in Publication Data

Beard, William, 1946–
    Persistence of double vision

    ISBN 0–88864–356–X

    1. Eastwood, Clint, 1930- — Criticism and interpretation. I. Title.
PN2287.E37B42 2000   791.43'092   C00–910318–X

Printed and bound in Canada by Houghton Boston, Saskatoon, Saskatchewan.
∞ Printed on acid-free paper.

The University of Alberta Press gratefully acknowledges the support received for
its program from the Canada Council for the Arts. The Press also acknowledges
the financial support of the Government of Canada through the Book Publishing
Industry Development Program for its publishing activities.

Contents

Acknowledgements

The third essay in this book ("Unforgiven: Anatomy of a Murderer") appeared in a slightly different form in *The Canadian Journal of Film Studies* 3:2 (Fall 1994): 41–62.

I would like to thank Garry Watson for his interest in, and helpful comments and suggestions about, this project, and Martin Lefebvre for some thought-provoking early discussions about Eastwood. Thanks also to Glenn Rollans, Leslie Vermeer, and Alan Brownoff at the University of Alberta Press for their prompt, friendly, and efficient work, and perhaps most of all to series editor Jonathan Hart for his encouragement and support.

Last, I must express my gratitude to my wife Wendy for her patience and editorial help, and to my children Michael and Anne for adding a human dimension to everything.

Introduction

There has been a considerable amount of writing about Clint Eastwood as a screen persona and as a filmmaker. Even at the newspaper-supplement level, this writing has generally been characterized by a certain thoughtfulness, as though this figure poses some special problem which needs to be addressed. In some sense, Eastwood has always seemed like a puzzle. *What* puzzle exactly has not always been clear, and indeed the question itself has often seemed to be shrouded in something of the mystery attending the persona itself; but there remains a sense that there is something unusual, something that needs explaining, about this figure who only seems to be monolithic. To a great extent, this sense has arisen from that blankness and "unknowableness" that has been cultivated in Eastwood's screen persona since its invention in Sergio Leone's Westerns and has been transported across many re-enactments in other genres and other situations—a quality of reserve and self-sufficient power apparently so innate that only a deliberate and detailed effort in a number of later films has been able to deconstruct even minimally. But the puzzlement has arisen partly from the strategy of Eastwood the filmmaker (if not always director then always producer-demiurge) of maintaining a kind of ironic shadow to accompany the heroic screen persona. The Eastwood persona represents probably the single strongest icon of heroic masculinity in popular cinema over the past quarter-century. But how odd it is that this icon should be continually, almost systematically, hedged round by reflexive and deconstructive elements whose action undercuts its stature. This undercutting only very rarely compromises the figure's heroic stature, but why is it there at all?

I'm not sure anyone can answer that question, but I do think that a catalogue of some of its most important iterations across Eastwood's cinema is illuminating—and that is one of my aims here. Most of the critical writing on Eastwood has tacitly acknowledged this strange phenomenon, but little of it has addressed it directly. In particular I think that looking through this prism of the films' irony, or proto-deconstruction, brings a useful perspective to a fundamental issue about Eastwood which *has* been directly, and widely, addressed: namely the construction of masculinity in his persona and in his work. And this too is a principal focus of the essays presented here (if "focus" is a word that can be applied to a somewhat disparate and idiosyncratic set of observations).

I ought to say something in general about what this book is, and what it is not. *Persistence of Double Vision* is a collection of meditations and close readings prompted by a widespread, recurring set of thoughts which Eastwood's films have stimulated in me. It is not a systematic survey or film-by-film commentary, although I am aware that it sometimes betrays an instinct to move in that direction. Academic writing about Eastwood could really use a thorough survey, in my view, since much of the existing survey-type literature either adopts the fannish "Films of Clint Eastwood" genre (high on illustrations, production details and career history and low on analysis) or tries to perform analytic commentary as a complement to biographical study (Richard Schickel's book is a prominent recent example). There has recently been a trio of middle-range books dealing analytically with Eastwood's cinema (by Edward Gallafent, Laurence Knapp, and Daniel O'Brien), but these again have been for the fan—albeit of the more thoughtful variety—rather than academic in orientation. Paul Smith's book makes an effort to reflect a wide spectrum of Eastwood's output and is as academic as a book can get; but it can't give real attention to everything. A properly systematic interpretive survey would be an enormous task and would probably result in an enormous book.

The enormity is because Eastwood's filmography is such a vast and heterogeneous thing. There are films in which he appears under the direction of a filmmaker of strong personality; yet Eastwood is an actor-persona of such stature that he needs to be considered almost as a co-author (the early spaghetti westerns directed by

Sergio Leone are the best examples, but many of the slightly later Don Siegel-directed films also qualify). There are films in which he appears under routine direction in routine big-budget Hollywood movies (*Paint Your Wagon* or *Where Eagles Dare*, for example—these movies are clustered near the beginning of Eastwood's career as a Hollywood star). There are films in which, by virtue of his power to choose his projects and his position as absolute boss of his own production company, Malpaso, he is in charge of his own persona, but the direction is in other hands. This category is large and highly variable, stretching from early Westerns like *Hang 'em High* and *Joe Kidd* through the Dirty Harry follow-ups *Magnum Force*, *The Enforcer*, and *The Dead Pool*, through satirical or farcical vehicles like *Every Which Way But Loose*, *City Heat*, and *Pink Cadillac*, all the way to distinctive one-offs like *Tightrope* (Richard Tuggle) and *In the Line of Fire* (Wolfgang Petersen) which seem very much to belong in the Eastwood "canon." There are films which Eastwood has directed but not appeared in (*Breezy*, *Bird*, *Midnight in the Garden of Good and Evil*) or has appeared in a secondary role (*A Perfect World*). And then of course there are the films he has both starred in and directed. But these too range from the relatively routine and uninteresting (e.g., *The Eiger Sanction*, *Foxfire*, *The Rookie*) to the moderately interesting (e.g., *Play Misty for Me*, *Sudden Impact*, *Pale Rider*, *Heartbreak Ridge*), to the interesting and accomplished (e.g., *High Plains Drifter*, *The Outlaw Josey Wales*, *The Gauntlet*, *Bronco Billy*, *Honkytonk Man*, *White Hunter, Black Heart*, *The Bridges of Madison County*), to the masterly (*Unforgiven*).

Most of my attention in this volume has gone to films in the latter categories. It is these films that one can just how complex a figure Eastwood has been in Hollywood history over the past quarter-century. In particular, it is here that those characteristics of self-questioning and schizoid double-vision are most to be found. And it is here too that one can see most clearly just how persistent has been Eastwood's auteur-like return to certain character-types, certain narrative and thematic configurations, certain tropes of action and style. Eastwood is unique in his dual position as overpowering cinematic persona-icon and creative filmmaker; as gigantic reflector, perpetuator, and even producer of mainstream cultural and ideological values; and as idiosyncratic, complex manipulator of the narrative environment(s) he has inhabited. This utterly strange dualism—as a figure who is simultaneously marmoreally powerful and compulsively self-deconstructing—is a source of endless fascination to me. I have approached this multifaceted topic both from a crypto-auteurist standpoint and from the angle of Eastwood's place as an icon of masculine power (as a performer, that is), and have tried to chart his journey from distant and disdainful figure of violence through prosocial hero-of-ideology to a kind of self-accusation and self-destruction of his heroic persona. While recognizing cultural-studies theorizations of masculinity in Hollywood, I have not attempted any theoretical intervention myself, but rather simply drawn some general terms and attitudes into what is essentially a study of the *cinema* of a particular director, producer, and star.

In trying to "place" that cinema, I have felt it useful to contextualize Eastwood within the evolution of Hollywood cinema as an aesthetic and ideological medium. At a number of points I have undertaken sweeping generalizations, classifications, and miniature surveys of the Eastwood films I feel best reflect the phenomena I am trying to describe. But I have also approached the topic through many detailed readings of individual films—most extensively of two films, *Unforgiven* and *A Perfect World*. I would also assert that these two films are, not coincidentally, Eastwood's best; and among the reasons why they are his best are the multitude of ways in which they comment upon, sum up, and even ruthlessly demolish some of the most crucial features of Eastwood's identity as a screen icon and cultural presence across his career. Finally, I have made some comments on Eastwood the director as a cinematic stylist.

But I am quite conscious of what *isn't* in this book. Important areas of the Eastwood phenomenon are simply left out. One example is the "orangutan movies" *Every Which Way But Loose* and *Any Which Way You Can* (neither directed by Eastwood). These were huge popular successes, among the biggest of Eastwood's career, and if I can scarcely bear to watch them I am conscious that they contain a meaningful slewing of the Eastwood persona (one upon which Paul Smith has commented interestingly) that is not seen anywhere else in his work. Then there are the Don Siegel movies, which are almost completely ignored here except for *The Beguiled* and *Dirty Harry*. Siegel was in fact almost as important in helping to create the Eastwood persona as Sergio Leone was; and almost all of the Eastwood films directed by Siegel were made at Malpaso under Eastwood's umbrella control. Certainly *Coogan's*

Bluff and *Escape from Alcatraz* are as important for the construction of the Eastwood persona as several of the movies that are discussed here. Neither do the Leone films get any non-generalized reading. Furthermore, a number of important films directed by Eastwood receive only scattered and piecemeal treatments (*Bird, White Hunter, Black Heart* and *The Bridges of Madison County* are examples).

There are topics, too, which I skirt around but address only partially or not at all. I am thinking particularly of the role of black characters in Eastwood's films, which topic I do not open at all. Even more interesting and complex is the question of the role of women characters — especially the persona's geological movement from a largely solitary figure to a figure who seeks to have a meaningful relationship with a woman (a movement which mainstream newspaper and magazine feature articles certainly noted) — which I touch upon but do not explore fully. And I have not even minimally entered upon any production discourse, either of the general and specific production background of any of the films or of the famous oscillation (also discovered in the mainstream press) between "personal" and "commercial" projects. This kind of information and analysis is already widely available.

Some of what *is* here may seem somewhat disconnected or arbitrary also. I can only say that it is these subjects which presented themselves to me and these subjects where I thought I most had something to contribute. The first essay, "Between Classical and Postmodern," discusses Eastwood's place within the global changes affecting Hollywood as a cultural institution from the 1960s to the 1990s. The peculiar nature of the movie environment around 1970s, when traditional or classical Hollywood cinema was undergoing a profound crisis, was of the utmost importance both to the construction of the Eastwood character as a figure of heroic power and to the way in which he was generally received. Moreover, as this period of negativity and ideological crisis eventually gave way to the more comfortable forms of Reaganite postmodern reassurance, Eastwood's cultural role changed in unique ways to accommodate and even to help produce that change. The next essay, "Heroic Deconstruction," surveys Eastwood's films to trace the specifics of his evolving power-masculinity over this period, and especially the doubled or shadowed construction of heroism in these films. Eastwood's recurring pattern of self-questioning is seen throughout as a kind of sideways recognition of the mythic artificiality and ultimate "impossibility" of the heroic figure and heroism itself. This process is seen at accelerate during the late 1980s, culminating in two important films of the early 1990s which have the effect of summarizing and raising to a higher power of self-consciousness what is now an outright critique of heroic masculinity. These are *Unforgiven* (in the realm of the violent action hero) and *A Perfect World* (in the realm of the Good Father). Each film is given an extended analysis in a separate essay.

Unforgiven receives a detailed close reading in the third essay, "Anatomy of a Murderer." This examination tries to unravel the film's complex weave of themes and commentaries on both the Western as a genre and, even more reflexively, the place which Eastwood himself has had in that genre as a figure of transcendental violence. Then the fourth essay, "Eastwood the Father," turns to that other aspect developed in Eastwood's masculine heroism: the cluster of more social and "human" roles which encompass everything from relationships of affection with other people to leadership of a community, and especially the large and suggestive number of roles casting him as a father or father-substitute. *A Perfect World* is the culmination of this thematization of actual and symbolic fatherhood, just as *Unforgiven* is of the transcendental-killer Eastwood figure, and it too is given a detailed reading, in the fifth essay, "There Is No Good Father." The sixth essay, "Postscripts of Disavowal," looks at two of Eastwood's most recent films, *Absolute Power* and *True Crime*, as further entries into this discourse of fatherhood and heroism, but now as regressing in significant ways from the position of *A Perfect World*.

The next essay, "He Who Lives by the Sword," looks back to two of Eastwood's early Hollywood films, *The Beguiled* (directed by Don Siegel) and *Play Misty for Me* (Eastwood's first film as a director), to find him presenting himself both as filmmaker and as persona in an unfamiliar guise: "woman's man" instead of "man's man." These two films take his persona, which at this point (1971) was defined as a figure of omnipotent violence in the world of masculine struggle, and place him in a quite different context—the context of heterosexual relationships—where his heroic violence is virtually reconfigured as heroic sexual desirability. But in this new context, his power is drastically imperilled and the catastrophes that enmesh him are presented in ways that are partly hysterically anxious and partly uncomfortably self-critical. In their unusual and never-to-be-repeated way, *The Beguiled* and *Play Misty for Me* offer a peculiarly self-deconstructing vision at the very outset of Eastwood's Hollywood career. Finally, I consider the visual style of Eastwood the director. This essay is entitled "Eastwood as *Auteur* and *Metteur-en-scène*"—a title which refers, perhaps somewhat obscurely, back to the old *Cahiers du cinéma* debates of the 1950s about which filmmakers were true creators (*auteurs*) and which were only talented visual stagers (*metteurs-en-scène*). Many of the "authorial" aspects of Eastwood's creative career are, I think, demonstrated, even if only in passing, in the earlier essays. Thus, this essay is devoted to the (again, rather scattered and various) characteristics of Eastwood as a visual stager of the dramas under his hand as a director—and to a kind of auteurist consideration of what elements Eastwood the filmmaker might have drawn from the two directors for whom he has always expressed his own gratitude: Sergio Leone and Don Siegel.

1
Between Classical and Postmodern

Everybody would agree that there's only one Clint Eastwood. But what is it that makes him different? Because, as a screen presence, he *is* different: not only in the way that all individuals and even all movie stars are different, but in an extra way. For a start, there is the sheer size of his persona. He conveys a monolithic solidity, a self-sufficiency, a bigger-than-life authority, which emanates not just from his marmoreal physical presence but from a refusal to accommodate or reveal himself to the outside world—a kind of magisterial disdain. Or at least, this is the nature of his primary persona, unveiled in Sergio Leone's "spaghetti westerns" in the mid 1960s and imported into a Hollywood environment in the succeeding decade. It is a persona which, however much modified and even softened in later years, is always present in Eastwood's screen appearances—certainly in the metatextual consciousness of his viewers with their history of Eastwood-watching. This persona, whether in the amoral wastelands of Leone's westerns or the urban cesspools of the Dirty Harry films, moves with a mysterious solitude and self-reliance. Moreover he possesses, apparently as a result of all these characteristics, an absolute mastery of violence: he is supreme and terrible in combat, seeming to carry some talismanic invincibility, some mark of a higher power. In this he recalls the heroes of ancient myth, who partake of a godlike sphere and are unknowable except through their awe-inspiring deeds. This almost-superhuman dimension I will call "transcendent." It is, again, an absolutely crucial and constitutive aspect of the Eastwood *ur*-persona.

1

This persona is first constituted in a deliberately exaggerated and "impossible" way (in the Leone and early Hollywood westerns, in *Dirty Harry*); later in Eastwood's career, it may appear in especially self-conscious, incongruous, or unexpected forms and contexts, commenting upon its essential self through an exaggeration, ironization, or contradiction of existing traits. This metatextual life is a familiar feature of postmodern Hollywood personae: the disintegration of classical realist narrative creates a space for just such an enhanced life outside the diminished narrative. Eastwood's arrival and evolution coincides historically with this development. But also his work has positioned itself across the gap between Hollywood classicism and Hollywood postmodernism in a unique way, drawing upon both classical substance and postmodern pastiche to create a persona more ironized and impossible than a classical hero of masculinity like John Wayne, more substantial and authoritative than a postmodern one like Arnold Schwarzenegger. In effect, the Eastwood persona is both flat and not-flat; mythically enlarged and two-dimensional; but with a suggestion of hidden depths and primordial authenticity.

Classical Hollywood cinema—the cinema, that is, of mainstream Hollywood from World War One to sometime in the 1970s—is, generally speaking, bound by conventions of realism and naturalism. When Eastwood entered its besieged ruins during its last stand, he had only one or two predecessors who could consistently show these qualities of mythic size and impermeability: John Wayne and (perhaps) Gary Cooper. These two were narrative personae of a uniquely authoritative iconic stature, powerful and taciturn, exerting a moral influence that was connected with their physical size, their granite strength of countenance, and their preference for action rather than words. Eastwood shares with them an unvarnished quality, a rough-hewn directness and honesty, an apparent lack of polish that has given rise to criticism about their limitations as actors, but which is also readable as a scorn for pretense, creating an impression of figures too large and authentic to stoop to artifice. In this sense, Eastwood could (and can) be seen as a persona in a Hollywood-cinematic tradition, albeit one with an extremely small membership. To put it another way, Eastwood has always had some of the qualities that could be associated with the project of classical Hollywood heroism, even if he began as an anti-classical, anti-realist hero; and these underlying qualities of substantiality and moral presence enabled him in the later 1970s and afterwards to re-emerge, to an important degree, *as* a classical hero.

To understand just what position Eastwood occupies in the broad context of the Hollywood environment past and present—and to understand why and how his presence has been meaningful and has helped to alter the cinematic landscape—it will be useful to journey briefly through the historical evolutions of Hollywood narrative, especially to look at Hollywood cinema's transformation from classicism to postmodernism. The classical project[1] is one in which obstacles are overcome, goals achieved, and problems solved by protagonists whose ultimate achievement is to master the narrative and navigate through its perils to a satisfactory conclusion. All of this occurs in the environment of a self-enclosed and autonomous "realist" fiction—hence the widespread term *classical realism*. The underlying aims and values of these narratives are basically congruent with dominant ideology, and work (most often unconsciously) to explicate and rationalize that ideology. They align matters so that what is good for the sympathetic central characters is identical with what is good for the society as a whole, so that the solutions of personal dilemmas are magically interchangeable with the answers to social problems. This is a world in which difficulties, however tortuous and apparently insuperable, exist against an unspoken background assumption that somehow they will be resolved and that it is only a matter of time before the "natural" condition of right and order is established. Historically, the period in which Hollywood classicism can be seen in its purest form is the 1930s (ironically, since the relatively untroubled work of ideological reinforcement was going on during the huge economic and social crisis of the Depression). Towards the end of World War Two, classical narrative began to get more complicated and difficult (one symptom of this is *film noir*), and during the 1950s and '60s the process became ever more complicated and difficult—incidentally giving rise to what I would count as the most interesting and aesthetically productive period of Hollywood history between 1945 and 1960.[2]

The classical hero who most resembles Eastwood is John Wayne. They are often compared, and Eastwood is frequently identified as Wayne's "natural" successor—a successor to a precious crown of American kingliness to which there can be very few pretenders. The extent of their joint dominance is suggested by the fact that Wayne was in the top ten box-office attractions twenty-five out of twenty-six years between 1949 and 1974, and Eastwood has appeared there twenty-one times over his career.[3] The two of them ranked easily first and second in polls to determine America's favourite movie star in 1993, 1994 and 1995 (when Eastwood was over sixty and Wayne had been dead for a decade and a half).[4] As with Eastwood, Wayne's principal quality depends on self-assurance, imperviousness to wayward influence, and power. Wayne's power sustains the dominant ideology but is also derived from it. In many of his post-war westerns and in the many roles which placed him in the armed services, he is a warrior and an enforcer of order. And this order is both social and moral—indeed it is the almost complete conjunction of social and moral order which allows his position as hero of ideology. Wayne's heroic stature is coterminous with his individual mastery, but the individual qualities that allow him to rise above others are also the expression of a social ideology of individualism: the ideology which holds that the specialness of America lies precisely in its creation of a *society* where individualist values hold the seat of honour. The Wayne persona acts not only to defend this society, but as the single best example of what it is defending.[5] His power transcends that of ordinary men, but insofar as it is in itself transcendent it is so by virtue of the special transcendental virtues of American ideology (and American society) as a whole.

At the climax of Wayne's career, some of his most powerful roles embroiled him in true crises of ideology. In films such as Ford's *The Searchers* (1956) and *The Man Who Shot Liberty Valance* (1962), we may see the very substance of ideological wholeness in the process of crumbling away, and the efforts necessary to restore it as desperate ones. Here Wayne stands on the verge of an agonistic classicism in crisis, and it is one of the peculiar strengths of *The Searchers* in particular that it should present Wayne (of all figures!) almost dissolving into the pathological, society-less protagonist who was to achieve dominance in the Hollywood of the decade 1967–77. Of course, most of Wayne's roles during the 1950s and afterwards were of a less conflicted, more straightfor- wardly affirmative kind, although the advancing crisis of classicism rendered him more and more marginal (*The Green Berets*, which he directed himself in 1968, is an unintentionally eloquent testimony to the impossibility of his classical heroism in the seminal classicophobic narrative environment of Vietnam).

Eventually, at the end of the 1960s, the contradictions and skepticism which had been growing inside Hollywood narrative for twenty-five years reached such a pitch that the entire structure tottered and collapsed. I believe we may speak definitively of this period, the decade between the late 1960s and late 1970s (specifically from *Bonnie and Clyde* [1967] to *Star Wars* [1977]), as the one which unfolds the final crisis and failure of classicism.[6] With an unequalled anguish and pessimism, this period stages over and over again the breakdown of classical narrative and thematic order. On the one hand are the many stories in which the protagonists are simply unable to solve the problems, unable to triumph or even sometimes to survive. Instead they fail— messily, ignominiously, often didactically—as if to show that the paradigm of classical victory has not simply disintegrated but has been replaced by an antitype of equally systematic and certain failure. A handful of examples will serve to recall this syndrome: *Midnight Cowboy, They Shoot Horses, Don't They?, Five Easy Pieces, McCabe and Mrs. Miller, Deliverance, The Conversation, Chinatown, The Parallax View, Dog Day Afternoon, Night Moves.* On the other hand, there remains a kind of story in which the hero still triumphs. But he (and in this kind of film it is inevitably "he") does so against a background of social decay and alienation and through a mastery and dispensation of the pervasive violence engulfing so many of the movies of the period, rather than through a suffering of that violence. Here we find such films as *Dirty Harry, The French Connection, Straw Dogs, Walking Tall, Death Wish,* and to some extent the *Godfather* movies and *Taxi Driver.*[7] Both categories of film depict a society where crime and greed are pervasive and all political projects are corrupt, but in the second type, heroes still retain the power to enact an isolated solution, to impose a regressive, violent, individual version of natural justice where society so signally failed to do so.[8] But even here, where the classical project of the victory of the individual protagonist still keeps a foothold, it is a victory over a blasted and desolate social landscape and in defiance of the classical alignment of hero and society.

Eastwood's intervention into this world falls basically in the second category. I would say "always" rather than "basically" were it not for those two strange films of 1971, *The Beguiled* and *Play Misty for Me.* In these films, the impassively distant Eastwood character is disconcerted or defeated at the hands of women characters; his vulnerability seems to stem exactly from the necessity of surrendering some of his unreachable distance just to get into a sexual relationship. But in a way, even these films confirm the persona's masculine transcendence, since they both turn on the idea that this most invincible of warriors may paradoxically be disabled in male-female conflict in a way he would—by definition—never be in a male-male confrontation. Certainly the spectacle of an Eastwood who is in any way weak, confused, or inadequate in the landscape of pure masculine conflict is unthinkable throughout this period. Masculine power is Eastwood's *sine qua non* in this primary phase, and its strength is all the more impressive because it occurs in a narrative environment where heroism has become unstable and incredibly difficult. The classical hero's prosocial stance has been made more or less impossible by the climate of moral chaos, and the sense that the timeless ideological truths of American specialness, individual potential, and social optimism have actually collapsed under the weight of assassinations, Vietnam, social disharmony, Watergate, and all the rest. It is an age more metonymically represented by neurotic figures like Dustin Hoffman, Jack Nicholson, Al Pacino, Gene Hackman, Elliott Gould, and others of the first category above—actors of an unprepossessing, certainly not heroic, appearance and a nervous, sometimes overly talkative, manner. The contrast between these figures and the laconic, slow-moving Eastwood is extreme. Like other figures of the second category, this Eastwood persona will not surrender mastery of the narrative; he insists upon maintaining the charisma of dominant masculine power. But in this post-classical context, the dominant masculine hero must reconfigure his position. When there is no centre, he must retreat to the margins; when he is unable truly to create an order to mirror the ideal of society, he must retreat to maintaining himself as an ordered being. He is a hero in exile. His recognition of the corruption of the world, and his truth to himself, must give rise to a veneer of disdain which viewers can recognize as a form of insight.

Disdain for his adversaries, disdain for the world, is indeed what remains to a hero whose mastery has no worthy object on which to practise, no worthwhile structure outside himself to sustain. We are all familiar with the snort of contempt and the flat dismissal John Wayne so often directed towards the weak and compromising, those who could not see the clear structure of moral truth and the straight, forceful path to its fulfillment. Eastwood has his equivalent of this—and it is a huge escalation, at its most extreme a withering death-glance, a cold sneer of disgust, a pitiless emotional removal from the scene. From the historical standpoint of classical Hollywood heroism it is quite astonishing that such a refusal to be included in the social fabric in any fashion, so cruel and detached, should inspire such a surge of recognition and welcome as it did in viewers of the time. The good fight, the fight that John Wayne always won, could not be won anymore: it had been lost definitively. Whoever pretended to win such a fight was either lying or deluded, and it was a virtue of Eastwood (and Charles Bronson, and all the other, smaller incarnations of heroic contempt) that he recognized the fight was fixed and the whole stage corrupted and manipulated. What a *smart* man, a *strong* man, must do is not play by the rules and not be taken in by the charade of official morality. This spectacle—a skeptical and consequently ruthless hero as a figure who had seen through the tired old shibboleths of self-sacrifice and devotion to the common good—appealed to audiences in the 1960s and '70s, and was another precise symptom of the death of classicism.

Eastwood arrived in Hollywood during this wholesale dismantling of prosocial heroism, armed with the knowledge (gained with Leone) of how to present heroic power in the total absence of any kind of social project.⁹ Leone's decadent European skepticism totally incinerates all idealist social beliefs and leaves the gunfighting hero—whose constitutional function hitherto has been to enable the good community—stranded in a literal and figurative wasteland with no interest to uphold but his own. The hero's mastery, no longer connected with a grand ideological project and denuded of classical camouflage, instead takes the form of a mysterious transcendent power. This deliberate simplification, occlusion, mystification of the origins and nature of the hero's power lends a unique flavour to Eastwood as persona, in Leone's films and afterwards.¹⁰ And its success is made easier in every sense through the removal of the persona both from ideological tasks and from the entangling paraphernalia of realist accountability and plausibility. In Hollywood, Eastwood in his westerns carried the mystification and transcendence to higher degrees of stylization, sharpening and distilling the component of frightening lethal violence; while as Dirty Harry he transported some of this essence into the constitutionally more realist world of the urban crime film. The Eastwood persona did, of course, still emulate one crucial facet of the classical hero: he vanquished the forces arrayed against him and emerged triumphant—unlike the tortured and defeated characters played by Pacino, Nicholson, and others. But he sidestepped the skepticism attached to any kind of classical-realist heroism precisely by refusing to contemplate the epistemology of his heroic powers and by reverting to a regressive, even primitive, anti-rationalism regarding the nature of transcendent-violent masculinity. Instead of ideological reinforcement through violent mastery, he could offer viewers violent mastery pure and simple, as an expression of alienated individual *ressentiment* and the revenge of each against all, with its origins lying in unknowable subconscious mystery rather than in the discredited rationalist structures of social harmony. Thus, initially at least, the Eastwood persona could act either as a quasi-supernatural mythic force of violence (in the westerns) or as the lethal agent of a generalized regressive anger masquerading as law-enforcement (in the cop films)—in both cases evading skepticism by a tacit acknowledgement of its own separateness from realist ideology, its deliberate self-mythification.

So it has been a central feature of Eastwood's persona (and this has surely been important in his cinematic survival through the various cultural upheavals over the years of his career) that the project of its heroism has always been accompanied by markers of the implausibility, unnaturalness, and indeed impossibility of its own existence. Audiences since the 1970s have been unable to believe in a *classical* heroic masculinity, but the required display of masculine power remains as forceful as before—perhaps more so to compensate for the disappearance of the patriarchal reassurances of classical ideology. This schizophrenic condition has been exactly answered by Eastwood's status as a hero who is in some way impossible; meanwhile the impossibility of the *viewer*'s wishes can be disavowed through removing the whole question of believability into the mystery and unknowableness of the persona's heroic nature. Eastwood's "markers of impossibility," in other words, serve to enable the construction and consumption of masculine-heroic values by a sidelong admission of their status as fantasy-objects, just as surely as the neo-innocent good guys and bad guys of *Star Wars* could function once more as idealist types because of the simultaneous pervasiveness of irony and techno-fetishism as disclaimers guaranteeing sophistication.

Here, in fact, we have the moment of Hollywood's shift from mortally wounded classicism to postmodernism. After ten years of foreclosure and defeat, the culture simply could not tolerate any more. America is a famously forward-looking, active, and problem-solving culture, and a notoriously unreflective and unself-knowing one—peculiarly unfitted, in other words, to accept any kind of final limitation, still less defeat. The catastrophe of ideology expressed in the films of this time could never make its wholesale destruction of the social project a cleansing prelude to a revolutionary new beginning of society, because that revolutionary new beginning had already happened, for all time, in 1776, and the result was a nation that was actually defined in terms of its ideal perfection. America was as good as any society could be; that notion survived even the cataclysms of the 1960s and '70s. Hence, if things were structurally really bad, there was no way they could get better. *Star Wars* finally showed the way out of this cul-de-sac by simply deserting the field entirely: removing itself to "a galaxy far, far away" and peopling itself with character-types whose utter inno cence and moral simplicity could only exist in the pre-adult narrative landscape of ultra-naïve classical forms represented by kids' matinee sci-fi serials from the 1930s and '40s. Travis Bickle, the psychotic hero of *Taxi Driver*, wants to clean away the filth and depravity of America's streets—a desire shared by many who could not escape the perception that America was foul and sick. But Bickle's quest is deluded and destructive, and even Harry Callahan's is grim and messy. *Star Wars*, on the other hand, is totally whistle-clean, bright and new. The brilliance of *Star Wars* didn't consist simply of bringing back anxiety-free good guys and bad guys and happy endings—though that was its principal gift—but in finding the precious formula to sell these discredited goods to a culture which desperately wanted to buy them but was prevented by its own extensive knowledge and experience of their inadequacy.

Classicism was what *Star Wars* offered once again; but a classicism that was *too* simple and innocent, a child's toy classicism that joined its adult viewers in slyly indulging in the certainties of classical optimism while always remaining totally aware at some level that the whole performance was really impossible, just an enjoyable game. (The resulting thinness of texture in the narrative was compensated for by the addition of lots of spectacle in the form of special effects and high-tech action sequences — another aspect of the formula we can recognize all too clearly twenty-plus years later.) This awareness of impossibility, this game-like quality, was something quite foreign to classicism *per se* — which is, again, fundamentally a *realist* form. *Star Wars*'s attributes of quotation and pastiche, of nostalgia and deliberately simple narrative regression, transformed classicism into something else, into a form of classicism to which no-one has yet given a name: neo-classicism or virtual classicism. This Hollywood neo-classicism is of course the same thing as Hollywood postmodernism, although what is always emphasized in commentary is this cinema's quotation/ pastiche/ games-playing and not its rescue of classical narrative and classical values (albeit in denatured and weightless guise). Postmodernism's famous "failure to believe in grand narratives" was actually directly staged in Hollywood in the agonized, we might even say "modernist," cinema of 1967–77. Hollywood-variety postmodernism, by contrast, almost always stages this disbelief in grand narrative *in conjunction with* the (classical) grand narrative itself — and both sides of the contradictory antithesis are consumed simultaneously and disavowingly. In other words, disbelief is a very important feature of Hollywood postmodernism that allows viewers something of the satisfactions of optimistic classical narrative, something of the (as Fredric Jameson might put it) utopianism, or (as a true skeptic might put it) the cowardly and lying opiates, of a cinema of coherence and meaning. If anyone was fitted to the schizoid requirements of such a cinema, it was Clint Eastwood.

The be-as-a-child strategy of Lucas and Spielberg, born fully formed in *Star Wars* and *Close Encounters of the Third Kind* (also 1977), opened the door to the realm of comic-book superheroes, quickly exploited by *Superman* (1978) — and eventually by *Conan the Barbarian* (1984), which effectively introduced Schwarzenegger the superhero. Hence the genesis of Hollywood postmodernism's new breed of heroic figures, whose hypermasculinity is accompanied by its own ironic disavowal. Schwarzenegger and Stallone (to go no further) are not just big, strong men; they are *really* big, *too* strong men. Either as cause or as symptom, they exist in the virtual-neoclassical action-movie narrative environment of pastiche and spectacle, where realist ideological drama has given way to flatness and fragmentation, and where both narrative/ideological problems and their solutions are equally insubstantial. Nothing is truly at stake in these narratives, just as the characters of their heroes are quite drained of the universal subjectivity their classical ancestors (like Wayne and Cooper) were made to bear.[11] The self-consciousness of these figures, the awareness of their cartoon exaggeration and flatness which the films display, is in striking contrast to the complete absence of these qualities in even the largest of classical-realist heroes and to the accompanying sense that in mastering their narratives, classical heroes were re-enacting the victory of a still-holistic ideology of values.[12]

Perhaps we can now see more clearly how Eastwood is placed at exactly the conjunction of these two eras, and how he embodies crucial aspects of both of them. In the sphere of masculine heroism, in fact, it is difficult to see how we could have gotten from Wayne to Schwarzenegger *except* by going through Eastwood.[13] The larger-than-life classical heroism of Wayne gives way to the transcendentalism and covert impossibility of the Eastwood persona; this in turn is followed by the frank comic-book exaggerations of Schwarzenegger's musculature and in some way overt impossibility of *his* persona. And when we move from Wayne's stainless moral rectitude in the application of heroic strength (however questionably grounded) to Schwarzenegger's undisguised contempt in the exercise of overwhelmingly superior physical force, we do so via the Man With No Name's casual homicides and Harry Callahan's do-you-feel-lucky-punk?-isms. Eastwood's early strategy—namely to detach masculine power from prosocial classicism and to reconfigure it as a free-floating hypermasculinity belonging to a transcendent individual—helped to open the door to the postmodern Hollywood strategy of reimporting social projects: that is, equally reconfiguring them as flat and hypertrophic forms. This too is a route to *Star Wars* and its innumerable children (from *Raiders of the Lost Ark* and *Rambo* all the way to *Batman* and *Terminator 2*), wherein markers designating "heroic" and "villainous" are colourfully manipulated around a map designating "social salvation" and "social catastrophe." Now the holistic project of classical ideology is reassembled as well as the hero, but with all of its components flattened and insubstantial, plainly fictionalized and constructed. This is pre-eminently the world of Schwarzenegger and Stallone, and it is increasingly full of postmodern (anti-classical) reflexivity and perspectives which "bare the device." In this environment, Schwarzenegger and Stallone assume the mantle of the ideological hero, indeed often more wholly and straightforwardly than Eastwood has ever done. But they remain postmodern ideological heroes, heroes of a resimplified *faux-naïf* virtual-classicism which engulfs all their narratives and denies them either the gravity of classical heroes or the agonism of defenders of a classicism in crisis.

The Eastwood persona, however, seems always within reach of an original classical authenticity, even when cultural and narrative conditions have been such as to make a too-straightforward adoption of this authenticity an inadvisable option. Eastwood's starting point is that of a heroic persona who, amid the ruins of classicism, adopts the role of a regressive and uncommitted centre of masculine power within the socially nihilistic period of the 1970s. As the neo-optimism of proto-Reaganite postmodernism comes to take its place, Eastwood is able—unlike any other masculine-heroic persona of the period—to draw upon his hitherto necessarily suppressed capability of classical stature to reinvent himself as a reborn classical hero.[14] This transformation begins, pretty much explicitly, in *The Outlaw Josey Wales* (1976), where the Eastwood persona virtually resurrects the dominant, authoritative cowboy hero and reinvests him with his old task of enabling the good community (here itself also reconstituted *ab nihilo*). But for Eastwood the tasks of heroic masculinity, whether post-classically alienated or neo-classically prosocial, are never straightforward or without questions. And when the Eastwood persona performs a reflexive or self-questioning act, the underlying proto-classical substance of the persona always gives that act an importance and a disturbing dimension which the postmodern quasi-Brechtianisms of a Schwarzenegger can never have. When the Eastwood figure asks the viewer whether it is itself possible, the question is real (Schwarzenegger is always-already impossible and understood to be such). Eastwood's films have incessantly asked this question about the persona in one way or another throughout his career; and as his persona's heroic masculinity progressed towards the dissolutions of age and second thoughts, the films have increasingly also asked the question of whether, possible or not, it was even desirable.

Eastwood's films are magnetic to any auteur-oriented approach because they combine a relentless restaging and repetition of persona-characteristics, narrative forms, and individual tropes with a constant juggling and reconfiguring of these same elements to see them in a different light. It is strange and fascinating, too, to see films, and a persona, which are simultaneously so prominent in ideology and dominant commodity culture and yet so persistent in a project of self-definition and self-deconstruction. The Eastwood hero has progressed from monolithic lethal self-interest through several interesting phases of redefinition and accommodation in the direction of a more "human" and/or prosocial heroism, and has eventually carried the always-visible process of self-questioning all the way through to virtual self-demolition. What follows is an attempt to describe and map this development in a rough fashion, first through some thoughts about Eastwood's "basic" persona, and subsequently through a process of looking at a succession of individual films or groups of films and examining them for both the nature of their heroic personae and for their accompanying "impossibility."

2

Heroic Deconstruction

or, Is Clint Eastwood Possible?

●TRANSCENDENCE

As a movie star, Eastwood deliberately sought from the beginning to embody a quality of transcendence—a removal of his heroic character from ordinary life and limitations. This search led in turn to an investigation of the very nature of transcendent heroism in fiction: its naturalness or artifice, its necessity or non-necessity, its relationship to ordinary experience, its benefits and costs. This cluster of questions seem to me one of the most central and important in Eastwood's work. As 1970s ideological despair gave way to a wilful restoration of ideological wholeness during Reagan's presidency, Eastwood's films adjusted their bracketing dialectic to exactly those questions of open affirmation and repressed doubt seen to exist at the centre of American culture. It is as if the transcendent form of heroic power which western culture bestowed upon Eastwood at the outset of his successful career engendered in its carrier, inside the figure itself, a shadowy questioner or *memento mori* whose function was always to point to the blatant artifice of the figure, to its impossibility, and to what needed to be repressed in order for the figure to achieve transcendence. And yet this self-questioning rarely or never takes the form of fundamental self-mockery of a pure postmodern kind. Rather the dialectic of forces, heroic-transcendent and doubting respectively, results in a kind of permanent dilemma, a problem which never really goes away but is only renewed in a deeper and ever more puzzling way. To some extent, this oscilla-

15

tion may be seen clearly in individual films and cycles of films; so that, for example, the transcendence of the Dirty Harry films is answered in the self-deconstruction of films like *The Gauntlet*, *Tightrope,* and *In the Line of Fire*; the demon-avenger aspect of *High Plains Drifter* and *Pale Rider* is relentlessly demystified and deheroicized in *Unforgiven*; and, in a less precise fashion, the gung-ho leadership qualities presented in *Heartbreak Ridge* are thoroughly debunked in *White Hunter, Black Heart* or revealed as confection in *Bronco Billy*. But the process is actually much more complex. Every Eastwood film, even the most transcendent, also contains at least some small elements of its own deconstruction; and even the most deconstructive retains at least an image of the heroic transcendence which is the first motivator of its existence.

●THE MAN WITH NO NAME

The first manifestation of the essential Eastwood persona is a dual appearance in the overtly mythic world of the western and in (at least superficially) the more realist world of the contemporary urban crime-film—as, respectively, the Man With No Name and Dirty Harry. This composite figure is simultaneously transcendent and harshly down to earth. Indeed, it is exactly the combination of the cold-blooded use of power for personal reasons on the one hand and a mythic invincibility hitherto available only to more naïvely "good" characters on the other that constituted Eastwood in the first place and to some extent continually afterwards. Leone's westerns feature a physically dirty, morally self-interested protagonist who is at the same time the embodiment of the transcendental heroic abilities of the westerner. Moreover, these films are expressly attracted to the mythic perspectives seen to underly the genre itself, and their exaggeration of the dirt, the violence, and the evil may be seen not primarily as undermining the conventionalism of the western but rather as emphasizing its potential for lurid melodramatic contrast—hence the frequent, and apt, description of Leone's westerns as "operatic." Of course, this process of stretching, enlarging, and emphasizing (as well as a host of other Europeanizing factors) results also in a flattening of the narrative environment, a displacement of still quasi-realist elements and their replacement by the openly mythic elements of heightened spectacle, ritual, flattened and simplified character "types," cinematic formalism—

and an attendant self-awareness and reflexivity. (The resulting qualities of alienation and pastiche may be seen as prototypical, and no doubt partly productive, of the postmodernism that would reach Hollywood in force more than a decade later.) Simultaneously, the emphasis on dirt and violence, and the de-ethicizing of the hero and indeed of virtually all the characters, may be interpreted (although not correctly) as moves in the direction of a greater psychological and even historical authenticity—a movement *away* from the mythical stylizations of the genre.[1] Capping everything is a mordant sarcasm and a thick layer of indifference to human suffering appropriate in a decadent environment where the social optimism and personal idealism of the classical western is long dead. The films thus manage to be mythic and ironic at the same time—and to strike a particularly resonant chord in audiences skeptical of the received wisdom of decaying classical narrative forms while still looking for some form of transcendence.

As for the Man With No Name, his powers approach the supernatural—whether in his mastery of his gun, his implacable persistence, or his unkillableness—and these powers seem directly linked with his godlike or devilish unknowableness and his indifference and even cruelty. Using the terms of psychoanalysis, Dennis Bingham has argued that the innovation of this initial Eastwood persona is to have evacuated the moral and social realms of the western, even of classical cinema altogether, and to have existed purely as a wish-fulfilling ego-ideal.[2] Citing the character's invulnerability, his strange identitilessness, and his stolid imperviousness to all phenomena (even those which interest the viewer), Bingham identifies the character as the omnipotent agent of the individual viewer's wishes. Needless to say he embodies patriarchal masculinity; indeed, he *is* the phallus. His affectlessness is both the symptom of a narcissistic retreat into the ego and the enabler of disavowal of any consequences to others of the ego's act. For me this addresses the dreamlike invincibility of the character, his equally dreamlike indefiniteness of origin and identity, and above all that sense of freedom and power which his character creates for the identifying viewer. Nevertheless, I feel that the character's attachment to the uncanny draws attention to his status as ego stand-in which, to be pure, surely ought to be invisible. Moreover the mastery which he embodies is not, I believe, just a projection of spectator desire. It is also other, and greater, than the viewer; and the blankness which he manifests is not merely the desubjectivizing and dehistoricizing necessary to create a transparent ego-substitute, but the inscrutability of the demigod. Even at the outset, the Eastwood persona is split between the knowable and the unknowable, the desirable and the dangerous.

●THE COP

Harry Callahan

Dirty Harry Callahan transplants a number of these characteristics to the domestic contemporary world of the crime film. As a policeman Harry is *ipso facto* professionally dedicated to prosocial aims, and this would seem to contrast sharply with the purely personal motives of the Man With No Name. But neither Harry's desire to protect society nor the Man With No Name's appetite for winning the game seem like adequate explanations for their violent behaviour or their disdain for their enemies. Both characters, rather, need ultimately to affirm their mastery, their power, in the bluntest possible existential terms — by taking the lives of others in combat situations. As Christopher Frayling has recognized, this quality is in some measure an updating of Robert Warshow's definition of the western hero: a man who lives to assert his honour.[3] But no classical western ever permitted its hero such a naked display of violent dominance as Leone's films or the "cowboy cop" Harry Callahan exhibit.[4] This affirmation of masculine existential mastery is allowed to wear at least a loose disguise of ethics and morality through the films' repeated device of making the bad guys into monsters. So good cop Harry is contrasted with a large gallery of sickos, punks, and scum of the earth, while even the Man With No Name is morally preferable to psychotic Gian Maria Volonté and his snarling, drooling rabble of henchmen. But this apparent moral distinction also acts as an alibi allowing the spectacle of the exercise of power in the most direct forms: ritual humiliation enacted upon the psyche of the enemy and extreme violence enacted upon his body, both followed by gestures of machismo contempt for his defeated form. Here again is Bingham's invincible ego-agent. Yet it is striking that the wishes fulfilled through this agent should be so relentlessly those of domination through violence. The contempt this hero feels for his prey, the fear he inspires in them, the imperious authority he radiates towards them (all of which are experienced vicariously by the viewer, potentially even as a kind of fascist abasement), all tempt one to revise Warshaw's definition: this is a man who lives to assert his *power*.

The entry of a violently regressive and even primitive form of conflict resolution and order restoration into the tortured world of liberal defeat and disintegration in early '70s America seems historically inevitable from a present-day perspective. In this respect, Eastwood's Harry Callahan may be numbered with such other icons of the period as Charles Bronson in *Death Wish* and Joe Don Baker in *Walking Tall*; or, in a more conflicted way, with Gene Hackman in *The French Connection* and Robert De Niro in *Taxi Driver*. And yet the Eastwood persona was always distinguished from its contemporaries through the self-consciousness of its heroic image and through its striving for some articulate form of transcendence. It is clear that this char acteristic originated in the Leone films, but even in the original *Dirty Harry* (directed by Don Siegel) Eastwood is posed at the crucial moment in a low-angle silhouette, legs spread, oversized pistol in hand, dominating the scene like a demigod. His famous paragraph-long speech ("Do you feel lucky?") is marked as ritualistic both by its strategic placement and repetition in the film and by its oracular quality in emerging so continuously and impressively from the mouth of one who is normally as silent as a stone. These defining moments, and their increasingly more exaggerated and stylized descendants in subsequent Dirty Harry movies, are images of transcendence—not just heroism but hyper-heroism—and their self-consciousness becomes clearer and clearer as each film unfolds.

Indeed it is astonishing how quickly the nominally gritty-urban-realist character of Harry Callahan becomes self-consciously mythic and reflexive. The first sequel, *Magnum Force* (1973), features Harry as a hero-figure in the police department, inspiring gung-ho young officers in vigilante tactics: Harry is a mythic figure *in* the movie as well as for the viewer. Moreover, the film's thematic debating topic is the degree to which "good cops" (i.e., effective, violent cops who don't get hamstrung by legal niceties) are justified in taking the law into their own hands. The film thus forms a self-conscious rebuttal to the extra-textual liberal reviewers' objections to *Dirty Harry*:[5] again the offscreen status of the Harry phenomenon comes onscreen, transgressing realist-narrative boundaries and calling attention to its status as a constructed, rather than natural, phenomenon. *Magnum Force* also contains a striking sequence in which Harry and other cops perform a kind of "war game" on a shooting range. They must navigate through a landscape constructed of building facades (just like a movie set) shooting, or not shooting, at pop-up cardboard people-facades representing either "bad guys" or "innocent bystanders." The degree to which this scene again stages and replicates movie activity diegetically—even pointing ostentatiously to its physical falseness and characterological over-simplification—is remarkable, and its similarity to the "actual" narratives of the Harry movies inevitably undermines their realist substance and calls attention to *their* artifice through its own. The Harry series institutionalized narrative features—such as the opening set pieces in which Harry dispenses a violent riposte to crime, the speech which occurs near the beginning of the film and then again near the end, and Harry's extraordinary ordinance— that became ritualized markers of the character's mythic non-naturalism. The fetishizing of the handgun (an enthusiasm picked up immediately by much of Harry's *lumpen*-male audience) moves from initial exaggeration to ever-greater excesses of hyper-trophy. Harry is given a super-Magnum in *Magnum Force* and acquires a handgun enlarged to the brink of comedy in *Sudden Impact* (1983). The process again brings increasing mythification, increasing self-consciousness, and increasing visibility of constructedness. The phallic significance of handguns has always been an aspect of their representation, but it was left to Dirty Harry to raise this significance to a garish level of artifice where latent meanings rise so close to the surface of the narrative that realist conventions and their host ideology are imperilled.

When Eastwood finally directed a Dirty Harry movie himself, *Sudden Impact* (the fourth of the series), the result was predictably the most reflexive and self-conscious of all the films. *Sudden Impact* returns to the question of illegal vigilante violence and Harry's problematic relation to it; but where the contradictions of that subject are simply ignored in *Magnum Force*, here they are examined more deeply and the result is more troubled. The film's complexity derives from its concentration on the criminal who lies at the end of Harry's trail of detection, a woman named Jennifer Spencer, raped years earlier and now taking vengeance on the gang of perpetrators. She is simultaneously Harry's quarry and his counterpart in the business of dispensing summary homicidal justice to evildoers. (This doubling of the cop and his nominal antithesis the murderer is also found, in more radical form, in Eastwood's next film, *Tightrope*.) The anguish of this figure (an anguish which is expressed in her dark and violent paintings and in her haunted flashbacks), together with the cold-blooded execution style of the killings and the indication that the guilty ones were not all equally guilty, are important aspects that help to problematize the theme well past the point of a wholly satisfactory solution. Moreover, the role is played by Sondra Locke, heroine of four previous Eastwood films and Eastwood's real-life companion at the time, and hence already possessing sympathetic associations. Harry himself often seems a perfunctory and even marginal presence in this story, but when he does appear, it is in the most startlingly self-referential and quasi-parodic form yet. In the final big set piece where Harry performs the *ur*-Eastwood task of rescuing the girl from the gargoylish villain (although here the villain is pursuing the girl because she has been murdering all his friends and wants to murder him), he appears as a spectacularly backlit, silhouetted figure casting a long shadow, his wide-legged stance recalling the transcendent moment in the first movie and the monstrous dropsied handgun a prominent visual trope even at great distance. This image is so self-consciously mythic that no viewer can miss its reflexive artifice. At the end of *Sudden Impact* Harry has at last become the cartoon figure whose exaggerated anti-realist dimensions he had been flirting with since his birth; while at the same time the film's surrounding narrative has opened dark prospects of suffering and moral ambiguity which none of its predecessors (nor its sole, exhausted, successor *The Dead Pool*) ever approach. Harry's impossibility has never been clearer.

The Gauntlet (1977)

To that question, "is Harry Callahan possible?", *The Gauntlet* is perhaps Eastwood the filmmaker's most plainspoken "no," his most overt, ironically inflated demonstration of the preposterousness of Harry and every other cop action hero. The protagonist of *The Gauntlet* is a washed-up, quasi-alcoholic police detective named Shockley, who is deemed so incompetent by his corrupt bosses that they assign him to pick up and deliver a key witness whom they intend to murder en route to prevent her testimony which can tie them to organized crime. The witness is another marginal character, a prostitute with a messed-up life incongruously named Gus, but she is college-educated and as intellectually quick as Shockley is slow. Each of them discovers the other's virtues and a promise of personal renewal as they survive the successive assassination attempts that constitute the narrative. It is already somewhat daring of the film to present a version of the Eastwood cop who is stupid and derelict—daring in the sense that the essential transcendence of the persona is dangerously obscured. Of course, the character survives and triumphs over impossible odds in a violent environment, and it might be said that this fact alone is enough to reinstitute him as the transcendent hero. But *The Gauntlet*, one of the most reflexive and formally elegant films in the Eastwood canon, undermines the whole transcendental enterprise through a program of parodic excess that demonstrates over and over again how impossible the transcendent hero and the transcendent narrative really are.

The film proceeds principally through a handful of giant set-piece action scenes, each dramatizing an individual assassination attempt. The most important examples are the scene in which Shockley and Gus are trapped in a bungalow by a regiment of police; the scene in which their car is chased along mountain roads by a helicopter; and the final scene, in which their armoured bus must proceed past a literal gauntlet of massed police forces armed with shotguns and automatic weapons. The first and third of these especially are marked by a deliberate exaggeration of violent spectacle that is simultaneously cartoon-like and terrifying. The house surrounded by police is so absurdly riddled by bullets that it actually collapses entirely—yet Shockley survives unhurt. This is impossible and faintly comic, and yet the film never strikes these attitudes unambiguously or even openly. The gauntlet itself is so formalized, so doubly and triply "impossible," that the point is made inescapably. Shockley even provides the corrupt police with a map of his entry into the city and his route to city hall, where he intends to deliver his witness in precise fulfillment of his orders and in ritual defiance of the forces trying to destroy him. The armoured bus then proceeds in stately fashion through an inconceivable and interminable hail of fire all the way to the front steps of city hall. Once more Shockley survives. The boldness of the film's stylizations, its expansion and

explosion of the action-conventions of the genre, its sabotaging
of the transcendental project through exorbitant overstatement
are all characteristic of Eastwood's method of providing a
dialectic of opposition within his work.[6] The lines run in both
directions. Eastwood's physical presence inhabiting Shockley's
tattered mediocrity casts a retrospective, ironic shadow over all
of the Eastwood persona's more powerful protagonists; but by
the same process, something of the persona's heroic stature
necessarily works back into the antiheroic shell of the Shockley
character. Shockley, like so many of Eastwood's most interesting, most self-deconstructive protagonists (as, for example,
in their different ways *Bronco Billy*, *Honkytonk Man*, and
Unforgiven), is both Eastwood-persona and anti-Eastwood-
persona, myth and deconstruction, simultaneously.

Tightrope (1984)

The doublings and reflexivity of *Tightrope* are so manifest that
this film is always cited as evidence that Eastwood's cinematic
universe is more morally complicated than it perhaps appears to
its least-thoughtful viewers.[7] We have a cop unmistakably
similar to Dirty Harry, iconically speaking (i.e., played by
Eastwood), who has a taste for prostitutes and sadomasochistic
sex and who is attempting to solve a series of sex-murders perpe-
trated by a cop with a taste for prostitutes and sadomasochistic
sex. The doublings of Wes Block (Eastwood) and the murderer
are so explicit and extensive that the viewer is overtly encouraged to wonder whether Block himself might not be the
murderer. Like Harry, Block no longer has a wife, and alarming
scenarios now present themselves for any questions we might
have entertained about Harry's usually invisible sex life. Unlike
Harry, Block is a single father and has two daughters asking him
embarrassing questions about sex, which uncomfortably points
up the hypocrisy of his dual roles as guardian of law and family
and as nocturnal pleasure-hunter. The height of alarming cate-
gory-confusion occurs when the murderer gets hold of Block's
daughter and binds her with cords all too reminiscent of the
ones Block uses with his sex partners.

Thus the film sets up a landscape of moral conflict in which
the Eastwood persona is divided into "good" and "dark" sides,
and the "dark" facet is further emphasized by its embodiment in
a truly horrific *Doppelgänger*. It is noteworthy how powerfully

Eastwood has turned again to a similarly Manichean construction in some of his contemporary or later films—especially *Pale Rider*, *Unforgiven*, and *In the Line of Fire* (which employs the *Doppelgänger* even more centrally than *Tightrope*). *Tightrope* suggests that the Eastwood action hero may have a dark secret, that his essential self may somehow be complicit with exactly those forces he is ostensibly dedicated to defeating. The moral drama of the film is then given over to a battle to "save" Block himself from these forces and deliver him to a more human and loving set of principles—embodied in the film by the rape counsellor (Geneviève Bujold) with whom Block has a relationship. In the end, Block saves himself and vanquishes the *Doppelgänger* (after an elementally desperate struggle), and moral order is restored. In this respect, *Tightrope* remains a less troubling work than *Unforgiven*—and perhaps even *Pale Rider* and *In the Line of Fire*—since in those films the "dark" side is left to triumph to a far greater extent. Yet *Tightrope*, with its spectacle of a giving way to unholy destructive desires and its confounding of Eastwood's lethalness with a serial killer's, is quite unsettling enough to any uncritical reception of the Eastwood hero.

●THE WESTERN HERO
High Plains Drifter (1971)

It is hard to overestimate the debt of Eastwood's westerns to the Leone films that were their foundation. The earliest American feature westerns in which Eastwood appeared, such as *Hang 'em High* (1967), *Two Mules for Sister Sara* (1969), and *Joe Kidd* (1972), are strongly imitative of certain superficial features of the Leone films, especially the character and iconography of the Man With No Name. But the first western directed by Eastwood, *High Plains Drifter* (1972), shows a different, and deeper, degree of influence and transmutation altogether. This film seizes on Leone's wild stylizations and distentions of western convention as a starting point and goes on to exaggerate the ritual and mythic elements in the narrative still further. What was still metaphorical in Leone has become literal in Eastwood. In *A Fistful of Dollars,* the Eastwood character takes on an uncanny quality as a half-dozen rifle bullets are fired into his heart without effect; but he is not really immortal, only protected by hidden Ned-Kelly-like armour plating. In *High Plains Drifter*, however, this suggestion of the supernatural has become *literally* true: the Eastwood character is actually the spirit of a murdered town sheriff returned from the grave to enact a symbolic revenge.[8] The heavily marked air of invincibility surrounding the Man With No Name here becomes the literal, actual invincibility of a supernatural being; the disdain of Leone's character for a corrupt world becomes the implacable project of an avenging demigod; in short, Leone's daring stylizations in the direction of the explicitly mythic become Eastwood's even more daring literalizations of mythic suggestion. Dennis Bingham suggests that this more naked articulation of the persona's freedom from limitations merely liberates the figure to become more untouchable and ego like than ever. I feel rather that it represents an increase in self-consciousness and an undermining of the persona's effort-less ego-functionality. Moreover, through its initial grounding in the character's extended martyrdom by bullwhip and its culmi-nation in an explicitly infernal excess of revenge, the persona's actions are again (even hysterically) marked as other, beyond comprehension.

The whole of *High Plains Drifter* is visually distinguished, but at the conclusion of the film Eastwood the director creates his first great visual tour-de-force. The wholesale red-painting, and then the burning, of the town results in an astonishing iconic transformation of the town into an almost literally hellish land-scape—a gesture of stylization at least as extreme as anything in Leone (and that is saying something). Moreover, *High Plains Drifter* refers intertextually not only to Leone but to one of the monuments of the post-war western, *High Noon*, whose narra-tive also has a sheriff victimized by three gunmen amid the cowardly and corrupt inaction of the townspeople. Thus, in *High Plains Drifter*, Eastwood provides new "takes" on his film's immediate ancestors (spaghetti westerns) and also its more distant ones (classical Hollywood westerns), and resituates both the heroic protagonist and the narrative itself within a much more self-conscious context which calls attention to its own mythic artifice and abandonment of realism while emphasizing the transcendent power of both protagonist and narrative. The film's most crucial activity, in other words, is to de-naturalize its story and its hero, and to move both of them towards an occult and transcendental realm. This transformation from a generic western realism to mythic mystification provides a context of deliberate anti-realist exaggeration for the protagonist's unyielding otherworldly glare and death-dealing vengeance, and therefore creates an ironic distance on the Eastwood persona itself.

———

Eastwood's next western, *The Outlaw Josey Wales*, is a film of some significance both in itself and within the western genre. It is certainly a weighty and important appearance of the Eastwood heroic persona, but its role in Eastwood's career was to move the persona from post-classical anti-sociality back to a kind of reinvented classicism and prosociality. Consequently, it spends far less time exposing the impossibility of the Eastwood protagonist, working in fact rather in the opposite direction. For this reason, it is omitted in this mini-survey of the westerns and included instead in the later essay on concepts of fatherhood and leadership in Eastwood's cinema.

Bronco Billy (1980)

Bronco Billy is not a western, since it is set in the present day, but it might be called a meta-western. It exists in a tradition of films that place western elements in a modern setting, often with melancholy or tragic results. Culturally speaking, it is significant that *Bronco Billy* was released in the same year as two other examples of the type, *The Electric Horseman* and (somewhat more distantly related) *Urban Cowboy*. At the dawn of the 1980s, these films were all looking for a way to connect once more with what is felt to be the golden age of American ideological innocence, cinematically typified most purely in the naïve classical western. But it is virtually impossible to reinstitute the western as such: a twenty-year history of ever more disillusioned and finally nihilistic westerns forms an insuperable barrier. (Eastwood himself, probably the last substantial maker of westerns, has scattered his four projects over a twenty-year span.) Instead, a more direct form of expression is sought in the spectacle of the naïve cowboy transplanted into a modern environment, where his innocence is shown to be incongruent and even impossible, but where it finally stands as a reproach to our skepticism and a sweet reminder of our best instincts. *Bronco Billy* is certainly the most analytic and complex of these films, and once more it draws for much of its effect on the uncopyable reverberations and ironies of having the transcendent Eastwood persona available for a startlingly different reconfiguration.

It is not an exaggeration to say that Eastwood's whole meaning as western protagonist ever since the Leone films is based on a repudiation of the naïve cowboy hero. In every available dimension—iconic, narrative, thematic, ideological—the Eastwood persona receives a crucial part of its meaning through its violent difference from this figure. The "code of the West," the philosophy of honour and clean living, was already well into eclipse by the 1960s in mainstream big-screen westerns,[9] and it was precisely the Eastwood persona which inflicted the *coup de grâce* to these qualities by most perfectly embodying their complete antithesis. The transcendent Eastwood westerner is distinguished by ruthlessness rather than pity; vindictiveness rather than generosity; cold-blooded and indiscriminate rather than reluctant and selective violence; demonic rather than redemptive overtones. Instead of inspiring admiration and gratitude, the cruellest manifestations of the Eastwood persona inspire fear and a corrupt desire to watch violence practised upon people who are not us. This is not a complete characterization of this persona, but it is the most essential one in describing its relation to the foundational naïve hero of the genre.

To find, in *Bronco Billy*, the Eastwood persona inhabiting the character of its erstwhile antitype illuminates in both directions. Partly it reminds us of that never quite absent sense that Eastwood is capable of the substance and authenticity of classical heroism. But this reminder is conveyed within a context that qualifies and ironizes itself repeatedly. In *Bronco Billy,* the character's stance is not just classical but (one might say) super-classical, in that its classical qualities are overarticulated, exaggerated to the point of comedy, through their pointed placement within a contemporary environment where such qualities can never be "natural." Bronco Billy McCoy, head of a small-time travelling Wild West show, dresses like the ultimate dude-ranch cowboy, drives a huge red convertible with steerhorns on the hood and six-shooters for door handles, and in general is a walking parody of ultra-naïve cowboys from Tom Mix to Roy Rogers. His creed is to live straight and true, stay away from liquor and cigarettes, and be kind to women and children. He refers to the kids in his audience as "buckaroos" and "little pardners" and gives regular benefit performances at orphanages and asylums, never stopping for a moment in living and selling his cowboy's credo. At one point, when he and his troupe are bankrupt and prospectless, he even leads them in an attempted train robbery of hallucinatory ridiculousness. Billy is preposterous, but the innocence of his idealism, and his insistence that only by this route will individuals be able to find fulfillment, strikes a chord of recognition and assent even as it demonstrates its own impossibility. The film's amazing next step is to convert this representative of a historically extinct form of classical heroism from a deluded (if charming) freak of nature into a strategically self-constructed edifice. Billy, it transpires, is not at all the last of the cowboys but a former shoe salesman from New Jersey who has spent seven years in Folsom prison. Upon his release, he decided to pursue his boyhood dream of being a cowboy. This paragon of naïve American virtue and ideological purity has in fact invented and fabricated himself from the ground up. He is a second-hand subject, modelled on a stylized and obsolete cultural artifact. He has no authenticity except the authenticity of a *desire* for purity and wholeness—and indeed, it is this desire, this "dream," that Billy articulates late in the film as the human necessity for a morally exhausted American society in 1980.[10] The film's finale takes place in a gigantic tent sewn together out of American flags—another astonishing stroke of *mise en scène* on the scale of the conclusion of *High Plains Drifter*, and a decisive move in bodily lifting the film onto the level of metacommentary: the whole final tableau is literally enacted in a symbolic realm. Moreover, the essential irrationality and dislocation of this grand metaphor and the project it represents is encoded in the fact that the flags are woven by lunatics from an asylum.

  Bronco Billy, like so many post-*Star Wars* and Reagan-era films, addresses a profound cultural dilemma: on the one hand, the intellectual and emotional realization that classical ideology is definitively discredited; and on the other the despair-weary, nostalgic longing for the simple reassurance of ideological meaning and wholeness. The contradiction is short-circuited by camouflaging idealist structures as fictional or "toy" structures, thus both disavowing and preserving them. The result is postmodern pastiche. But *Bronco Billy* distinguishes itself from its contemporaries in two ways. Its articulation, and indeed thematization, of its own artificiality is far more self-acknowledging and explanatory than the purely latent virtuality of other films. It is true that in openly offering a recycled dead ideology in place of an organically alive one, and in then happily celebrating the fact, it participates in the pathology of cultural fantasy all too uncritically. But it has the merit at least of spelling out the necessity of abandoning all claims to authenticity and naturalness, and of substituting the frankly artificial. The other element the film has that others do not is the physical presence of the Eastwood persona. The proto-classical authority and power which it carries with it survives even its deconstruction through the personage of an ex-convict shoe salesman pretending to be a cowboy, and endows the character with a residue of substance underneath all of the artifice. The endemic confusions of Eastwoodian inter- and metatextuality are also fully operative. Like all of Eastwood's westerns, *Bronco Billy* presents Eastwood pretending to be a cowboy; but in this case, the film's actual narrative could be described in the same way—the (Eastwood) character pretending to be a cowboy. Such endlessly reflecting mirrors are a recurring feature of Eastwood's cinema, and of course help to further emphasize their textuality.

The film also casts light in that opposite direction, towards Eastwood's "really" transcendent roles. In an early scene, Billy stops a bank robbery in progress by pulling out his pistol and vanquishing the criminals, exactly as Dirty Harry would. Here, though, the event is more than half comic because Billy is ready to allow the robbery to take place without intervening until he sees a small child's piggy-bank broken by the thieves' violence. He goes on to exploit the media's interest in the event by putting in gratuitous plugs for his show. The satirical reflexivity here is very plain. In a bracketing (and much bitterer) scene later, Billy is humiliated by a local sheriff who challenges him to draw his gun and pours scorn on his pathetic pretensions: every viewer expects Billy—or rather the Eastwood persona—to respond to this humiliation with violence. But he does not. He backs down and swallows his pride. These two scenes are among the film's clearest statements of the difference between the mythic landscape normally inhabited by the Eastwood persona and the world of experience, and the latter scene in particular remains a highly disconcerting moment for adorers of Eastwood the figure of power.

In *Bronco Billy*, Clint Eastwood is clearly impossible—is in fact purposely self-constructed. In this case, he has to be constructed because, although he is impossible, he is necessary to the culture. Indeed, in this film Eastwood's persona has resumed the role of the western hero who enables the good community. But *Bronco Billy* resituates this structure in present-day America, bringing the mythic conventionalisms of the most visibly conventional of all western protagonists—the naïve cowboy hero—into a modern realist comedy where their contrivance and mechanism of cultural reassurance are blatant. As the cowboy hero of a classical western helps the good community to resist the forces inimical to it, so Billy will enable not just the members of his troupe and his diegetic audience but also the viewer of the film to resist the forces of skepticism and, indeed, history which would destroy their self-idealization. But in marking the conventional and artificial nature of every aspect of the process, the film calls attention to the degree to which both the idealization and the figure who enables it are willed, unnatural, self-serving.

Pale Rider (1985)

Pale Rider unfolds on a basis of intertextuality more extensive than that of any Eastwood film. If *High Plains Drifter* is a kind of demonic sequel to the canonic western *High Noon*, then *Pale Rider* is actually a detailed restaging—also demonic—of the canonic western *Shane* (1953). Moreover, *Pale Rider* has crucial features that look back specifically to *High Plains Drifter* and beyond that to the Leone films. *Shane*, of course, tells the generically central tale of a mysterious stranger who comes out of nowhere to aid a community of good settlers in their struggle against a predatory cattle baron, and in particular associates himself with an individual nuclear family. *Pale Rider* resets the action in a gold-mining community, with a corporate hydraulic mining operation and its hired guns acting as the bullying villains. The hero is a dark, mysterious stranger called the Preacher, who wears a clerical collar but whose demeanour is more satanic than godly. Once more the supernatural landscape of *High Plains Drifter* is revisited, as the Preacher is found to bear the scars of a half-dozen bullet holes on his torso in places which must surely have been fatal.[11] A further echo of the earlier film occurs when the Preacher once more confronts the man who shot him (a hired gun named Stockburn) and inflicts upon him the identical punishment—this time unambiguously fatal—in an Old-Testament-style act of vengeance. This quasi-supernatural hero arrives, Lohengrin-like, in answer to a young woman's prayer for help and is darkly (and explicitly) tied to scriptural writ, as his entry into town coincides with a reading of the lines from Revelations 6:8: "and behold a pale horse: and his name that sat on him was Death; and Hell followed with him." This latter image of the uncanny avenging spirit of death, bringing hell in his wake, is a striking feature of both these films and will occur again in *Unforgiven*; clearly it has the status of a preoccupation in Eastwood's westerns.[12] As we have seen, it has its roots in Leone, but Eastwood's version not only strongly stresses the supernatural transcendence of the figure and calls upon the ancient cultural rhetoric of Judeo-Christianity for further emphasis, but also morally problematizes the character by suspending him between the godlike agency of righteous justice and the demonic agency of hellish bloodletting. The contrast between this dark and menacing figure and that of the gentle, blond, buckskinned Shane is extreme. Where Shane's famous entrance into the film, riding out of a background of verdant mountains and momentarily framed between the antlers of a deer, symbolizes him virtually as an intervention from benevolent nature, the Preacher's cold, black silhouette emerges from the harsh snowy monochrome of a hostile landscape. There is a marked transformation from a soft organic world in *Shane* to a hard mineral one in *Pale Rider*, seen most clearly in the metamorphosis of *Shane*'s farmers, who are seeking to make the earth produce a rich bounty of food, into *Pale Rider*'s miners, who are merely attempting to dig material wealth in the form of gold out of the rock. This transformation is a deliberate movement of the western's centrally important community values from the quasi-spiritual one of making fruitful what was barren to the nakedly materialist one of a search for an innately useless substance with a high exchange value. Nor is this disconcerting and deflating shift away from traditional symbolic values recuperated by the film's contrast of the miners' "honest" individual hand labour with the mining company's ecologically devastating hydraulic methods. In every way, *Pale Rider* represents a harshening and problematizing of the classical generic project of *Shane*, and it continues the unsettling thematization of the Eastwood protagonist as a troubling figure whose mysterious transcendent source may be either good or evil—or, more probably, some unthinkable conflation of the two. The quotation from Revelations, the unfathomable mystery of the character,[13] the frightening aura of deadly power emanating from him, and the ritual violence he duly performs are set strikingly against his clearly prosocial, chivalric function in the *Shane*-narrative and the extra qualities of benevolent patriarch which he assumes with respect to the good community in *Pale Rider*.

In this respect, *Pale Rider* represents a kind of unsettled reshuffling of themes and tropes from *High Plains Drifter*, *The Outlaw Josey Wales,* and *Bronco Billy. High Plains Drifter* most definitively reverses the naïve-western pattern of the relation of hero and community: the transcendental cowboy hero arrives mysteriously from outside the community; but instead of saving it from the villains, he delivers it over to them and watches its destruction with extreme satisfaction before turning on the villains himself. The community is (mostly) just as bad as the villains, and he revenges himself upon each in turn in an efface-ment of any real distinction between the two. *High Plains Drifter* is thus a kind of radical extension of the revenge western typolo-gized by Will Wright's structural study of the genre,[14] wherein the hero begins in a position of alienation from, and even hatred for, society and only gradually works his way back to a prosocial func-tion. In *High Plains Drifter,* he not only never relinquishes his enmity for society, he positively acts as its scourge. The supernat-ural qualities of the character even suggest that he is a kind of divine scourge. This idea is stronger still in *Pale Rider*, where the hero has an explicitly biblical grounding and clerical signifiers; there is a distinct suggestion in the scenes of violent mastery that it is the wrath of Jehovah which is somehow being tapped. But in *Pale Rider,* this supernal violence is exercised only against the villains and very pointedly on behalf of the good community.[15] It is indeed as if the vengeful hero of *High Plains Drifter* were now returning a second time from death, and on this occasion not just exacting a private reckoning but additionally performing the clas-sical role of prosocial hero.

From this perspective, *The Outlaw Josey Wales* may be seen as a painstaking transformation of the revenge hero into a prosocial one (actually conforming fairly directly with Wright's "Vengeance Variation") and *Bronco Billy* as a return of the most naïve classical cowboy, with his prosocial function clearly emphasized but displaced into the present and pastiched. What *Pale Rider* does is simply, brazenly, to conflate the quasi-demonic vengeance figure with the prosocial figure, dragging in *Shane* as a narrative skeleton to emphasize further the congruence of the prosocial figure and the incongruence of the vengeful one. The resulting contradictions and thematic chaos are not papered over or argued away: they are allowed to stand intact in all their undecidability. *Pale Rider* may thus be described as an incoherent film. But its incoherence is, as it were, coherent within the overall patterns of Eastwood's cinema. It allows the Eastwood persona to be simultaneously prosocial and privately vengeful, godlike and demonic, redemptive and frightening, mortal and immortal, substantial and imaginary, classical and post-classical (among other contradictions) — all variants of the dichotomies of power and artifice, desirability and impossibility which we have been discussing throughout. Eastwood has never been concerned to suppress contradiction — rather the reverse — and *Pale Rider*'s willingness to allow itself to be incoherent is merely an exaggeration of a quasi-permanent condition. Superficially, this tolerance of contradictory opposites resembles what Robert Ray has described as a constitutional Hollywood strategy of never forcing viewers to choose but always providing them with the benefits of both sides of a dichotomy.[16] But if the catalogue of heroes who are both (for example) rebellious and prosocial would seem to include the Preacher, it is a project of virtually all those films to conceal and disavow their contradictions. From this vantage point the incoherence of *Pale Rider* is a positive virtue.

Unforgiven (1992)

Unforgiven is the culmination of all the contradictions specifically of the transcendent Eastwood western persona — the culmination because it attempts, more consciously even than *Bronco Billy*, to comprehend and articulate the contradictions rather than simply assert them and let them stand without comprehension and articulation. The next essay presents an extended close reading of the film, Eastwood's masterpiece as a filmmaker and one of the finest Hollywood films of the past quarter-century. Here, though, it will be useful to give a brief preview as a way of setting *Unforgiven* within the evolution of the heroic persona we have been examining. The film's protagonist,

William Munny, is a demonstratively schizoid personage, first a pious pig-farming widower and father who can't ride or shoot, later reverting to another incarnation of the Eastwood persona in its invincible demonic-violent form, as seen in both *High Plains Drifter* and *Pale Rider*. Splitting the character in this way is a way of marking out the contrast, and conflict, between the contradictory demands on the heroic persona to be good and prosocial on the one hand and transcendentally violent on the other—a move accompanied by a clear (indeed almost caricatured) ethical labelling of those two sides as respectively "good" and "bad." At the end of *Unforgiven*, the antiheroic "good" character disappears and is replaced by the transcendental-heroic "bad" Munny whose resemblance to the archetypal Eastwood persona is unmistakable.

As we have seen, earlier Eastwood westerns collectively mark a tortuous path through the central generic question of the relation of power and social responsibility. *High Plains Drifter*, in Leone-like and post-classical fashion, simply repudiates social responsibility except to a handful of marginal individuals and arrogates the exercise of transcendental power to the persona's project of quasi-demonic personal revenge. *Josey Wales* meticulously and conditionally reformulates the classical prosocial hero through a painful transformation of the vengeful demonic persona. *Bronco Billy* resurrects the classical cowboy whole and intact, and puts him in charge of renewing American individuals and culture, but more or less cancels his transcendent power by rendering it parodic, artificial, nonviolent, and now purely imaginary and inspirational. *Pale Rider* then brings back the powerful, mystically violent archetype and yokes it crudely and unceremoniously with the beneficent social redeemer. *Unforgiven* splits these juggled opposites of prosocial and transcendently masterful into the "good" and "bad" facets of the protagonist's character: the pig-farming Munny is good but not masterful, the legendary-killer Munny is masterful but absolutely not good. In the glimpses we get of this latter figure through reminiscences of the old days and through his behaviour at the end of the film, the bad Munny is demonic in corrosive and ugly ways never explored in the earlier Eastwood avatars. This character is difficult for even hardened lovers of Eastwood's killing power to recuperate without a good deal of misrecognition and disavowal. In a more detailed and painful way than ever before, an Eastwood film questions its own basis and the legitimacy of its own constitutive elements.

In a sense, *Unforgiven* thus undoes all the work Eastwood has done since his arrival from Leone-land. The film meticulously reverses the process of mystification whereby the persona was able to act with transcendent violence: the bad Munny, though still shrouded in darkness and hellfire and indistinct in its outlines, is demystified as a pathological creature whose transcendence equals the blasted, dysfunctional landscape of his psyche. And while the transcendental hero is reconfigured in terms of the sickness of a "real" subject, his powerful flatness as a mythical object is presented as a quality demanded by his audience and the culture in general. That "real" subject is a rounded, imperfect, vulnerable character, the good Munny. Or perhaps we should say that the good Munny, with his history and name and relationships (all those things of which Bingham notes the absence in the Leone-derived persona), is the window through which we may see the "real" subject, who is both sides of the character, the imperfect "good" and the demystified pathological "bad."

Instead of "real," we may call this subject simply "classical" and describe the reconsideration and reconfiguration of the Eastwood persona in *Unforgiven* as another reclamation of that genre-film classicism which Eastwood had assumed to different degrees in different films. "Classicism" here signifies not the generic structures of the classical western, which are definitely not reproduced straightforwardly in *Unforgiven*, but rather the larger model of Hollywood cinema in which a substantial, unironic ideological drama is enacted. *The Outlaw Josey Wales* installs Eastwood as the good hero in the western to a far greater extent, and attempts to humanize the persona's transcendent power in the process of bringing the character into a rounded classical world. Films as completely different as *Tightrope* and *Heartbreak Ridge* also present a rounded classical figure (although *Heartbreak Ridge* contains dangerously exaggerated elements of convention which place the persona closer to the ironic realm where most Eastwood heroes have to function). *Tightrope*, with its traumatic doubling and pervasive sense of crisis, may be the closest to *Unforgiven* as an example of agonized classicism, if very short of the latter film's symphonic complexity and maturity. In any case, in *Unforgiven* there is emphatically, absolutely unpostmodernly, something at stake, a moral perspective whose dimensions are neither pastiched nor diminished through the agencies of spectacle or flat hypertrophied characters. Almost miraculously, the film can incorporate and even thematize the transcendent violent Eastwood persona without transforming the narrative into the flattened territory of myth by the very presence of that persona.[17] In this respect, *Unforgiven* recreates the kind of late-classical conditions found during the 1950s, that period when the western was at its most complex and richly conflicted prior to a wholesale structural collapse.

Unforgiven, then, has the effect of a definitive report on the question of the transcendent Eastwood western hero's possibility. Earlier films had repeatedly presented the transcendent persona as constructed, artificial, hyperbolic, and hence impossible except in a mythic context. *Unforgiven* shows the persona as constructed (by different characters in the narrative, but also by us) *from* the ugliest forms of violence, destruction, and self-destruction— elements that can have no true appeal for the subject bearing them and can only exist as heroic or charismatic qualities through a pathological process of distortion in their reception and interpretation by others and by the culture.

●FICTITIOUS VICTORIES

Heartbreak Ridge (1987)

The nearest Eastwood has ever come to being a wholehearted hero of ideology is in *Heartbreak Ridge*, where he plays a marine gunnery sergeant training a platoon of undisciplined, smart-ass kids to be war heroes—a role they duly enact during the invasion of Grenada. Eastwood's role as Tom Highway, the aging, bemedalled veteran of Korea and Vietnam who drinks too much, gets into bar fights, and is constantly busted for insubordination, is a kind of tour de force of army-movie and populist-heroic clichés. The film unites the rambunctious roughhousing of the low-comic Eastwood (e.g., *Every Which Way But Loose*) with an overt patriotic posturing entirely in tune with the age. Particularly striking is the unification of the Eastwood hero and the American nation on the same exalted symbolic plane: the mythic persona of Eastwood acting out in a Stars-and-Stripes-marked landscape. The final scene of *Heartbreak Ridge*, featuring the Marine heroes in dress uniform welcomed home from Grenada by cheering, flag-waving crowds, transports the film to that realm of symbolic theatrical triumph which recalls the didactic mythicization of *Bronco Billy*'s last scene. In both instances we have the self-consciously artificial Eastwood hero delivering a myth-thirsty America from its ideological trauma by offering it a ritual symbolic spectacle of heroic mastery. In *Bronco Billy*, as we have seen, the ideology of heroic self-realization is explicitly artificial. In the case of *Heartbreak Ridge*, however, the constructedness is less overt. The film identifies America's myth-sickness: since World War Two the nation has "gone o-1-1"—has "tied" in Korea and lost in Vietnam. The sporting metaphor is perfectly consistent with the symbolic nature of the subject. The characterization of wars as won, lost, or tied, with the outcome determining whether America is in first place in the world league, has only a nominal relation to geopolitics but has an entirely real one with the score-keeping abstractions of American postmodern virtual history. Grenada itself was, of course, a Reaganite abstraction of exactly this kind, intended to wipe out the myth-defeat of Vietnam, a toy war and a toy victory as voodooistic as Rambo's or *Rocky IV*'s. The movie seizes eagerly on this symbolic process: after the success of the minuscule Grenada invasion, Highway claims that the US is "1-1-1." The film cannot be and is not unaware of the preposterousness of this claim. The "victory" in Grenada is not a real victory, but a theatrical, symbolic, artificial one. The conventionalism of the protagonist's character and his mission of transforming and shaping recruits is balanced with the artifice of the national narrative in Grenada; both are make believe. Eastwood offers a fictional victory as palliative for a real condition exactly as Reagan does, although the film manifests what one might call a naïve self-consciousness which habitually foregrounds the fictionality of the process and thus threatens to a greater extent the disavowal of history on which the project rests.

In the Line of Fire (1993)

In the Line of Fire—like *Tightrope* a significant Eastwood film not directed by Eastwood—enacts something similar, though in a far more skeptical and self-aware fashion. Here Eastwood plays Frank Horrigan, a Secret Service agent nearing retirement age, who had failed to prevent John Kennedy's shooting and is now enmeshed in tracking a new would-be presidential assassin. The opportunity, at the end of a career, to atone for an earlier catastrophic failure which has left deep and lasting psychological wounds uncannily recalls *Heartbreak Ridge*. In both films the protagonist occupies a markedly prosocial, one might say—pro*national*—profession and is clearly performing the symbolic work of the ideological hero; and in both cases the hero is attempting to compensate for and efface traumatic wounds to the national psyche (Vietnam, the Kennedy assassination). In these films (as in *Bronco Billy* with its Capraesque philosophy and flag-draped finale), the Eastwood hero is not trying to save just his honour or the girl or the family or the community, but the idea of a stainless and special America. But in both films the redemption, though perfectly executed, falls well short of the goal, and both films reveal (*In the Line of Fire* far more explicitly) the necessity of the shortfall and by extension the impossibility of the heroic project.

In the Line of Fire provides this perspective through two complementary strategies. The first is to juxtapose the historical actuality of the Kennedy assassination with the fictionality of the assassination which Eastwood does succeed in preventing. That is, Eastwood cannot prevent a real historical assassination creating real historical pain; he can only prevent a fictional assassination and create fictional redemption. He cannot really compensate for the loss of President Kennedy and the national innocence which perished with him; he can only present a theatrical spectacle in which he pretends to prevent a non-existent assassin from killing a non-existent president.

The film's second strategy lies inside rather than above the narrative and consists in the characterization of the would-be assassin, Mitch Leary (John Malkovich). Here again is *Tightrope*'s doubling. Like Horrigan, Leary is a federal government security agent; in fact, he is virtually his evil twin, as Horrigan's highly skilled masculine-violent expertise is professionally devoted to saving life while Leary's is devoted to taking it in CIA covert operations. Leary is Horrigan's dark side, as the CIA is America's. Leary is also the sociopathic product of America's ideological failure (sick America has trained him to kill innocent people), and self-consciously attributes his postmodern, post-ethical, post-ideological pathology to the hypocrisy of America which promised him idealist validation but gave him bloodstained *Realpolitik*. His personal interest in Horrigan is also part of his symbolic paradigm-war: he has identified Horrigan as, in effect, the last classical hero struggling unsuccessfully to sustain a holistic positive ideology of America. Horrigan has failed catastrophically already at Kennedy's assassination, and that failure can never be redeemed. Now he is wheezing and tattered and saddened, and though he persists in the struggle, he really has no chance against Leary. Leary has a diamond-bright intelligence, a limitless postmodern access to information, an astonishing ability to transform his physical appearance or change his venue with no warning. Leary's attitude towards the stolid, outmoded classical hero, trapped in the single iconic identity of Clint Eastwood, is one of pity. Leary too would have liked to be a heroic Eastwood persona, but morally bankrupt America would not allow it; and in fact, has not allowed it to Horrigan either, who failed (as it were) to be Eastwood when Kennedy was assassinated and will fail again. Leary sees the pathos of this diminished Eastwood persona and decides to help the old-timer in the interest of making their symbolic contest less one-sided. All that is left in Leary's view is (postmodernly) "the game": the exercise of intelligence and skill in a competition to demonstrate the ideological aridity of America an aridity so severe that it has deprived Leary of any subjectivity but a pathological one. Leary helps out ideological America's creaking, once-defeated champion Eastwood-Horrigan and repeatedly demonstrates that Horrigan can only have even a hope of defeating Leary through Leary's own aid.

If the Eastwood persona, displaying a flash of his old Leone cunning and trickery, is given finally too much aid, so that he actually foils the assassination—and moreover in at last "taking a bullet for the President" isn't even wounded on account of his bulletproof vest—the victory is still doubly compromised. Not only is the saved president a purely fictional one, but the film's mutually reflecting mirrors characterize the victory of the classical hero Eastwood-Horrigan as possible only in the context of and indeed through the agency of a postmodern manipulation and tolerance of obsolete items of classical machinery such as the Eastwood hero and the redemptive happy ending. In this respect, *In the Line of Fire* is a highly elegant formal construct whose narrative dispositions allow for the survival of a classical action as a "wish" of postmodern skepticism and for the persistence of a heroic Eastwood persona whose actions remain heroic but whose epistemological grounding is systematically deconstructed. The film is a blueprint of Eastwood's career-long cinematic achievement of staging a heroic presence in a series of anti-classical environments. *In the Line of Fire* juxtaposes the classical and the postmodern in an unusually dexterous fashion which again undertakes the Eastwoodian project of both constructing and deconstructing the heroic agent. The film's narrative reaches positive closure, the Eastwood persona defeats the villain, the President is saved; but the firm basis for the victory, and its solidly sustaining meaning, have crumbled underfoot, leaving a closure whose lifeblood has been denatured. More substantial and lingering is the sense of loss expressed in the film's most deeply felt scene, where Horrigan recalls the day of Kennedy's death, with its intoxicating fresh sunlight and bright air. Notwithstanding the film's fictionality, that was a *real* loss of a sort which the viewer can recognize, of a kind for which no narrative can compensate.

●OTHER LATE FILMS

One might add here that other Eastwood films have provided a further interesting perspective and redefinition of the hero: in films such as *Honkytonk Man* (in which Eastwood plays a tubercular country songwriter during the Depression) and *Bird* (a film about Charlie Parker in which Eastwood does not appear), the protagonist is an artist, a creator and performer, in both cases suffering from profound physical and psychological weaknesses, and in both cases dying at the end. The fact that these figures are creator/performers carries the project of reflexivity to another plane—after all, Eastwood the director and Eastwood the persona are creator/performers too—and this plane is in a sense more direct and less symbolic than the one occupied by the action hero. In this more literal context it is fascinating to see the powerful physical masculinity that has always characterized the Eastwood protagonist undermined by bodily weakness and giving way to mortality in a protracted and emphatic way.

White Hunter, Black Heart (1990)

In *White Hunter, Black Heart*, Eastwood again plays a creative artist, this time a film director. In its paraphrase of some of the circumstances surrounding John Huston's direction of *The African Queen* on location in 1951, the film introduces a dizzying *mise en abîme* in the spectacle of the visible actor Clint Eastwood under the invisible direction of Clint Eastwood mimicking the actions and mannerisms of director John Huston, a historical personage whose physical appearance and rhythms of speech we are familiar with because he too acted in many films. The protagonist of *White Hunter, Black Heart*, John Wilson, has no bodily frailties, but his moral weakness and reckless egotism (which have disastrous effects on others) are their spiritual equivalent and are moreover seen as inextricable from his charismatic courage and individualism. The film also depicts its protagonist's failure to act out his dream of mastery in real life, in the end substituting for it the "lying" and obviously artificial mastery of a Hollywood movie scenario. Wilfully pursuing his existential-romantic personal ambition to shoot an elephant, Wilson embarks upon a Hemingway-esque machismo quest to the detriment of the film he is supposed to be directing. Against the advice of everyone in the company, including the initially admiring young novelist he has lured along, he presses ahead, enlisting the aid of a prominent local native hunter whose primitive masculine virtues he idealizes. But in the event, Wilson acts rashly and the hunter is killed by an enraged elephant. Utterly crushed in spirit, Wilson returns to the movie, now calling for the script's original happy ending, which he had previously denounced as false and cowardly in a manifesto of his own creative philosophy. The heroic persona is deconstructed, and along with it the mythical activity of moviemaking. This hero is explicitly undesirable, his charismatic attraction and powerful individuality translated in the end as not only self deluding but destructive. In its own way, *White Hunter, Black Heart* is as devastatingly critical of the heroic Eastwood persona as *Unforgiven*. If the figure is indeed possible (and its possibility is partly enabled by its demythologization), it is not at all desirable. And one must of course add to this list of fallible artist/performer figures the character of Bronco Billy, explicitly rendered as a character whose heroism is constructed and not natural.

A Perfect World (1993)

A Perfect World is a powerful and complex film that sums up the Eastwood cinema's developing ideas about fatherhood, in particular that facet of the Eastwood persona that plays the Good Father, and is dealt with in detail in a later essay. But we may briefly note its further condemnation of the heroic stance as a kind of pathology. Here the protagonist's role is taken not by Eastwood but by Kevin Costner, and this fact must place the film apart from that line of works in which the Eastwood screen persona is a central constitutive element. Escaped convict Butch Haynes kidnaps eight-year-old Philip, and for most of two days they run from a manhunt while Butch acts as a charismatic-scary substitute male parent for the fatherless Philip while acting out his own childhood traumas. The situation moves through excitement and comedy to catastrophe as Philip shoots Butch and de-fathers himself a second time. Most important for our considerations here is the film's rendering of the heroic as a chimerical, wish-fulfilling function whose action is finally false and destructive rather than redemptive or enabling. It is noteworthy, too, that the role Eastwood takes in the film is the marginalized one of the aging Texas Ranger (another present-day cowboy) who chases Butch. He is revealed to have intervened in Butch's life at a crucial point in his adolescence in the hope of saving the boy from his abusive criminal father, but his action has in fact arguably set Butch on his path to disaster. The Eastwood character is unable to save Butch in the past or in the present; he can only look on helplessly as an FBI sniper shoots down the unarmed and wounded Butch. In many ways, *A Perfect World* is a sober, clear-eyed, and unmitigated confession of the impossibility of the heroic.

The Bridges of Madison County (1995)

The Bridges of Madison County signals a radical departure in at least one way: Eastwood, after a career of making films for and about men, has at last made a "women's picture." The story is of a middle-aged married woman who has sacrificed youth, personal dreams, and above all the ideal of romantic love for the prosaic life of a responsible wife and mother; who is confronted with and experiences the perfect fantasy of a lover; and who then renounces and banishes him so that she can return to her duty, while still cherishing him (and being cherished) *in absentia*. And this is precisely the story of a Bette Davis or Joan Fontaine movie of the 1930s or '40s, only with an actual affair instead of just a contemplated one as a marker of changing mores. What is of interest here is that the Eastwood persona—now a lover rather than a warrior, a woman's man rather than a man's man—has nevertheless retained its transcendent quality. Still the figure of fantasy, he is in *The Bridges of Madison County* even more imaginary and less present than in any of his earlier films. It is in keeping with the conventions of this particular brand of romantic melodrama that he should be renounced and sent away in order to be the better preserved as a cherished image and memory, that he can only exist as a fantasy because marriage would make him ordinary and prosaic. But it is equally in keeping with the mythologies of transcendence which have accompanied the Eastwood persona throughout its history in westerns and other masculine genres. The momentary appearance, banishment to imagination, and lifelong fetishization-in-absence of the gentle, poetic artist-photographer Robert Kincaid is another version of the uncanny arrival and departure of the otherworldly heroes of *High Plains Drifter* and *Pale Rider*—especially the latter, who comes in response to the need of women.[18] Kincaid is a gentle, knightly hero of courtly love, and his appearance caps that history of the Eastwood protagonist whose function was in part to deliver and safeguard vulnerable women. But as much as in any other Eastwood film, the persona's possibility is in question, because of his "perfect" or "fantasy" quality and his evanescent existence in imagination and memory.

●ENVOI

In retrospect, *Bronco Billy* was a harbinger of a long, slow trend in Eastwood's cinema to move the too-powerful, too-heroic essential persona from a narrative status of impossible transcendence to one of non-transcendence. *Bronco Billy* first presented the persona as self-constructed and culturally constructed. *Honkytonk Man* dips into realist waters, with the Eastwood protagonist appearing as a figure who suffers limitation, vulnerability, and helpless death. The period since the late 1980s has shown the persona's aging with its decline from the heroic masculine body into a rueful resignation in the face of decay and mortality. *Heartbreak Ridge*'s quasi-jingoistic patriotism features a last hurrah of the hardbody Eastwood persona: a kind of explicit farewell performance of Eastwood the warrior. Most of the films after this have become harsh in their judgement of the "essential" persona, when it has reappeared. *White Hunter, Black Heart*—another realist project but one which displays the persona as a figure of power—is a wholesale attack on the irresponsibility, self-delusion, and destructiveness of charismatic leadership, of the elite or transcendent individual. *Unforgiven* profoundly features what is probably the very last appearance of the persona as figure of transcendent violence; and in this appearance that persona is characterized as a nightmare of half-remembered horrors to be shunned or, when its return is unavoidable, as a homicidal maniac whose engine is the torment of a damned soul. After this, *In the Line of Fire* and *A Perfect World* have strongly elegiac qualities. The former film again has the Eastwood action hero reduced by age, still mourning for the loss (during his watch) of the bright ideals of American ideology, symbolized in the assassination of John Kennedy, and contented in the end with a retirement whose symbolic gold watch is the virtual frustration of virtual assassin. Here, and in *Heartbreak Ridge*, the retirement from the battle is also accompanied by the consolation of the love of a good woman, in effect the domestication of the masculine hero. *A Perfect World* pushes the Eastwood persona right out to the margins of irrelevance: not only is he old, but even when he was younger he failed to protect and lead effectively. At the centre of the film is an elaborate and agonized demonstration of the illusoriness and destructiveness of ideals of masculine heroism and in particular the model of the Good Father. The sense of loss pervading both of these films (indeed engulfing the second) persists in *The Bridges of Madison County*. Here the tone is more autumnal yet, with the action set in the past through a flashback from after the deaths of the participants and with the Eastwood figure in its heroic specialness yet more misty and insubstantial, and finally banished. Throughout this progress, Eastwood the filmmaker has appeared as a kind of Prospero renouncing his arts of magic, renouncing that transcendental heroic persona which formed the core of his cinema, and contemplating instead the transience and limitation of life, the complex demands of actuality which no heroic model can fulfill, the necessity of loss. He has felt, perhaps, that his own actorly persona can never definitively assume a quotidian dimension, that to reduce the persona simply to a kind of documentary ordinariness would be perverse and, moreover, irresponsible to the sometimes-guilty history of that persona. Instead, he has presided over its demythologization, its sometime prosecution, and the prospect of its death.[19]

3

Unf⬤rgiven

Anatomy of a Murderer

The narrative of *Unforgiven* passes back and forth, back and forth, over the process of hero creation and hero destruction, transcendent invincibility and vulnerable humanity, legend and experience. It incorporates in the most reflexive way the mechanisms of myth formation and the artistic discourses of transcendent heroic action. It explicitly dissects a number of conflicting moral imperatives more or less innate to the western and allows them to proliferate into contradiction in a manner characteristic of very few of the species. It examines the notion of "justice," a concept central to both the western and the history of the Eastwood persona, and finds it impossible even to see clearly, let alone to institute through heroic and violent means as the genre and the persona require. And it attacks head on the problem of violence itself in the genre and the heroic action-narrative in general—and in particular the necessity of violence to the proper constitution of the Eastwood persona as it has existed in this context and is understood by its devotees in the audience. It also includes some features specifically recalling earlier Eastwood westerns and thus turns itself into a commentary on those films and an act of visible reflexivity. Seen in this way, it is the most disturbing of all Eastwood's films in the trouble it creates for those who would read the heroic activity of the genre as a whole or the Eastwood persona specifically in an ideologically or morally comfortable way.

The film begins in the realm of literary narrative, as a rolling title describes the marriage of a young woman to William

Munny, a "known thief and murderer, a man of notoriously vicious and intemperate disposition," and her subsequent death from smallpox. The widower has two children and raises pigs for a living. As *The Outlaw Josey Wales* traced Eastwood's career from peace-loving sodbuster to man of violence and back to peaceful community leader, so *Unforgiven* traces a similar trajectory—but in an inverted and ironic way. In the time prior to the narrative, Munny was a terrible and arbitrary killer. Then he was tamed and called to sobriety and virtue as a husband, father, and home-steader. Then, a widower and frustrated hog-farmer, he consciously decides to return to violence for one occasion, as a mercenary, to provide a more secure base for his own enterprise and his chil-dren's well-being. Then he undergoes a further metamorphosis from a hired assassin to a maddened figure of elemental demonic destruction. And at last—after the end of the narrative—he returns to the role of ordinary citizen: the final title tells us he is said to have moved to San Francisco and prospered in the dry-goods trade. The pattern of inversion is even clearer if we compare *Unforgiven* to *Bronco Billy*. In that film, Billy consciously moves from his prosaic life as a New Jersey shoe salesman into the tran-scendental realm he has always aspired to by becoming a western hero; William Munny reveals the transcendental realm of western heroism to be a place of horror and escapes from it to find a distinctly unheroic apotheosis in becoming, as it were, a shoe salesman.

The Eastwood persona similarly undergoes a transformation. At first, and for a considerable time, Munny is depicted in anti-heroic terms. Stumbling face-first into the mud trying to catch disease-ridden pigs, unable to hit anything with his pistol at target practice, incapable of mounting or riding his horse without a struggle or a fall, complaining of missing his bed as he tries to sleep under the stars, later shaken with ague and fever, looking irresolute and submitting almost without a struggle to the brutal beating administered by the town sheriff, Little Bill Daggett (Gene Hackman)—through most of the film, Munny is the antithesis of the contemptuous master of homicidal violence of Eastwood's prime persona. Particularly telling is his failure to control the two most important tokens of individual power in the western, his gun and his horse. But we also understand that however short the Eastwood protagonist may fall initially or inci-dentally from his most powerful archetype, in the end he will turn and become himself. One can almost feel audiences waiting for this moment to arrive in *Unforgiven*. And it finally does come, as Munny, propelled into drunken ferocity by the death of his friend Ned Logan (Morgan Freeman), unleashes his towering anger on a saloon full of cowboys. The scene is heavily inflected visually through its staging in murky torchlit darkness: in the midst of a thunderstorm, with the menacing figure of Eastwood often merely a frightening silhouette, his face reduced to a pool of shadow in which is visible only a murderous glint in the eye. Here he once more becomes the figure of superhuman death-dealing vengeance, as in *High Plains Drifter* and again in *Pale Rider*. The dark and boiling landscape, the portents in the heavens, add a supernal quality to the persona's intervention, mark it as above ordinary experience and comprehension. But now the action is more unambiguously hellish and demonic than ever before. Little Bill's agonized last words, before Munny executes him with a shotgun blast directly to the face, are "I'll see you in hell, William Munny"; Munny signifies his agreement. He is avenging the death of his friend—a good man—and also perhaps punishing a system which allows violence against women. But that sense of righting a wrong and restoring a "correct" hierarchy, so important to the achievement of moral balance and the validation of individual power in both the general sphere of the action hero and in the western in particular, is absent in this scene of carnage. The heroic Eastwood persona's virtually contractual requirement to exact a vengeance which also has the alibi of justice is mimed in *Unforgiven*—but in such a way as to expose it as an act of regurgitative bloodlust born out of despair and not the godlike anger of a transcendental personage acting from some realm beyond normal humanity.

Eastwood's presence in the film thus departs from his archetypal persona in two separate ways: first, through its status as an antitype in the person of the "good" Munny; and second, as an exaggeration and specifically a monstrofication in the "bad" Munny. In her overview of the western in film and literature, Jane Tompkins has argued that cowboy heroes take silence and action as absolute goods, and that they and the genre are at war with women's words and especially an historically female articulation of inner feeling.[1] The taciturnity of the western hero, his repressive unwillingness to admit to an inner emotional life which might include anything "soft," his attempt (as Tompkins puts it) to turn into something as hard and eternal as the land-scape itself, his crystallization into a potent *agent*—these features are more starkly visible in the Eastwood persona than in any previous important western hero. Indeed, it might be argued that the persona's special quality of enclosedness and unknowability, his air of being almost constituted through superhuman violent action or the ever-present anticipation of such action, is a final distillation of these pervasive characteristics of the western protagonist.[2] In its presentation of the dual William Munny, *Unforgiven* makes a significant commentary both on the western's traditional war of men's silence and women's words and on Eastwood's own history as a silent hero. It does this by widening the gap between the two aspects of the protagonist to such an extent that they become virtual caricatures of traditionally anti-thetical character types, and certainly caricatured inversions of each other. (Exaggeration of persona traits or anti-traits to the point of caricature has of course been a consistent tool of self-consciousness throughout Eastwood's career as a filmmaker— *High Plains Drifter*, *The Gauntlet*, *Bronco Billy*, *Sudden Impact* and *Pale Rider* furnishing the clearest examples.) The good Munny is not merely an example of the "civilized" frontier male (non-violent agrarian *paterfamilias*) but is marked as a specifically and particularly feminized one. He piously repeats the temperance-and-decency creed of his dead wife as a series of homiletic principles learned by rote and constantly refers to her interven-tion in his life as a powerfully transforming moment. He is an uxorious widower, in fact. His difference from the Eastwood of the earlier westerns is sometimes so extreme as to be comic, although the character's moral regeneration—or rather its inven-tion from scratch—is also genuine.

But if the good Munny represents an occasionally amusing effacement of the persona's familiar characteristics, the bad Munny is formed rather by an *exaggeration* of those same traits of powerful violence which are absent in the pig-farmer. The figure being exaggerated here is, of course, the Man With No Name, and even more exactly the Eastwood transcendent-killer of *High Plains Drifter* and *Pale Rider*. The sense that both of the latter characters are returned from the dead is now paraphrased in the bad Munny's resurrection from a long period of human subjec-tivity represented by the good Munny. This figure of transcendent violence is produced in *Unforgiven* through a process that is just as portentous and awe-inspiring as it is in the two previous films, but now represented in terms of psychic dysfunction and ugly violence rather than of a mysterious higher power. *High Plains Drifter*'s project of personal vengeance against a whole community is repeated in *Unforgiven*—even down to the torchlit setting and the fact that the revenge is enacted on behalf of a victim whipped to death. The earlier film's elevation of the Eastwood character literally to a supernatural plane, and his vengeance to a kind of Old Testament judgement day, serves to underline the omnipotent violence of the Eastwood persona and ground any discomfort attaching to his violence in a principle of divine justice, albeit of the most vengeful variety. Something similar happens in *Pale Rider*, where the Preacher again appears to be returning from the dead and is specifically identified as Death riding on a pale horse, with Hell following after him. This figure then proceeds to ground his violent acts, disconnectedly, both in an acting-out of personal vengeance and in defending the weak virtuous community.

One might say that in *Unforgiven* these two sides of the Preacher's character have been reified, in deconstructed form, into the two sides of William Munny. Where the Preacher saves the good community from predators, the good Munny weakly covers his mercenary project in the transparent veil of a response to the victimization of women. Meanwhile, in contrast to the demonic power displayed by the Preacher (and the protagonist of *High Plains Drifter*), the practice and spectacle of the bad Munny's violence is demystified. Similarly, the motive to repay in kind violence inflicted upon him by the villains—a feature of both *High Plains Drifter* and *Pale Rider*—becomes in *Unforgiven* a terrible desire to revenge a friend whose death can most fitly be traced to Munny's own initiative in involving the friend in the first place and to the difference between Munny's willingness and Ned's unwillingness to kill. Munny's anger, in other words, is more truly directed at himself than at his victims. Deprived of cloudy supernatural origins and bearing a history of truly monstrous crimes, Munny can no longer be interpreted as perhaps good, perhaps bad—or an impenetrable combination of the two. Here, the implications and consequences of the persona's murderous violence are troubling in a way that is never seen in the earlier films. As for masculine taciturnity, the earlier Eastwood western heroes, from Leone to *Pale*

Rider, possess this quality in abundance: when Eastwood speaks — briefly — it is harsh, hoarse, and highly compressed. But in *Unforgiven*, words have retreated even further, into a lost unfathomable pit of pre-verbal, pre-conceptual experience. Munny is quizzed several times about his earlier deeds of violence, and his answer is typically, "I don't remember, mostly I was drunk." This is disconcerting, for however mysterious the acts of the persona must necessarily appear to the rest of us, it is essential that the hero himself have some knowledge of them. Here the persona's silence does not signify hidden depths or (as Tompkins has it) a desire to be solid, complete, and safe from change,[3] but only a swirling unconscious abyss of murderous compulsions, in which the subject is seized and controlled as much as the victims and in which silence proceeds from incomprehension and oblivion rather than any transcendence of the affective world. This is certainly auto-critique.

The doubling or splitting of the protagonist into human/ superhuman, antiheroic/heroic, or good/bad facets has, then, the effect of laying the Eastwood persona open to a deconstruction which is at once anti-mythic and — despite the elements of caricature — humanizing. Endowing the transcendent-destructive hero with a history and a personality, a mind and a conscience, making him a creature who not only acts omnipotently but feels and is acted upon, puts large cracks into the previously rock-like, monolithic imperviousness of the Eastwood western persona.[4] Munny, in his doubled state, is both unfeeling ego-projection and feeling subject. The inferno of violence he is capable of bringing into the world is ugly and abhorrent, without redeeming qualities. In a handful of scattered scenes, he confides to Ned that he is haunted by the horror of his earlier deeds; these memories are surreally imprinted in his mind as the details of a series of terrible atrocities — atrocities he committed himself. In the delirium brought on by the fever and his beating, he cries aloud that he is afraid of dying and that he saw in a dream the face of his beloved wife covered with worms. This quality of human anguish is never even suggested in *High Plains Drifter* or *Pale Rider*, or any of Eastwood's other transcendental-heroic films. Images such as those tormenting Munny will not be purged from his mind by any feat of heroic action; indeed, the opposite is the case as he finds himself re-performing just those deeds that have created this agony. Whatever satisfaction is to be gained in killing Little Bill, or in automatically performing an act of terrible violence in response to personal pain, has been demonstrated to be ultimately useless and self-destructive even while that revenge is enacted. The emotional rewards of vengeance—for the protagonist and above all for the viewer—have never been more clearly indicated as ugly and horrifying, at least not within the vengeance-filled world of Eastwood's films.

But even before the frightening concluding scenes of the film, this Eastwood character has been morally compromised. This is not just a matter of Munny's earlier inhumanness, that earlier devilish self which we have never seen, which he himself cannot even remember and whose difference from his present self he and Ned keep superstitiously asserting. It is perhaps even more crucially a matter of what can only be described as the criminality of the reformed Munny: the criminality, that is, of engaging in assassination for hire. We may recall that a number of Eastwood's earliest movie western protagonists were mercenary killers and bounty hunters, and that in those roles the occupation did not constitute a moral difficulty for viewers. The Leone universe was morally arid, and cynical self-interest was as high a value as any available. But in *Unforgiven*, the essential moral structure of the classical western is once more present. Like so many westerns before it, the film debates the values of community versus individual, justified versus unjustified violence, and the place of heroic transcendence in a frontier environment balanced between institutional rigidity and anti-social anarchy. In presenting these terms in all their potential contradictoriness, it interrogates the genre as a whole, but it does so from within—it is not an anti-western. The moral and ideological status of Munny's career, past and present, is a question of real importance, not a post-ethical dead end or nihilistic gesture of style as in Leone's and other truly "decadent" westerns (including perhaps *High Plains Drifter*). Munny's polarization between the extremes of prosaic-virtuous pig-farmer and family man and poetic-satanic legendary killer is a demonstration, stylized but genuine, of just this question of moral status. But perhaps the greatest difficulty is created by the decision of the good Munny to undertake, in a kind of rational Lockean fashion, a single considered expedition into the murderous territory of the bad Munny—a territory that has belongs exclusively to the drunken, irrational savagery of the damned soul.

This is, in fact, to dabble in the practice of satanic evil for sound commercial reasons—an insupportable contradiction. And the contradiction is brought home once the killing starts, beginning indelibly with the murder of the young cowboy Davey by a botched long-range rifle shot. No one can deny the intense moral discomfort created by this scene. It is a touchstone of the film's desire to create "difficulty" that the painfulness and moral compromise of Munny's actions are not in any way flinched from or covered over. The rationale that this murder is punishment for the attack on the prostitute is feeble, and is understood to be feeble. Ned Logan, the designated marksman, refuses to shoot the cowboy, and this is presented as the decent and human thing to do. Later, the would-be desperado the Schofield Kid (Jaimz Woolvett), after shooting the second cowboy in an outhouse, renounces violence and declares his desire for a peaceful, unheroic life; this too is presented sympathetically. Only William Munny will cool-headedly go ahead with the shooting of Davey; only he can accept the moral burden of the killing expedition even in the face of its ugly consequences. He is going to kill two strangers strictly for money. Of course the money is to be devoted to his children, to providing a solid material basis for his attempts to preserve the values of family and honest toil. But is this sufficient reason for premeditated murder? No, clearly no. In this way, even the good Munny is presented as a criminal. This criminality remains a difficulty right through to the end of the film, and in burying it together with his horrifying reversion to evil under a future of prosperous respectability, the rather smug concluding title only emphasizes the scandal of his actions. Like the Martin Landau character in Woody Allen's *Crimes and Misdemeanors*, William Munny simply gets away with murder.

That he should get away with killing while Ned dies horribly for *not* killing creates the moral abyss into which Munny plunges in forsaking his "good" self and embracing again his "bad" one. Here lies an additional perspective on the film's cryptic title. Of course, the title's primary significance refers to that Old Testament ethic which demands punishment instead of forgiveness: the prostitutes demand punishment of Thirsty and Davey, the law itself in the form of Little Bill demands punishment (and punishes Ned), and of course, ultimately, Munny demands punishment for the death of Ned. Each of these punishments is seriously flawed from the perspective of fitness or balance, and all fail to embody the ideal of "justice," which is in each instance distorted and tainted by revenge. Forswearing vengeance, meeting evil with good, a Christian perspective such as that propounded by Munny's wife Claudia, is pushed aside in this rubric—and the consequences presented by the film are dreadful.

One might go further, however. In attempting Munny's regeneration, in pulling him out of the maelstrom of nihilistic compulsive violence and drunken self-obliteration into a world of principle and language and family and human self-recognition, Claudia *forgives* him. The act of forgiveness produces the (feminine) redemptive result of self-forgiveness. In addressing at last the buried consciousness of horror and guilt, the fiery cycle of repression and violence whose first victim is the perpetrator is broken, and the functional person William Munny (the "good") is dredged up into view. Once established in the social world of human relationships, gainful occupation, the code of civility and "decency," Munny is happier than before. Even after the death of his wife, and despite the rather naïve and rudimentary nature of the precepts upon which he leans, he continues forthrightly in the same path. The process that pushes him back off that path begins with a condition of economic hardship and the unfulfilling nature of his labour. Pig-farming is dirty, frustrating, humiliating, and profitless. The temptation to move into another form of paid work—killing for hire—is very strong, when that work suffers none of the drawbacks just enumerated. In drawing Ned Logan into the business, Munny wishes not only to provide himself with a dependable co-worker but to give himself a degree of orientation in this strange endeavour. Ned, like Munny (and like the Eastwood persona too), is a former hellraiser, now a respectable freeholding family man.[5] As the film proceeds, Ned develops into Munny's anchor to the world, his reassurance that he has forsaken the old ways (which Ned also witnessed), and his guarantee that his actions have some foothold in a worthwhile life-pattern, in decency and fellow-feeling. But Munny makes the mistake first of returning to killing (however different his motives this time) and second of pulling Ned with him. When this happens, the result is different from what was anticipated (this too is morally instructive). It is Ned who is punished for the transgression, a transgression he did not truly commit; Munny does everything and goes free, and gets paid to boot. It is not just that any notion of a higher system of justice and moral equilibrium is derisorily contradicted by this development. The death of Ned is also Munny's personal loss of his "good" self, his loss of Claudia's forgiveness and his own self-forgiveness. When he walks into Greely's to kill Skinny and Little Bill, he is a creature who has lost salvation, a damned soul, "unforgiven."

Previously I said that *Unforgiven* was not an anti-western. It might be described instead as a peculiar late flowering of the kind of complex western that arose as the famous "moral clarity" of the genre began to be cast into doubt and the entire system to be undermined. I am thinking here of such films of the 1950s and '60s as John Ford's *The Searchers* (1956) and *The Man Who Shot Liberty Valance* (1962), of Anthony Mann's westerns of the same period—especially *Bend of the River* (1952), *The Naked Spur* (1953), and *Man of the West* (1958)—or of the early Sam Peckinpah film *Ride the High Country* (1962). These films, among many others, formed a final stage in the development of the classical western, a last historical outpost of the antinomic moral and social dualities that organized the genre[6] before the onset of complete alienation, pastiche, and open deconstruction as practised by the spaghetti westerns and Hollywood anti-classical post-westerns like *Butch Cassidy and the Sundance Kid* (1969), *Little Big Man* (1970), and *McCabe and Mrs Miller* (1971). Eastwood's own westerns have, in a way, progressed *back* from the Leone anti-western abyss (most clearly represented in *High Plains Drifter*) and towards some reconstitution of the terms of the classical western. *Josey Wales* in effect reinvents the positive cowboy hero out of the ashes of the criminal which that figure had virtually become by the 1970s, while *Pale Rider*'s gestures towards the canonical western *Shane* are unmistakable, if not always coherent, and signal a wish to draw upon the moral resonance of the classical genre. Then *Unforgiven* unfolds a systematic restaging, and reproblematizing, of archetypal western issues and narrative and character configurations, with the extra inclusion of the Eastwood persona itself. It is definitely a very late, if not "decadent," arrival on the western stage, indicative of boundary-destroying forces of violence and cynicism that threaten the stability and even the existence of the genre. A broad pattern of generic social context and narrative and character alignments is very much to the fore in the film, so that, more than in any previous Eastwood film (and to an extent rare in any western of the past twenty-five years), *Unforgiven* represents an extended, self-conscious intervention into and commentary upon the history of the genre. The presence, to greater or lesser degree, of such topics as agrarian economy, capitalist enterprise and commodity ownership, law and law enforcement and their relation to moral order in the world, the place and value of women in a "man's" environment, and of course the nature and constitution of heroism on the frontier, mark the film as a deliberately large and systematic contribution to the western genre.

Let us turn our attention, then, to the social environment in which Munny acts. No justification is offered for his earlier atrocities; none is possible. His subsequent crimes, however, both the mercenary and the passionate, occur within a context of mores and institutions, not legend. The cause of the immediate action is the assault by two cowboys upon Delilah (Anna Thompson), a prostitute working in a brothel run by the saloon-keeper Skinny Dubois in the town of Big Whiskey, Wyoming. A cowboy named Thirsty Thurston cuts up the face of the young and inexperienced Delilah for giggling at the small size of his penis; his younger friend Davey holds her while the attack takes place. The sheriff Little Bill first proposes to settle accounts by bullwhipping the perpetrators. Skinny objects that this will do nothing to compensate him for his damaged property: Delilah is now permanently scarred and will have trouble attracting customers; Skinny's investment of capital will be lost. Little Bill sees the justice of this argument and imposes a fine instead of corporal punishment: in the spring Skinny will get five ponies from Thirsty, two from Davey. The senior and most vocal of the brothel women, Strawberry Alice (Frances Fisher), is angry about this arrangement. Delilah is cut up, Skinny receives horses in compensation, but there is no justice for Delilah. Little Bill defends his decision by saying that the cowboys were just carried away—they are not "given to wickedness in a general way." "You mean like whores?" Alice asks bitterly.

It is clear that Alice is angry not merely on behalf of Delilah but also because this crime exemplifies the abject status of all the prostitutes, including herself, who are treated as commodities pure and simple, and are not defended in their own right as citizens by the law. The truth of her arguments is plain to the viewer. These women have a legal status greatly inferior to that of men such as Skinny; they are disposed of by the law as property; and the law stands revealed as a guarantor of (male) property rights rather than of moral justice for all citizens. At this moment, the film actually becomes virtually Marxist and feminist. Alice's response is to organize a property-driven reparation, or rather revenge, on behalf of the women, to compensate for the law's unwillingness to provide one. A bounty of $1000, collected from the women's savings, is put upon the heads of the two cowboys. News of the contract is spread through the institutional structure of the brothel itself, as the women quietly convey it to their customers. In a strategy of considerable ironic equity, the material incentives of property (i.e., money) are thus employed to invert the actions of the materialist system of law.

But despite its satisfying element of "justice," Alice's plan is also morally flawed. If ponies or a bullwhipping are insufficient counterbalance for the lasting injury to Delilah, then summary death for the perpetrators swings the balance too far the other way. Of course, the symbolic dimension of the crime and its unsatisfactory punishment, the suffering and subjection of all the women and their lack of redress before the law, need to be considered. In this light, the contract is nothing less than a political act—a terrorist symbolic protest against oppression. On the other hand, the whole pretext for the operation is to compensate for a specific crime and the suffering of a specific victim. Neither Delilah's scars nor her memory of violence will disappear, however, nor will her condition of powerlessness improve. She herself is conspicuously quiet when voices are raised for vengeance on her behalf, and the film gives no indication that she takes any satisfaction from the project—if anything, it suggests the reverse. The cowboys, too, present complexities. Although Thirsty's actions were ugly and unpardonable, Davey scarcely knew what he was doing and is certainly less guilty (their respective physical iconography confirms this distinction: Thirsty is ugly and mean-looking, Davey is sweet and innocent-looking). Moreover, Davey later makes a gesture of repentance and reconciliation when he brings an especially fine extra pony, not for Skinny but for Delilah. Alice leads the prostitutes in a mud-throwing rejection of this offer, again without consulting Delilah. Then, of course, it is Davey who suffers the most agonizing death, gutshot by Munny at long distance. The two purest victims of the film, Delilah and Davey, are exactly those who are not consulted or paid attention to: they are merely props in a movement of larger forces.

The attempt to balance the first injustice clearly results in a second one. (The same configuration is repeated when, in attempting to right *this* injustice—the murders of Davey and Thirsty—Little Bill whips Ned to death. The wrong person dies at the hands of "justice," the "eye for an eye" system shown to be all too fallible. This liberal attitude is the same as that which argues for Claudia's feminine Christian forgiveness and against the bad Munny's masculine Old Testament vengefulness, as seen in the final scenes.) Yet Alice's initial arguments are never answered; the institutional prejudices of the law remain. Alice's remedy, which is to punish violent aggression with even more violent counter-aggression and not stop to make nice distinctions or worry about the rights of the perpetrators, strikingly resembles the rationale employed by so many Eastwood protagonists in earlier films. Many of these earlier Eastwood films even foreground the same initial crime: a brutal male attack on a woman in the sexual arena. But when the Eastwood persona of *Unforgiven* comes nominally to the rescue of a woman with an act of revenging violence, the action has been qualified and undermined beyond recognition.

There is another discourse of law and power in the film, namely that which revolves around Little Bill Daggett. This character is advanced across the template of a generic archetype in a fashion parallel to that of the Eastwood persona. But whereas William Munny is a twisted avatar of the lone hero who comes from outside the community to rescue it from bullying force, Little Bill more recognizably represents the "duly constituted authority" whose mission is to render the community safe from *arbitrary* authority, that is, the individual, self-interested exercise of violence in an as-yet-unstable frontier society. *Unforgiven* complicates and enriches its already intricate balance of thematic elements by making Little Bill a figure just as contradictory, and virtually as charismatic, as the Eastwood persona himself. As we have seen, Little Bill and the law he stands for are morally compromised in the film by their commitment to the clearly marked excesses of patriarchal capitalism. The alignment of Little Bill with the employer/proprietor Skinny and against the employee/chattel Alice reveals not the corruption of Little Bill but an underlying problem in the constitution of the community—and not merely the old charge of greedy materialism traditionally levelled by those westerns which criticize the community for engaging in commerce rather than settlement. Greedy materialism it is, and of a noxious oppressive kind; but it is also depicted as perfectly in keeping with the regular practice of capitalist values and the law which must protect them. The film does not suggest for a moment that capitalist practice as such is evil and ought to be abolished, nor does it advocate a return to values associated with nature, the wilderness, or the free individual, as most westerns which condemn the materialism of the community do. It merely reveals an ethical fissure in a community that operates according to laws of property and exchange, claims to be constituted justly, and yet discriminates against certain classes of citizens (in this case, women). That the community's excluded class should be female is another of the film's meaningful complications, for in the western, women have traditionally served to embody the community's stability, its collectivity of mutual support and nurture, and some of its most crucial nascent institutions such as schools, churches, and families. And that these women should turn for redress to hired guns is yet another twist, when women in the western are famous for denouncing guns and killing. Of course, these women are prostitutes, and thus clearly related to the female sub-species of individualist-oriented "dance-hall girls" rather than to the dominant species of communitarian schoolmarms and pioneer wives and mothers; but their collective solidarity and concern for rights reconnects them to the predominant community-directed type.[7]

In this context, Little Bill has an "impossible" task: to enforce the laws of the community in an ideologically unconflicted way when the construction of the community is such as to reveal the irremediable conflicts in ideology. This impossibility is revealed in perhaps the film's most adroit metaphor—the sheriff's own house, which he is building himself. This edifice is its owner's pride and joy, and yet its construction is comically inept, all crooked angles and leaky surfaces.[8] The house is clearly a symbol of community values and the community project, and the fact that Bill is proudly building it himself signifies his leadership in the undertaking and his idealistic commitment to it. But the project and the leadership are both defective, full of holes. As Skinny comes to tell him of the prostitutes' contract, Bill bangs his thumb with a hammer; the torrential downpour that accom-

panies the arrival of Munny, Ned, and the Kid in town leaks in
buckets through Bill's roof. Bill is not good at building. What he
is good at is violence. The beatings he administers first to
English Bob (Richard Harris), then to Munny, and finally, fatally,
to Ned Logan, are all attempts to enforce the law of the community. But they are excessive; the violence is accompanied by too
much sadistic zest. Moreover, they do not have a sound basis of
justification: the law in whose name they are carried out is not
what it is supposed to be. These brutal examples of law enforcement resemble too much the offences they are supposed to
prevent, just as the judgement that punishes the two cowboys in
commodity terms merely reaffirms Delilah's commodity status.

This system of law is linked to another configuration of
topics in the film: those of masculine violence as such and the
range of mythicizing discourses about that violence, together
with their means of formation and distribution. The character
who focusses this set of topics is travelling writer W.W.
Beauchamp (Saul Rubinek), an Eastern author of penny dread-
fuls glorifying the violent legends of the Old West. He arrives as
the Boswell of English Bob, then moves along to become the
chronicler of Little Bill when the sheriff proves to be the
stronger "hero," and in the end is making inquiries of the
strongest of all, William Munny, after the slaughter in the
saloon. His iconic features—bowler hat, waistcoat, spectacles
and sidewhiskers—signify civilization and education, as does his
nervous bumbling when faced with any indication that his
subject might actually involve him directly rather than
remaining as passive narrative material (in one scene he even
wets himself in fear). Beauchamp is fascinated with murderous
violence and its structuring codes in a manner disguised as
scholarly but suggesting rather a passionate inner compulsion:
in fact, he is riveted upon the display of power with the thirst of
a fascist acolyte. This characterization may replicate popular
culture's scorn for book learning and intellectuals, particularly
when juxtaposed with men of action, and here Beauchamp not
only embodies all the usual sins of his kind but adds the extra
one of a sneaking desire to feast upon the charismatic acts of
violence performed by these authentic men without incurring
any of the attendant danger. But our contempt as viewers for
this character ought not to be too gleeful, for Beauchamp,
however ignominious he may appear, acts as the representative

agent of the western as a narrative project, *Unforgiven* itself as a story framed by a teller, and those in the audience who consume the tale with avidity. When Beauchamp, fuelled by an appetite for scenes of bloodletting and displays of violent mastery, narrativizes the actual events of western history for the pleasure of his readers, he is an emblem of the activity of the western genre. And more particularly when he will tell the story of Munny's homicidal rampage in Greely's Saloon, he will be an emblem of the very film we are watching. For how is our appetite for the spectacle of Eastwood killing people different from Beauchamp's appetite and that of his readers? And how is any film which mythicizes or pleasingly distorts the exercise of violence different from Beauchamp's stories? In plain terms, the western is criticized as a distortion of history and experience, and its consumption is equated with the corrupt craving of viewers for the spectacle of triumphalist power and violence. And no westerns have depended more on this craving than Eastwood's.

This is the result, but the articulation of the question is complex and meticulous. Beauchamp's journey from English Bob to Little Bill involves the mapping of an entire sub-discourse. The imperial blowhard English Bob, who gives himself civilized airs, is fully prepared to encourage Beauchamp in the idealist clichés of melodrama which he brings from the literary world of the cities. In these terms, Bob becomes "the Duke of Death" and engages in six-gun duels with villains to preserve the honour of women. This style of narrative is, like the power of English Bob himself, destroyed by Little Bill. At first amiably and then with a certain fatuous enthusiasm, Bill takes it upon himself to deflate "the Duck of Death" and all the assumptions that go with him. The violent altercations of the frontier have nothing to do with honour and striking picturesque attitudes; they have nothing to do even with being quick on the draw or a dead shot. Bill's revisionist account of the night English Bob shot Two-Gun Corcoran in the Bluebottle Saloon is an extended debunking of idealist attitudes. It depicts a world of falling-down drunkenness, guns going off by accident or misfiring, and an absolute disregard on all sides for principles of fair play. Bill goes on to offer his own systemic analysis: the most important quality in a gunfight is cool-headedness, the absence of disabling fear; a simple innate quality of character—"sand" or "grit"—replaces the elaborately acquired rituals of the showdown. Life is a shambles of accident and ugliness rather than an embodiment of the orderliness of idealist narrative. This perspective is demythicizing, a substitution of *Realpolitik* for ideology. It is true that Bill then wishes to attach a certain moral schema to this quality, which he himself possesses to a high degree. The average miscreant whom he pulverizes is described as lacking in backbone and conviction; a handy example is provided by the prevaricating, fever-wracked William Munny, whom Bill kicks all around Greely's Saloon while orating to Beauchamp about his victim's deficiencies of character. And of course, Little Bill is a sheriff—a professional with a nominally prosocial job to do.

In the context of the genre, and to employ Robert Warshow's terms (140), the movement from English Bob's discourse to Little Bill's pushes the western from the sphere of the honourable hero who must shoot only under certain stringent conditions, towards the western's antitype, the gangster film, presided over by a protagonist whose distinction resides merely in his *willingness* to shoot, a quality of daring. It also reproduces a movement from the naïve classical movie western to a late stage of the genre's evolution in which more problematic and antiheroic qualities assume predominance. In *Unforgiven,* that stage gives way to a further evolution yet: namely to the hellish and mindless all-consuming force of destruction embodied in the person of William Munny, a force which Little Bill is quite unable to comprehend. Indeed, no one can comprehend it, not even Munny himself. Beauchamp does not comprehend it either, but he recognizes it instantly as an escalation in the scale and intensity of violence, and he is magnetically drawn to it. Munny represents a more potent concentration of force than Little Bill; Eastwood trumps all predecessors in his command of the sources of violence and its dispensation. Here in fact we have a complete recapitulation of the development of the western as a genre, up to and including the present film. Beauchamp's narrative subject progresses from naïve through decadent and into a final stage of distilled, meaningless violence. These stages correspond respectively to the early and classical western; to the later western in both its "complex" Hollywood and "decadent" Italian and post-Italian forms; and finally to Eastwood's own quasi-demonic westerns, where the protagonist's power of violence exceeds any kind of explanation. The genre's history is thus presented as an ever-growing appetite for pure violence increas-

ingly detached from any moral context or justification. Its logical
end lies in the Eastwood persona as a figure of occult, uncontrol-
lable violence—in an unexamined way the Eastwood of *High
Plains Drifter* or *Pale Rider*, and in a now fully conscious and sick-
ened way, the bad William Munny. The Eastwood persona's killing
spree in the saloon, his barefaced executions of Skinny, Little Bill,
and the wounded deputies—and also his earlier legendary deeds
of dynamiting trains full of women and children, blowing some
poor man's teeth out the back of his neck, and so on—are
presented as insupportably awful. They remain charismatic for
the viewer, as Beauchamp's attitude demonstrates, but they are
insupportable. Again, the terms in which the final scene recapitu-
lates the scenes of vengeful devastation in *High Plains Drifter* and
Pale Rider (torchlight and darkness, silhouettes, Eastwood's
basilisk stare of death) constitute a powerful critique of the principle of violence in Eastwood's work. And of course *Unforgiven*
repeatedly lays bare its *own* contradictions.

The violent actions of the Eastwood persona, then, are framed
and commented upon through their juxtaposition with
Beauchamp's project of narrativization. But they are also illuminated from another angle, namely the perspective provided by
the Schofield Kid. The nature of the transcendental western hero
is one of Beauchamp's subjects: English Bob, Little Bill and
Munny represent its three evolutionary stages. The Schofield
Kid, too, has a preconception of heroic action, and equally for
him it takes place within the arena of violence. But the Kid's
homicidal models are unburdened with either the moral code of
English Bob's discourse of violence or the institutional justification
of Little Bill's. The Kid is impressed by the legend of William
Munny, whom the Kid understands to be a "meaner-than-hell
cold-blooded damn killer" and "the meanest god-damned son of a
bitch alive." In this heroic model, the brutal act of killing successfully constitutes the appeal; the absence of moral or legal
rationalizations is an additional enticement rather than a handicap. The Kid, as his name implies, is very young, and his a
attitude is seen at once to be immature. The very naïveté of the
Kid's attraction to the purest and least-encumbered manifestation of violence seems to go right to the heart of the matter,
however, in its rejection of any form of disguise or adulteration of
instinctive appetite. In this, he simply mirrors the naked, unillu-
sioned, or "decadent" tastes of late- or post-western viewers. But

just as Little Bill's compromised status is exemplified in his house, so the ignorance of the Kid's views is demonstrated in the metaphor of his comic shortsightedness. He is literally blind to what the world is really like. His ambition to be a killer exists in a vacuum of knowledge. When he finally experiences killing closely enough to see it—that is, when he shoots Thirsty at point-blank range in the outhouse—all glamour vanishes and he is properly appalled. Munny's earlier shooting of Davey, although it happens at too great a range for the Kid to see it, arguably acts as just this kind of eye-opener for the viewer. But the Munny who shoots Davey is not yet the legendary killer. That character—the transcendental hero—has yet to be presented to us, and his final arrival in the film is postponed until the viewer is properly equipped to interpret him. As a matter of fact, the bad Munny is exactly as the Kid has described him; but the actual presence of that character is far more troubling than his legend consumed imaginatively at a distance. Reading all this in a reflexive context, we may see that the Kid's gushing admiration for the idea of killing is the equivalent of the viewer's admiration for the Eastwood persona as killer. Eastwood is a hero to at least a certain class of viewers merely by reason of his violent potency, not at all by virtue of any moral or prosocial alibis which might attach to his persona. At the end of *Unforgiven*, Eastwood once again provides viewers with the spectacle of homicidal mastery: he is a "meaner-than-hell cold-blooded damn killer." And once again the spectacle has the power to thrill the viewer. Of course, it is only a representation of killing, not real killing. But the viewer who will enjoy the spectacle without second thoughts, or without an accompanying twinge of horror in the knowledge of everything the film has shown as accompanying this kind of action, is another naïve Schofield Kid. The film critiques the charisma of pure violence just as it critiques the attractions of violence masquerading as honour or justice.

Thus *Unforgiven* deconstructs the Eastwood persona and the Eastwood fan. But it does so in the curious two-handed way that is characteristic of Eastwood films. Munny is shown striding into the saloon, uttering the hoarse Eastwood warnings and brutal gnomic pronouncements[9] with which we are all familiar, killing five men, and riding out of town amidst hellfire, rain, and thunderbolts. His action has been elaborately qualified well before its enactment: in the haunted memories of earlier violence Munny has expressed to Ned by the foreshadowing light of their campfires, in the anguish of his dream of the angel of death and his desperate desire that his children never know of his deeds, and in the abyss of drink-sodden oblivion in which the crimes were committed and sealed off from conscious knowledge. But the film does not make the character pay with his life, or the lives of his children, or even with the failure of his mission of revenge. Such outcomes would counter the violence even more strongly, would completely cancel any pleasure in the spectacle for the viewer. The last contradiction of *Unforgiven* is that it too is an example of what it is questioning. Even the most deconstructive Eastwood film (and *Unforgiven* probably is that) retains what is deconstructed: the transcendental-heroic Eastwood persona. The films do not supplant a heroic discourse with an anti-heroic one. Rather they present both contradictory discourses side by side. They problematize and do not resolve.

Unforgiven asks us to look at the Eastwood persona in a new way—and not just the persona of this film, but that of all the others in which it is a conduit for violence. In his lethal Eastwood-whisper during the final scene, Munny acknowledges himself as "killer of women and children": "I guess I've killed just about everything that walked or crawled at one time or another." When Beauchamp asks him—in a piece of dialogue that virtually repeats a scene from *Josey Wales*—what his strategy was in shooting down his opponents, Munny denies any strategy whatever: "I was lucky in the order. But then I've always been lucky when it comes to killing folks." This blank statement is a chilling judgement on every Eastwood character who ever shot a man down.[10] Here there is no personal martyrdom to revenge upon evil men and a cowardly community, as in *High Plains Drifter*, and no crusade to lead on behalf of defenceless victims, as in *Pale Rider*. Nor is the protagonist untouchable and unknowable in his personal makeup, above the mere humanity of his surroundings, as in the Leone westerns and many of the subsequent films. In *Unforgiven*, the earlier persona's transcendental qualities, its ego-invincibility, and its mysterious unreadable positioning between justice and damnation are all resituated in an updated moral discourse where each remains recognizable but where all the most basic constitutive traits are brought into question. The film calls upon the viewing ego to unfree itself and recognize its place in the world; it calls upon the savage, oblivious instinct for violence to remember that it cannot inflict punishment without putting itself too into hell; it calls upon the ideological action of the genre itself to unmask itself and renounce its disavowal of contradiction. More than any other Eastwood film, *Unforgiven* represents a confession on the part of both the filmmaker and the persona of their doubts and uncertainty, of the spectre of bad conscience haunting them, and of their basis in a moral dilemma whose conflicting terms cannot be reconciled.

Eastwood the Father

4

As the process of his development as transcendental violent hero was unfolding, another form of heroic masculinity began to take shape in Eastwood's gallery. The first avatar of the heroic male was essentially solitary, and if he acted in a prosocial way it was incidentally, or because the community's interest happened to overlap with his own. Even Harry Callahan, nominally a public servant dedicated to safeguarding the community, seems motivated more by a will to power over his contemptible quarry than by than by any tenderness towards the commonwealth. Nevertheless this distant, transcendent figure began to discover the obligation to lead others, not merely to defend but to enable, shape, even create as a social group those with whom he came in contact. In this of course he merely replicated the movement of so many "reluctant" American heroes, who needed to be tempted and cajoled from their magnificent individual mastery into an alignment with the best interests of society: this is the path of the most archetypal heroes of American westerns, action narratives, and other dramas of heroic masculine agency.[1] The Eastwood hero, though, had farther to come than most, since his separation from ordinary humanity was so much more extreme, even to his constitution as an uncanny, quasi-supernatural being. Within the larger context of masculinity, one might say that Eastwood was discovering new answers to the question of what it was to be an ideal heroic male. If the first answer—the one embodied in the violent transcendent hero – was simply to have invincible power, the subsequent ones were more shaded and complex. Certainly they entailed some kind of a transfer to prosociality, but they also turned towards the potentially thorny issues of the hero's opening of his affections towards others, especially women and children, in family or family-like contexts. They involved a diminution of psychological distance and the correlative increase of human subjectivity; they introduced the idea of responsibility, and also the necessity of some kind of limitation and the possibility of some kind of failure.

This transformation can be described in another way as well. To move from transcendental socially alienated solitude to prosocial heroism was for Eastwood not only to replicate the conversion to communal values of the classical male individualist hero, it was actually to move from post- or anti-classicism back to classicism, to become a kind of classical hero. As we have seen, the last years of the 1970s brought a shift throughout the whole of Hollywood culture in this direction, through the means of a "light" postmodern neo-classicism as demonstrated in *Star Wars*. This particular option, however, was particularly difficult for Eastwood to follow. He did, in fact, move in a number of his projects of this period (*The Gauntlet, Every Which Way But Loose, Bronco Billy, Any Which Way You Can*—all 1977–80) towards humour, overt self-ironization, and even pastiche. But there was always something slightly lumbering about Eastwood's attempts to lighten up and become more proto-postmodernly supple and self-parodying, even if he was adroit enough in the best of these efforts to incorporate a charming self-consciousness about the *ur-*persona's mass and lack of maneuverability. Even at the 1980s and '90s height of comic-book postmodern hypermasculinity, Eastwood was never as good a Schwarzenegger as Schwarzenegger was and basically only dabbled in this area. It was other forces (Ronald Reagan, George Bush, standup comedians, the media—the culture itself) which created Eastwood most powerfully in this realm, as a parody of transcendent masculine power. Certainly the irony which helped to constitute the transcendent Eastwood persona ever since Leone was crucial to its success during its post-classical beginnings; and it proved equally valuable once the shift to neo-classicism/ postmodernism began. But in truth it was the *authority* of Eastwood's screen persona which allowed him to do something which very few male superstars of the period between the late 1970s and the 1990s could do: namely, become truly a classical protagonist in the heroic tradition of John Wayne. Eastwood began this transformation very self-consciously in *The*

Outlaw Josey Wales (1976), where his persona constructed a bridge between his Man With No Name transcendent separateness and a prosocial care for others which would ultimately place him in the role of a father or father-substitute.[2]

The male leader of a community becomes its metaphorical father, particularly in a patriarchal society, and Eastwood is rather pointedly this kind of metaphorical father in a number of his films (for example, *The Outlaw Josey Wales*, *Bronco Billy*, *Heartbreak Ridge*, and *White Hunter, Black Heart*). Here, the persona acts as patriarchal saviour to a group of individuals or a community or as masculine role-model for younger males, either in a professional capacity or within a more personal context. There is also a persistent and intriguing occurrence of a more literal fatherhood in his cinema. This can take the form of actual parenthood (*Tightrope*, *Unforgiven*, *Absolute Power*, *True Crime*), but with strange frequency, it is a kind of substitute fatherhood. In films like *Honkytonk Man*, *Pale Rider*, and *A Perfect World*, Eastwood acts explicitly as a substitute parent, standing in for an actual parent in some crucial way. Here again he can function as a role model or act in the place of a father who is inadequate or absent. Looking at all three of these forms together—metaphorical, literal, and substitute—we can see a cluster of themes and attitudes that has grown into something significant for Eastwood, both as persona and as filmmaker. This cluster has become perhaps the most important vehicle for Eastwood's "other" sphere—the sphere, that is, which contrasts with and counterbalances the mythic, transcendent, violent one.[3] The films stretch across a spectrum from attempts to bring the transcendent violent hero into closer contact with humanity and into a prosocial role (*Josey Wales*, *Pale Rider*, *Unforgiven*) to narratives in which the Eastwood persona moves all the way to non-transcendent humanity (*Honkytonk Man*, *A Perfect World*), with various points in between.

Another way to look at this phenomenon in Eastwood's cinema might be to classify this potentially humanizing and de-transcending father-relation as a subset of a larger category of all of the humanizing personal relations of the persona. This would extend the field to include not only paternal or quasi-parental relationships but also those of friendship and (even more important) romance. If I choose to concentrate on the "fatherly" varieties here, it is with the understanding that the larger super-category needs to be evoked at times. In *Heartbreak Ridge*, for example, the persona's problem of a history of failure is one that exists simultaneously in his heroic-violent soldier's guise (Korea and Vietnam) and in his "human" husbandly one (his broken marriage); his rehabilitation requires a redeeming victory in both fields. His domestic success is every bit as important as his "fatherly" success as a recruit-trainer, and in fact the two roles are seen as somehow related. This is even clearer in *Tightrope*, where the Dirty-Harry-descended cop hero is meaningfully conflated with a far more "human" protagonist—imperfect, vulnerable, needing help and correction—and the humanity is embodied in his relationship both with his children and with a woman. In *Unforgiven*, the persona's "human" self is again produced both by his status as a father-provider and by his relationship with the woman who converted him from hellish transcendence and bore him the children; Munny's drama is precisely the opposition and tension between his guise as violent-transcendent and his guise as widower and father. *In the Line of Fire*, like *Heartbreak Ridge*, plays off the aging persona's defeats and victories in the realm of battle with a gracefully rueful ("human") recognition of his physical decline, which is then consoled by the romantic interest of a woman. Although there is no role whatever in this film for fatherhood in any form, the contrast between the heroic sphere and the human sphere is just the same as it is where fatherhood *is* part of the picture. In short, there is something slightly artificial about dividing the fatherly from the romantic Eastwood persona. But at the same time, the configurations and variations of this father-function are so insistent that they invite a separate treatment.

Perhaps the most curious and fascinating feature of the "fatherhood" array is the way in which Eastwood has brought to it the same qualities of shadowy contradiction, disavowal and deconstruction we have seen him bring to the "impossible" transcendent hero. To begin with, Eastwood is concerned with "the Good Father"—an idealization of the paternal and patriarchal role—and its contrasts with the weaker and more limited fatherhood of "ordinary" or "realistic" fathers. The Good Father has something like the same relation to the weaker, ordinary variety that transcendental heroism has with "ordinary" or "realistic" heroism. The Good Father rarely makes an appearance in Eastwood's cinema without some hint or presence of the weaker, limited one or some equivalent. In some of the films (mostly later ones) the two functions are actually combined, to produce a doubled, self-contradictory, or deconstructed father-figure. Just as the violent transcendental hero is presented simultaneously as an unquestionable (super)natural force and as an artificial, constructed one, so the Eastwood-father is simultaneously a father and not a father, a protector and not a protector, a nurturer and not a nurturer. In both cases what we find is a persona who is simultaneously a sterling success and a mirage or failure, a charismatic figure of power and a fraud. One can probably say that, at the most fundamental level, the double vision expressed here is exactly the same in both transcendent and "fatherly" realms. So many of the "fatherly" contradictions feature a contrast between the father-figure as a particularly gifted (in fact a heroic) personage and as someone crucially lacking in some fundamental way—a lack which is very often coincident with an *absence*. Eastwood fathers, in other words, are either not really fathers but metaphorical father-leaders or father-substitutes, or else are really fathers but are somehow not there.

Only rarely in Eastwood's cinema, then, is fatherhood allowed to exist in any kind of straightforwardly good or successful way, without some kind of shadow or negation. And from this swirl of contradictions, compensations, and disavowals emerges a construct of ideas on fatherhood in the most inclusive sense of the term. What follows is a film-to-film account of some of the most important stages in the evolution of this construct, confining itself to films in which Eastwood himself plays the part of the father-figure. The picture that emerges stretches over a very large territory and exhibits a startling range of attitudes. When *A Perfect World* arrived in 1993, it was possible to see in Eastwood's cinema the culmination of a movement towards self-questioning and self-deconstruction—a kind of summary and "final" statement on these ideas of fatherhood which was a companion-piece to the equivalent summary on the subject of the transcendent violent hero that had been represented by *Unforgiven*. But in the last few years, this film, which at first seemed a teleological endpoint, has emerged instead as another way-station (albeit still the most important one of all). For Eastwood has returned to the question, disconcertingly but absorbingly, in two films—*Absolute Power* (1997) and *True Crime* (1999)—which seem to go backwards in their attitudes and presentation of the question. *A Perfect World* remains nevertheless Eastwood the filmmaker's most extensive and concentrated examination of the topic of fatherhood. But in it, he himself takes a secondary role and the central father-figure is played by Kevin Costner. It is one of his very best films, a profound self-examining meditation of ideas which have shifted and percolated through his cinema to an increasing degree throughout the 1980s and '90s. Partly because of Eastwood's more marginal screen presence, but more importantly because I believe it demands and rewards a detailed close reading, it is excluded from the present essay and given one of its own, immediately following. *Absolute Power* and *True Crime*, fascinating regressive postludes to *A Perfect World*'s "final statement," then have a little space to themselves in a short essay.

———

We may begin by looking again briefly at the Eastwood hero at his most transcendentally violent—in *High Plains Drifter*—and noting his stance with respect to prosociality and community leadership. Of course, at base this film is so far from being prosocial that it may actually be called *anti*social, the hero's main activity being to mete out a pitiless punishment for the inhabitants of the community, and the community itself being founded on principles of corruption and greed. The marshal-returned-from-the-dead was once upon a time the good enabler of the community, but his prosociality was rewarded with the most agonizing and public death carried out exactly by the agents of that community on whose behalf he had been acting. In this extreme revision, in fact inversion, of the western's basic model of the relation of hero and community, *High Plains Drifter* makes its own contribution to the cancerous 1970s post-classical collapse of the genre, flanked by such other terminal westerns as *The Wild Bunch* (1969), *Little Big Man* (1970), *Soldier Blue* (1970), *Monte Walsh* (1970), *McCabe and Mrs Miller* (1971), *Doc* (1971), *The Great Northfield Minnesota Raid* (1972), *Bad Company* (1972), *Ulzana's Raid* (1972), and *Pat Garrett and Billy the Kid* (1973).

But the avenging-spirit protagonist is not completely indiscriminate; he spares and even befriends a few people. Indeed, he delights in exalting the lowly and the outcast over the venal and treacherous burghers of the town—specifically some Indians who are being bullied with casual venomous racism by the store-keeper, and a despised dwarf whom Eastwood appoints as the new sheriff. These people for whom the violent Eastwood hero stands up are particularly designed to be as far removed from any established or enfranchised social group as can be imagined. It is a strategy for presenting the transcendent hero not only as a figure of violence but also as a patriarchal dispenser of favours, a drastic moral rectifier of perverted social hierarchies—not only a merciless scourge of the wicked for reasons of personal revenge but also a saviour of the downtrodden for reasons of disinterested justice. Certainly the justice very decisively takes a back seat to the revenge, but it is there, sketched in.[4] Even in a sketched-in form, however, it is still necessary to distance the protagonist from any hint that he is an "official hero" in a project which is devoted to destroying the idea of a viable official community. Consequently, the beneficiaries of his power must be aggressively characterized as being outside, or beneath, any such society.[5]

———

The film in which the leaderly and fatherly Eastwood emerges most definitively is *The Outlaw Josey Wales*. This development is very much related to the persona's important shift from post-classical to classical status. *Josey Wales* dates from 1976, the last year of what I have suggested is a decade of anti- or post-classi-cism in Hollywood. It was the year of one of the most potent of all post-classical movies, *Taxi Driver*, and of end-of-the-line westerns such as *Buffalo Bill and the Indians* and *The Shootist* (which depicted the death of John Wayne), as well as the menacing *The Missouri Breaks*. But there were also definite signs in 1976 that some kind of thaw was in the offing. *The Missouri Breaks* ends with the death of the terrifying Marlon Brando assassin and the survival of (what passes for) the good guys. *All the President's Men* reverts to the classical-closure structure of the detective movie even as it is suffused with anti-classical shivers of dark paranoia. Above all, *Rocky* shows its protagonist progressing from paradigmatic anti-classical hopelessness (ugly streets and meat-packing plants, violence and dead end despair) right back to a pure classical-type triumph through individual energy and optimism. *Rocky* actually treks overland from post-classical pessimism to neo-classical optimism—as opposed to teleporting there instantly like *Star Wars*—and as a result, it is a more arduous journey and leaves more traces of where it came from and what a desperate effort of will was required. *The Outlaw Josey Wales* is another film of this kind.

Even more than *Rocky*, Eastwood's film emphasizes its starting point in anti-classicism. The murder of the protagonist's wife and child, and his vengeful response of turning into a murderous vigilante irregular, essentially duplicates the skeleton-structure of, for example, Charles Bronson's *Death Wish* (1974), where the peace-loving *paterfamilias* responds to a terrible crime against his wife and child by going on a narrative-long[6] rampage of assassination. And of course, in this respect it also resembles *High Plains Drifter*.

Indeed, it is fascinating to examine the complex similarities and differences between the nameless hero of that film and Josey Wales: to see the survivals and repetitions of that figure's transcendental violent mastery together with the humanizing subjectivization which finally softens its pitiless fury and brings the character into a classical commitment to others. From this standpoint, *The Outlaw Josey Wales* gives a biography to the Man With No Name—it gives him his reasons for violence, rather than wrapping that violence in mystery. It shows him as initially having occupied the status of (classical) realist humanity as an "ordinary" man, and then it shows his production as transcendental violent figure through the wicked deeds of other men and his perpetuation in that role through the stereotyping actions of society as a whole. And these reasons, this connection to "ordinary" humanity, allow him to escape from what can now be seen not just as a potently violent mystery but also as a solitary prison of hurt and hate. In this way, the Eastwood persona's lethal separateness is laboriously assembled and then disassembled, and his mysterious transcendent violence is subjected to at least a part of the same process which it undergoes in *Unforgiven*. But unlike that film, *Josey Wales* leaves its hero finally in a position to enjoy both halves of his newly presented persona. He can feel an attachment to others and take his place among humanity, but he does not have to surrender his violent mastery. He can emerge from the traumatic pain that creates his transcendent power without really losing that power. And what this process does, among other things, is to assert again the classical order: a problem is solved, difficulties are overcome, the narrative ends in wholeness with

the protagonist in command of the scene, having acted successfully on behalf of the community.

If the Eastwood hero needs to be reconfigured for classicism,
so does the community. *Josey Wales* still presents the mainstream
or dominant community in post-classical terms. It is engaged in
a civil war (*the* Civil War), in which the cruelest human impulses
receive opportunity and encouragement and in which social
institutions are reduced to their most oppressively arbitrary
form as a ruthless killing-machine during the war and the
despotic martial law of the victors after it. This is indeed a
savage metaphorical picture of the contemporary American
social landscape, but it is one which, in the wake of Vietnam and
the internecine wars between counterculture and silent
majority and between black and white, had become quite
familiar by 1976. As that alienated civil chaos had required the
mystical violence of the transcendent Eastwood hero, so a
humanized Eastwood hero requires a new society if he is to be
reconciled to it and act as its communal leader. And so the
community that Josey forms and founds accretes around him
gradually and accidentally, consisting of outcasts, misfits,
orphans, leftovers, and derelicts. It is a kind of augmentation of
the tiny group the hero had favoured in *High Plains Drifter*—
right down to the presence of Indians, virtually exterminated as
a race by dominant white culture, and in *Josey Wales* vagrants
even from their own society. *Josey's* society consists so wholly of
those unacceptable to existing society that the film and the
protagonist will not be contaminated by the perceived moral
bankruptcy of that society and by the dangers still inherent in
reviving an idealist prosocial project. And their ultimate place of
constitution as a miniature society is in the Indian Territory: for
any new America which they might represent must get outside
America in order to reconstitute itself afresh.

And so to fatherhood. Josey is presented at the beginning
very pointedly as a family man, and the most poignant of his
sufferings in the first scenes comes as he sees his small son's arm
fall out of his burial sack and he must gently replace it. His tow-
headed boy is beautiful and dear, but as he is not there long
enough for us to get to know him in the slightest, his importance is, necessarily, primarily symbolic. Eastwood begins, then,
symbolically, as a father, and the film proceeds to describe a
trajectory whereby the atrocious effacement of his family makes

him the solitary transcendent killer; only then is he *re*constructed as the symbolic father of a new community. It is notable that the process begins with Josey acting as a substitute father to a young blond fellow-rebel named Jamie—a boy, we can clearly see, just like the one his own might have grown into. When the lad is wounded, Josey tends him with fatherly solicitude, and Jamie's admiration for him and the intimacy created by a closeness to death prompt the boy to start talking about his own father. His white shirt is beautifully embroidered with flowers—a sign, ordinarily, of a mother's love and care. But Jamie reveals that it was his father who had painstakingly sewn it and begged his son not to tell anyone lest the father be thought too tender and womanish. Clearly this fatherly tenderness sounds a chord in the Eastwood character, who recognizes such soft feelings because he is capable of them himself and is willing almost to occupy that position with respect to this son-substitute. It is an extraordinary moment, one of the most touching in the film, and it places Eastwood the terrible killer in close juxtaposition with a male fatherly love that has about it something explicitly female. In the context of heroic masculinity, this is something indeed. But shortly after this the boy dies, and Eastwood the substitute father is robbed of his child a second time. Already the idea is present: fatherhood is loss.

By this time, Josey is a wanted and hunted man, whose escapes and the bodies of his vanquished pursuers make him a legendary fearsome outlaw. The Eastwood of "do you feel lucky?" and "make my day" is very much visible in this figure, whose trademark (along with a frightening curtness of speech) is the particularly foul gesture of spitting a stream of tobacco juice onto the fallen form of his enemy. This nasty little ritual is even played for laughs—the film's clearest demonstration of the degree to which it is still dependent on the transcendent hero's attitudes of arrogance and contempt. But even as this violent scenario is unfolding, Eastwood's new community is slowly assembling. It materializes gradually out of the social void—the wandering old Indian Lone Watie, a wisecracking chorus to Josey's heroic deeds; a young Indian woman whom he liberates from the tyranny of her white "employer"; then the mother-and-daughter rump of a family of Kansas jayhawkers whose male head has been killed by Missouri irregulars (like Josey) and whose permanently missing son/brother they are in search of; and finally even an entire ghost town whose only remaining inhabitants are a troupe of unemployed gamblers and saloon entertainers. For all of these people, Josey represents a kind of centre around which they coalesce, somehow a "natural" leader, somehow the missing patriarch.

It is as a patriarch that he goes to parley with the patriarch of the still-free Indians in the territory, the impressively stone-faced and gigantic Ten Bears. These two equally larger-than-life, deathly serious and laconic male heroes then embark on an earthshaking exchange of ritual speeches (in some ways reminiscent of Harry Callahan's) in which each offers the other his "word of life" or "word of death." Drawing now from stereotypes of Indian nobility and heightened simple rhetoric, Eastwood is confirmed in his heroic stature even as he acts as the representative of a community and offers to sacrifice his life for it. He is simultaneously beckoned gently to fill in role of the missing male in the jayhawker family. Only instead of being the husband of the mother and the father of the daughter, he will be the son of the mother and the husband of the daughter, the patriarch taking a wife who is presented as hardly more than a child. Thus he will be husband and father simultaneously and integrate himself into both the nuclear family and the family of humanity without giving up his heroic loftiness.

———

Bronco Billy represents another step along the road to fatherly leadership. Once again Eastwood, heading up a rag-tag band of Wild West Show performers, is presented as the leader of a community of misfits. The small band of performers resembles the new community of *The Outlaw Josey Wales*. There is an Indian couple, a ringmaster, a young man who does lariat tricks, and a prop man—and of course Billy himself, who is a trick rider and knife thrower. The comic incongruities and failures of this act are legion: the Chief is constantly getting bitten by his own rattlesnakes, Billy goes through endless quantities of pretty female assistants who don't like having knives thrown at them, the prop man has lost a hand trying to do a trick with a shotgun, the lariat boy turns out to be a draft-dodger, and on a more muted level, the ringmaster is black. One further character is added, a spoiled heiress on the run straight out of *It Happened One Night*[7] whose life is blighted by her posture of arid skepticism and sophistication. All of the members of his little "family" are (in the end successfully) encouraged by Billy to live out their inmost best desires for themselves and thus to achieve human wholeness through the nurturing ideals of cowboy mythology. Billy is in fact more self-consciously a leader, with responsibilities to regulate and protect and provide a good example, than any Eastwood character.

Just as Billy's position as cowboy hero is undercut by the complete artificiality of his New Jersey shoe-salesman origins, so is his role as enabling father and chief mythmaker. *Bronco Billy* emphasizes more distinctly than ever Eastwood's new role as good patriarch: the authority figure who enables the community through the purity of his faith and example, who defines and enforces the belief system of the whole group, who ensures the (American) structure that allows all individuals to be what they most ideally and self-realizingly want to be. But no distinction is made between historical fact and the consistent acting out of a willed, historically preposterous set of desires. Such a destabilization of authority may be necessary in a postmodern environment where "grand narratives" are disbelieved; but skepticism is precisely the enemy in *Bronco Billy*, where authenticity may be re-achieved simply by willing a re-belief in grand narrative. In this deliberately self-hypnotizing fashion, Billy not only enables himself to be a "real" cowboy hero, but the Chief to be a "real" Indian and Miss Lily to be a "real" woman. Fatherhood, symbolic communal fatherhood, means enabling your children to achieve an idealized wholeness and "authenticity" through their own belief in themselves—no matter how artificial that ideal or belief may be. This representation of the symbolic father as a fiction is in keeping with the whole project of representing Eastwood's heroism in this way, but it has a particular pre-resonance from the later standpoint of *A Perfect World*, where the fictions of Good Fatherhood will become agonizing and destructive.

Yet in *Bronco Billy* the leader's powers of command depend on no one but himself. Even *Josey Wales* at a certain point needs the help of a woman (the jayhawker daughter Laura Lee) to coax him into humanity and hence to a truer relationship with his flock.[8] But Billy has engendered himself parthenogenetically, and his commitment to and affection for his little band springs from nothing but his self-belief. The women in his life, far from being his collaborators in this process, seem potentially to be its enemies; they seem to have aroused more than a little hostility. He actually shot his wife after finding her in bed with his best friend, and the subsequent nubile women of the troupe, including Miss Lily, are required to spin head over heels tied to a wheel in skimpy cowgirl dress while he throws knives at them. Like many aspects of the film, these quasi-misogynies have a farcical tone, but the knife-throwing routine in particular is clearly symbolic: any potential partner of Billy's must be willing to submit to this process as a token of her eager assent to Billy's benevolent patriarchy.[9]

———

Both *The Outlaw Josey Wales* and *Bronco Billy* deal with Eastwood as a symbolic social father, a metamorphosis of the heroic condition from individualist to communal ends, where efficacy comes not only from an active, violent defence of the group but also from example. In *Honkytonk Man* (1982), Eastwood takes a further, crucial step: to embody his persona in dimensions smaller and more naturalistic than his usual scale, and to bring his "fatherhood" into the intimate confines of the individual family. Set in the rural dustbowl poverty of the Great Depression, the film evokes the left-leaning populism of Walker Evans, James Agee, and *The Grapes of Wrath* as well as the anti-heroic, observational realism of a documentarist or at least a non-commercial cinema. Its hero, Red Stovall (Eastwood), is a peripatetic, alcoholic, fatally tubercular country-and-western singer, and the film's central relationship is that between him and his twelve-year-old nephew Whit, who has been sent by the boy's mother to accompany her ailing brother on a picaresque trip to Nashville for his one real shot at fame and fortune. In the event, this is an apotheosis which can only occur posthumously, as the dying Red fails his audition and must be content with cutting a few last recordings. Whit's relation to his uncle is that of adoring acolyte and part-time nursemaid. As the film sets Red up as the unsteady head of a tiny ramshackle group consisting of his underage nephew, for a while Whit's old grandfather, and then an orphaned and comically ambitious young woman escaping from indentured servitude, the outlines of *Josey Wales* and *Bronco Billy* again become faintly visible: Eastwood as patriarch of the community of misfits.

But *Honkytonk Man* seems intent upon contradicting the dominant model of the Eastwood persona through an almost didactic antithesis. In place of the persona's habitual transcendence—present even in *Bronco Billy* albeit as a pastiche—the film insists upon his human frailty and his bodily weakness and mortality. And though his footloose life has a powerful appearance of freedom and glamour to the young Whit, these characteristics too are marked in the end by their limitation and insubstantiality. What does emerge is the powerful bond between the man and the boy, and the configuration whereby the boy can be dazzled and carried away by the man's example and then become aware of its imperfect and mortal dimensions.

Two details are striking here. First is the fact that Red is not Whit's real father, but his seldom-seen uncle and *substitute* or quasi-ideal father. Whit's real father is a pinched-faced, profoundly defeated little sharecropper whose tendency is always to limit and deny and in whose eventual acquiescence to Whit's journey may be seen both his failure to be the traditional strong male or even to stick by his convictions and also the hopeless underlying recognition that his wife's judgement, or even his son's, can hardly be worse than his own. By contrast, Red is a much-reduced version of the Freudian "family romance" noble or famous father, the exciting adventurer and conqueror. The second detail is that, having removed the character of Whit from actual filiality with respect to the Eastwood persona, Eastwood the filmmaker then casts *his own son* Kyle in the role of Whit, thus affirming metatextually just that kinship which the text denies. Eastwood is thus a substitute father to the boy onscreen and a real father to him offscreen. The ambiguities and blurred outlines of this relationship-which-is-not-a-relationship are, I believe, absolutely characteristic of Eastwood the filmmaker, who constantly proposes contradictory principals, muddies clear boundaries and categories, and cultivates thematically a kind of persistence of double vision throughout his work. Here and in virtually all of the films we are considering, Eastwood both is and is not the father—just as in his transcendent-violent roles he both is and is not good, invincible, or "real."

Within these terms, what Whit has to learn from his uncle—and what Red has to teach—is a version of masculinity, male maturity. This cluster of strategies and values begins with the idea of freedom and independence, of personal self-actualization. Red's freedom from the grinding constrictions of "working" life, his glamorous role as performer-artist (Eastwood's own calling as well), are part of this quality. Then, by treating the adolescent Whit like an adult, Red in effect makes him one. He thrusts power, control, upon the boy: he insists that Whit drive the car, gives him all sorts of responsibilities, and even arranges for him to lose his virginity in a whorehouse. He also initiates him into the mysteries of chicken-stealing, evading the law, and collecting on bad debts — and also racial mixing in a blues-and-marijuana-sodden "colored" bar where Red sits in with the black musicians and demonstrates the authenticity of his musical populism. Virtually all of this activity demonstrates another characteristic of the masculinity being conveyed: it is unconventional, rebelliously free, on the road, "cowboy" (a quality heightened by the "harmless" illegality of much of it). To be a man is to act freely, to pursue your desires lustily, bursting the bonds of social conformity and the petty restrictions of the law. (In the latter case, though, only mild offences are permitted, and even they are ruled to a degree by underlying principles of natural justice.)

There is a further horizon of manhood in the film, however, one that is also the condition of adulthood: the horizon of transience, loss, and mortality. This perspective is present in shadowy form right from the beginning, in the poverty and hopelessness of Whit's nuclear family and in the racking tubercular cough and terrible weakness of Red himself. Although the film moves into cheerier, and even farcical, realms, the shadow of that perspective never fades entirely. It is given an additional social dimension by the presence of Grandpa, whose glowing youthful memories of the great Cherokee Strip landrush of 1893 are evoked on the very historical spot itself (as the group passes through it) — now just another piece of desolate dustbowl scrubland, its talismanic hope faded as completely as the youth of the rememberer. Here it is not only the promise of life to the young and vital which is drained, but that of the nation itself and its ideology of the endless bountiful frontier. Such a letdown cannot help but infect the joyous lessons of male freedom taking place simultaneously. And of course, most agonizingly, there is the long, painful, mortal decline of Red himself. The end of the road (coterminous with the goal of Nashville) is death, death rather than fulfillment.

Red hacks and coughs, collapses, cannot perform properly, is terribly racked with disease, and dies. If this *telos* is not exactly a judgement on his ideology of masculine freedom, it is at least a profoundly limiting accompaniment. Of course all lives end in death, even all "heroic" male lives; everyone knows that. But American ideology, and especially dominant Hollywood ideology, is devoted to the occlusion and denial of that fact, has bitterly resisted the de-heroicization brought by mortality; and one might say that the transcendental Eastwood persona has represented a particularly pointed resistance.[10] In *Honkytonk Man*, Eastwood as artist-performer, the object of youthful male adoration, teaching a life of absolute mobility and freedom, is dragged back down to earth in most emphatic fashion. Even before his last mortal agony, the character has expressed profound regrets regarding some crucial aspects of his free male life: it has deprived him of any deep and lasting relationship with a woman. In a quietly intense scene which operates structurally as a kind of culmination of ideas subtly percolating through the film, Red tells Whit about the one woman he might have made a life with, but whom he abandoned after luring her away from her husband and children—and lost. He had even left her pregnant, but had decided not to intrude upon his daughter's life later on. The life which throughout the film has often appeared such a perfect small model of ideal maleness is now revealed as having a large hole at the centre, an absence of the vital quality of love. Moreover, the substitute father Red is revealed to be a real, but absconded, father—and to have been capable of substitute-fathering Whit only because he has abandoned his real child. Death—the ultimate "failure"—ends this life; but its very essence can seem retrospectively to have been loss and absence.

This is, in fact, the shadow of negation at the heart of the film. The Eastwood persona's charismatic aspects—a diminished and limited version of its transcendental-heroic aspects—are revealed to be founded upon a failure of and exile from the truest humanity. Heroic solitude here is, as broadly sketched in *Josey Wales* and exhaustively analyzed in *Unforgiven*, a bad consequence of personal dysfunction. And in the realm of fatherhood we find in the most explicit way yet the strange and suggestive configuration of the failures of real fatherhood and their attempted redemptions in the dimension of idealized charismatic substitute-fatherhood. This dialectic often seems to say that as a real father the heroic Eastwood persona is in some way a failure, perhaps even a complete failure; but as a heroic model he compensates with the special things he can provide as a substitute father, things which no real father can give. In this configuration, though, there seems to be a kind of disavowal—a disavowal of the reality of failed fatherhood, and a substitute of what I have previously called "fictitious victories." But in the both/and, simultaneous-opposites fashion that characterizes so much of Eastwood's cinema, those disavowals and fake substitutes are sometimes actually revealed or at least suggested as such. This is certainly the case in the Eastwood films that most intensely dramatize these ideas: *Honkytonk Man, Unforgiven, A Perfect World,* and (more furtively) *True Crime.*

———

Tightrope offers another version of this shadow-failure. In this film, the Eastwood character is an actual parent, and his fatherhood becomes a thematic issue—not the central one, it is true, but still of some importance in the narrative. Wes Block is a divorced single father (Eastwood's condition at the time of the film). His wife has deserted him for another man—an action characterized as selfish and irresponsible—leaving Block to fulfill the role of Good Parent. The elder of his two daughters, Amanda, is played by Eastwood's then twelve-year-old daughter Alison, creating a metatextual perspective just as intriguing as the ones offered earlier by *Honkytonk Man* and later by *True Crime.* This is especially the case since his daughters personify Block's "respectable" life, just as the Bourbon Street prostitutes whom he engages in sadomasochistic sex with and who are then murdered by his *Doppelgänger* represent his hidden or dark side. Since the murderer's ultimate act is to bind and menace Alison, there ensues a traumatic confusion of the two sides of Block's nature and the faint but intolerable suggestion of the presence of sadistic sexual impulses towards his own daughter. The film at no point suggests that Block might actually have such desires, and indeed the developments just mentioned are presented rather as an appalled glimpse of where transgressive desire might finally lead if it is not defeated[11] and the degree to which it exists absolutely in enmity to the values of family love. At the end of the film the ultimate threats are allayed, the murderer killed, the protagonist set on the road to health and wholeness; but the dark perspectives the film has so insistently offered refuse to be completely dispelled and continue to haunt the Eastwood persona across the whole of its filmography, past and future.

Tightrope's explicit doubling also depicts once more the gap between Eastwood the hero and Eastwood the humanized father and family man—those dialectic opposites which he has contrasted, differentiated, and tried or failed to reconcile throughout his cinema. It is a subtle and indirect depiction, because Eastwood the hero is scarcely in evidence in this film. But one of that persona's most instantly recognizable symbolic forms, the cop, is. Eastwood playing a cop always evokes the stereotype of Dirty Harry, and as we have already seen, Eastwood the filmmaker plays with that stereotype ironically in *The Gauntlet* and self-critically in the present film. In *Tightrope,* the cop is (and how familiar this configuration is becoming) both a good cop and a bad cop: a fine, honest, talented officer who gets results and a flawed, corrupt cop who is not above using his position to abet his perverted sexual appetites and whose hypocrisy is the rationale for the murderer's horrifying crimes. The character's compromised cop-life is then the source of the dreadful threat to his good and wholesome family-life; the cop's charismatic and heroic generic association with a world of violence and masculine supremacy is set against the dysfunction this reflects or creates in the world of relationships and human connection in general. But in *Tightrope*, again, all the familiar oppositions are systematically short-circuited and confused. Very faintly we have the pattern presented in so many Eastwood films: the hero is a hero, but his heroic status must be accompanied by some kind of loss or renunciation or failure in his life as a human being. Except that in *Tightrope*, he is not much of a hero to begin with and his human dysfunction has spread into his professional cop-hero side. Meanwhile, even in the wholesome world of his fatherhood, the Good Parent is revealed as harbouring very un-Good-Parent-like, kinky sexual tastes which lay his wholesome home open to a terrible desecration by forces which are in effect the logical extreme of those tastes.

———

Pale Rider returns decisively to the figure of the Eastwood heroic transcendental-killer persona in its western-genre guise and also raises again some of the issues of prosocial leadership and substitute fatherhood which *High Plains Drifter* and *The Outlaw Josey Wales* touched upon. If *Josey Wales* painstakingly engineered the humanization of this figure, *Pale Rider* casts it firmly back into transcendental mystery and awesome frightening violence. But it also constitutes the persona explicitly as a prosocial entity, evoked by a prayer from one who, as both a child and a female, is doubly marked as the purest type of human value in the community requiring protection.

Pale Rider's model, *Shane*, is perhaps the definitive Hollywood-movie expression of the agonized longing for idealized heroic masculinity on the part of the pre-adolescent male. The character of Shane is virtually willed into existence by the young boy Joey as a properly transcendent figure of masculine power and heroic resplendence, which will compensate for his actual father's worthy and realistically limited failure to achieve this plane. One of the striking changes made in *Pale Rider*'s restaging of the story is the recasting of the boy's role into a girl's, and the transformation of the boy's longing for a powerful male saviour into the girl's (additionally) for a lover. This is, of course, to add an entirely new dimension to the hero-worship of the original and to conflate the pre-sexual boy's desire for an idealized figure who will resolve the wracking masculine conflicts inside and outside himself with, literally, the answer to a maiden's prayer. The relationship here of the Eastwood hero and the maiden in distress is a kind of strangely twisted version of the one in *The Outlaw Josey Wales*, where Eastwood rescues and ultimately mates with a woman young enough to be his daughter. Here, he is the knight in shining armour (lethally dour, in fact) whom the girl takes for her fantasy saviour-lover, but who is determined instead to act as her substitute father—even taking a quick departing tumble with her mother by way of emphasis. (No doubt the latter development is another of the film's many rather dislocated paraphrases of *Shane*, in which there is a subsurface attraction between Shane and Marion Starrett, little Joey's mother.)

Moreover, the family lacks a "true" father, for the Michael Moriarty character who is the equivalent of Joe Starrett in *Shane* is merely wooing the girl's mother, let down by her long-gone husband (himself another absconded and inadequate father). The Preacher thus becomes even more powerfully than in the original the substitute-father, the ideally powerful mature male, to this fractured and incomplete nuclear family. In *Pale Rider,* the Eastwood persona acts simultaneously as a figure of transcendental—in this case almost demonic—power and as both saviour of the community and lover of the woman. He is both separate (markedly, indeed supernaturally, so) and a leader of the good society. The contradictions of this simultaneity are left to lie untended throughout the film, another example of the filmmaker's willingness to tolerate (or blindness to) rough edges and allow potentially self-paralyzing questions to remain unresolved.

———

In *Heartbreak Ridge*, Eastwood's commander-patriarch Sgt. Highway must strip the rebellious, good-for-nothing young marines in his new platoon of their immature selfishness and mould them into a team of *men* in his own image. It is strange to watch the reversal of *Honkytonk Man*'s education of freedom and the effacement of *Josey Wales*'s and *Bronco Billy*'s "misfit" individualism by the hard military conformity and violent certainties enforced by Highway. Contradictory to the point of incoherence as it is, *Heartbreak Ridge* also forms the definitive statement of that educative role performed by the transcendental Eastwood hero as well as the fatherly one. How to kill somebody successfully is his lesson. Harry Callahan is often the masculine-heroic role-model and educator of his partners—a role which extends to other Eastwood "cop" movies such as *The Rookie* (1990) and *In the Line of Fire*.[12] But much more than the cop movies, *Heartbreak Ridge* presents this education in masculine violence as having a social utility. The movie gives the contradictions of being masculinely *strong* and socially *responsible* another Hollywood expression (of innumerably many), but later Eastwood films will return to this problem with much greater insight and self-consciousness, not to say self-criticism. Highway's barroom misdemeanors and the platoon's shirking recalcitrance are revisited with far more penetration in *A Perfect World*'s combination of criminality and "fun."

The most widely remarked aspect of this film (at the time and now) is the fifty-something Eastwood hero's belated accommodation to feminine culture. The spectacle of this trash-mouthed, brawling, hypermasculine hard case reading women's magazines to discover the reasons for the failure of his relationship with his wife and pick up tips on how to win her back gets a good laugh from all sides of the gender-politics spectrum. It is the clear signal that now the warrior persona does not exclude a kinder, gentler Eastwood, and that the synthesis between the heroic and the human, which has been a constant topic in his cinema, has reached a point of equilibrium. In this respect, it is a "grown up" coda to a development that has certainly had its points of masculine anxiety and even hysteria (*The Beguiled* and *Play Misty for Me*) and has always seen at least a potential difficulty in bringing the powerfully separate hero down to earth. The romantic lyricism of this development, unabashed at times, is set next to a treatment of the warrior-leader theme which is bellicose enough and displays its own moments of anguish and loss (Korea, Vietnam), but which is also covered in a thick coat of comedy, often of the lowest variety. *Heartbreak Ridge* offers a kind of confused union of the leader-father hero of ideology with the humanized vulnerable husband, both descending elegiacally into the vale of years, and yet surrounded by the ironies of virtual victory and the farce of caricature and low comedy.

White Hunter, Black Heart again presents the communal father, this time a film director, as a charismatic individual who follows a creed of heroic specialness, a creed which he attempts to teach to a younger sidekick. The difference is that the narrative eventually reveals this specifically masculine specialness, charisma, leadership, to be lunatic megalomania, destructive both to the community of which the protagonist is supposed to be the good patriarch and to exactly those values of individual difference and separation which the hero's existential quest pursues. In the end, the hero is completely defeated and subdued, rightly rejected by his erstwhile protegé, crushed under a burden of guilt which his actions have prompted, and relapsing into the role of purveyor of "Hollywood" false-happy-ending movies.

———

It is one of *Unforgiven*'s central premises that the amalgamation of the transcendental hero and the humanized subject—that activity which so many Eastwood films circle around—is flatly impossible. There can be no softening of the first, while the second has no heroic dimension whatever. And in working out this premise, the film also makes a commentary on Eastwood the father. For the reformed William Munny is a "good family man." As the "bad" Munny is a representation of Eastwood the transcendental killer, so the "good" Munny is a representation of Eastwood the husband (widower) and father. A woman has redeemed the transcendental killer from his solitude and pain (as in *The Outlaw Josey Wales*), and this time the removal of his mysterious separateness has rendered him a human subject of a particularly limited and quotidian kind. She has not wooed him gently towards a modification of his heroic separateness, allowing something of both states to exist together, but has persuaded him to repudiate it completely, in exactly the teetotalling, testifying temperance way she has gotten him to renounce alcohol. His new humanized self has survived the death of his wife and is continued in his attempts to live an ordinary life and care for his children. Indeed, it is his role as a father, his desire to provide for his children, which apparently forms the most important motive for Munny's bounty-seeking assassination expedition.

The attempt to be a better father by acting violently, although it does in fact generate income and (after the end of the action) set the family up in more comfortable circumstances, nevertheless is shown to be traumatic and indefensible. Not only does it require the reformed Munny to regress to the inferno of self-hatred and indiscriminate bloodletting, it also puts into question the moral platitudes which position the health and even the existence of the domestic sphere upon a basis of necessary masculine violence. *Unforgiven* represents "being strong for the family" as every bit as destructive and self-destructive an activity as *The Godfather, Part II* does — except that *Unforgiven*'s final title indicates the possibility that Munny can (with dreadful irony) resume full status as father and pillar of the community after sinking into such irredeemable hellish depths. While with one hand the film depicts transcendental heroic violence as ugly and self-annihilating, with the other it remorselessly traces the masculine agency of the "good" father to the same tainted roots. Also deconstructed, of course, is the Eastwood hero who offers in his transcendent heroism a fatherly example to a younger man — a role recurring at intervals from *The Outlaw Josey Wales* to *The Rookie* by way of *Honkytonk Man, Heartbreak Ridge,* and *White*

Hunter, Black Heart. Here the "protegé" is the immature, myopic, and at last utterly disillusioned Schofield Kid, a would-be lethal killer who will, one imagines, be happy to take up a life of pig-farming after his experiences here.

5

A Perfect World

There is No Good Father

As *Unforgiven* represents a kind of summation and final insight into Eastwood's persona of transcendent violence and its relation to connected ideas such as charismatic power, prosocial action, the family, and community, so *A Perfect World* is a kind of big re-examination of the cluster of thoughts and feelings surrounding fatherhood in Eastwood's work. Like *Unforgiven*, too, *A Perfect World* has the inestimable benefit of a complex, intelligent, self-conscious script (by John Lee Hancock), whose level of understanding and articulation far surpasses the less clear-sighted level of the scripts for even many of Eastwood's most interesting films. *A Perfect World*, of course, lacks *Unforgiven*'s mythic resonance, for heroic violence and transcendent power have after all had an absolute centrality in Eastwood's cinematic career which fatherhood has never quite attained. Nevertheless, the later film is astonishing in its ability to gather together and capture with piercing affective power the longings and contradictions which have (we can now see) underlain that "softer" side of Eastwood's masculinity project.

Affect is certainly the key to this film. Although there are crime, chase-and-escape, violence, death, and many of the other features of the "hard" action movie, the narrative is essentially a melodrama and not a landscape for charismatic mastery. It centres on longing and loss, rather than doing and overcoming, and its central characters are almost deterministically circumscribed by their social positions and personal histories, not at all free to act from a stance of idealized male-heroic separateness. The failure and lack which so characterize the narrative's central agents are instead familiar, classically, from the more "feminine" forms of melodrama with their bounded, helpless, and self-sacrificing characters (many of them female)—and yet no Eastwood film is more wholly dominated by male characters and the explicit subject of masculinity.

As in *Honkytonk Man*, the two central characters are a mature man and a young boy, on a cross-country car journey together in which the boy, removed from his mother-centred family, learns lessons about manhood and the big world from a substitute father. Indeed, the parallels with *Honkytonk Man* are remarkably detailed. They are both road movies of picaresque structure. In both films, the older man occupies a "glamorous" role of freedom from social constraint (the one is a singer-performer, the other an escaped criminal), and Eastwood's character is nicknamed "Red." In both cases the "son" receives an education in the tools of power (the car, the gun), although *Honkytonk Man*'s chicken-stealing and jail-breaking hijinks are repeated in a much more serious and consequent form in *A Perfect World*. In both films, the lessons of masculinity are transformed into prospects of loss and emptiness; in *Honkytonk Man* the older male wishes to be received into the temple of the Grand Old Opry, while in *A Perfect World* he is heading for a fantasy world of freedom and father-wholeness in Alaska. Most importantly, both narratives end with the awesome and drawn-out spectacle of the death of the "father" with the "son" looking on. There are specific echoes of other Eastwood films in *A Perfect World* (notably *Tightrope*), but its relation to *Honkytonk Man* is extended and intense; it seems in fact to revisit and restage *Honkytonk Man* in a much more thoughtful and self-knowing way—as *Unforgiven* revisits and restages *High Plains Drifter* and *Pale Rider*.

A Perfect World not only displaces the Eastwood persona from the world of transcendent violence, it displaces it entirely. The central masculine role, of the escaped convict Butch Haynes, is taken by Kevin Costner rather than Eastwood, while Eastwood himself is removed to the secondary role of the aging, Geritol-drinking sheriff Red Barnett. Here Eastwood is again the "cowboy cop" (in Stetson and cowboy boots, looking like the hero of *Coogan's Bluff* at retirement age), trying to right the moral imbalances of society—but now the imbalances are shown to be far too complex ever to be righted in such a simple fashion, and virtually all of this character's projects end in failure. (The self-parodying cowboy iconography also recalls *Bronco Billy*.) Indeed,

Eastwood's inability specifically to be the strong good father is overdetermined here: not only is he not diegetically the substitute father of the vulnerable eight-year-old boy Philip (that is, he is not Butch), but it is eventually revealed that he has *tried* to act as the substitute father of the traumatized Butch and has failed absolutely in that role.

Butch is the film's central, agonized subject, who is in the narrative's thematic doubling and redoubling both archetypal son in search of a father and father in search of a son. In the first instance he is the good father, rescuing Philip's mother from the rape his fellow-escapee Jerry Pugh is about to perpetrate—like so many versions of the Eastwood hero have done in so many earlier films. He protects Philip's mother, and Philip. But imme diately afterwards he needs to trick the boy, and he does so by evoking a cops-and-robbers scenario. As Philip holds a (real) gun on the convicts, Butch says: "Point it at me...now say 'Stick 'em up!'" Then, in the friendliest way, he abducts Philip. Butch's relation with this boy is thus, from the beginning, formed of an inextricable knot of affectionate and instrumental, protective and pathological, motives. As the action unfolds, Butch's relation with Philip becomes more and more obviously impulsive and compulsive; he uses it to try to work through, or act out, his most deeply rooted emotional wounds.

Butch's trauma stems from his childhood experience in a dysfunctional nuclear family. His father had abandoned him and his mother when Butch was six. Butch's mother was a Bourbon Street prostitute in New Orleans (like the erstwhile Eastwood's "dates" and assassin's victims of *Tightrope*), bringing Butch up essentially in a brothel after the departure of her husband. When one of her customers tried to hurt her, Butch (aged eight, the same as Philip) killed him. Suffering from tertiary syphilis, she committed suicide when Butch was twelve, whereupon the father reappeared. Shortly thereafter, Butch stole a Ford (the father's favourite car and the make which Butch insists on stealing at the beginning of the movie); when he was caught, he received a very harsh four-year prison sentence during which he "learned to be a criminal." Butch's hither-and-yon father has managed to plant the seeds of an idealized father-son relationship, and even after their last meeting has sent Butch a postcard inviting Butch to visit him in Alaska and get to know him when he is older. This picture of a loving but absent and undependable father is counterpoised with other testimony, however: Barnett had the young Butch sent to prison after the theft to get him away from his father, who was not only a habitual criminal but a wife-and-child-beater, and Butch also tells Philip flatly that both their fathers are "no good." Butch's feelings for both of his parents are a horrific mess of love and hatred, longing and disappointment. He is quite unable to get away from the obsessively recurring mirage of an ideal boyhood, an ideal father—precisely those things he never had, but which have never ceased to act as objects of profound desire and which are powerfully reactivated by the encounter with Philip.

Philip appears to him as another version of himself as a child. Philip and his mother have also been abandoned by the father, and the fatherless family is left (in Butch's mind at least) crippled and especially incapable of giving Philip the kind of upbringing he needs. Philip's mother is strictly religious, and her beliefs cause her to forbid Philip and his sisters any indulgence in commercial "fun" or any participation in festivals such as Halloween (which is underway as the action takes place).[1] Butch's role is then to provide those things which Philip's mother cannot; to ensure that Philip will take his place as a "normal" boy in the "normal" world and will not have to be tortured by loss and exclusion from whole-ness as Butch has been. But such normality and wholeness are actually nowhere to be found: Butch does not have them, Philip does not have them, Barnett cannot provide them for Butch, and Butch cannot provide them for Philip. The attempt to institute them leads merely to grotesque distortions of behaviour: condemning an adolescent to a long prison sentence in order to remove him from a bad environment, dragging a boy from his home, and introducing him to "normal" pleasures while on the run from a police manhunt. Butch cannot help Philip any more than he can help himself to recover the lost "normal" childhood, the lost "normal" father, he never had.

The culmination of Butch's agony occurs when he and Philip are invited into the house of some black sharecroppers, Max and Lottie, a fifty-something couple, and their grandson Cleve, whom they are bringing up. Cleve immediately appears as another Butch-Philip, a child with no or substitute parents, and Butch befriends him and flips him playfully head over heels, "fathering" him as he has done with Philip. But now Butch plunges into a maelstrom of overpowering primal feelings. First he sees Max casually hit Cleve hard on the head for some trivial cause; then he discovers an old record of bagpipe music, which his mother and the other women used to play at the bordello when he was a child. The radio now betrays to everyone Butch's fugitive status, and in his nervousness Max gives Cleve an even harder blow. Father, mother, violence, nostalgia, the uncovering of the subject's criminal impossibility of normality, all these in succession precipitate Butch's crisis. Cleve is young Butch, beaten by his father with no protection from his mother—only now it is the mature Butch, a full-blown male, who will revenge his childhood self on his father. He puts his gun to Max's head and demands that he tell Cleve that he loves him. Max does this, Butch exclaims "God, that's beautiful!," puts on the record of bagpipe music, and prepares to execute the tied-up Max. He tells Cleve to look away and tells Philip that he can stay or wait in the car: "You're old enough to think for yourself." When Lottie begins to pray, he duct-tapes all their mouths. The terrified Philip picks up Butch's gun (resuming the posture he held in their first meeting) and shoots Butch.

Butch's attempt to kill Max[2] is the emblem and full unfolding of the pathology of his condition. Love is his desire; he yearns to get love and give it as a son/father. But it is too late: his childhood and his father are gone. Moreover, his attempts to reinstitute the ideal condition all take place under the sign of the criminal violence which defines him and which he must always re-enact, however much he may wish to avoid it. Butch's criminality originates in his childhood relations with his parents, either directly (the killing of his mother's assailant) or indirectly (the father-imitative theft of the car; the prison term which Barnett, acting as substitute father, gets for him by virtue of the theft and in order to keep him away from his real father). We might even say that Butch's criminality *is* his wounded-child-ness; his crimes and his twisted attempts to realize his dreams and punish their shattering are one and the same. Butch's abduction of Philip is criminal but is also an attempt to act out his needs; his punishment of Cleve's grandfather is a starker, more anguished and violent, expression of the same condition. He suffers from the abused child syndrome: the nurturer is the abuser, and therefore his desire is to love and kill the same person. Butch has replicated the schizoid pathology of this condition in his own life: he is a loving criminal, a nurturing abductor, one who would enact father-son closeness by murdering the father. Finally, Butch arranges (consciously or not) that his child alter-ego, Philip, will kill Butch, who is now acting the role of his own father.

For Butch, Philip is himself as a child; Butch will now do for Philip and for his child self what never was properly done for him. He will give Philip good times and freedom, show him the world. He steals a Ford and takes Philip for a long ride in it, at the end of which he will disappear from Butch's life — and will thus reproduce his own childhood experience for Philip to a far greater extent than he ever wanted to. Philip's experience of this entire chain of events is not the enabling education in masculine maturity which Butch half-intends it as. Philip is of course a major character in the film himself, almost as important as Butch, in fact. And his perspective on the action is maintained throughout the narrative, showing us both the ways in which his experience diverges from what Butch wants for him and the ways it approaches Butch's own childhood more than is comfortable. The film emphasizes Philip's vulnerability at every point. His strict upbringing has left him more than usually ill-at-ease with the outside world. The way in which his dreams of a more "normal" childhood are invaded and appropriated by Butch is profoundly unsettling. Whether the absence of Philip's father has led him to identify all the things he misses in his world (carnivals, cotton-candy, Halloween, the "fun" which he supposes other children have) with a truant masculine parent is something the film does not tell us. But it is certain that Butch moves into just such a space in Philip's life. The boy's defencelessness is not only against the violent and frightening things that happen but also against Butch's powerful appeals to his affections and his desire for a parent with Butch's attitudes. The parallel and simultaneous representation of Philip's and Butch's longings and half-despairing hopes is in fact devastating as it unfolds and climaxes in the amplified melodrama of Butch's death.

Butch endeavours to be as loving, providing, and protective towards Philip as he possibly can be. Treating the boy like a real person, he draws him out, attempts to give him subjectivity, status and independence, emphasizes their emotional kinship ("We got a lot in common, Philip: both of us is handsome devils...and neither one of us had a daddy worth a damn"). Philip's *lack* is the basis on which Butch reaches out to him; that lack is what Butch sees as constituting them, and is simultaneously what Butch wants to underline and efface through his presence. Butch's own emotional strategies, many inherited from his father, are now extended to Philip. As they barrel down the road, Butch explains that the car is a "time machine": the road ahead is the future, the road behind is the past. Taking Philip along on a criminal enterprise, in flight from the law and society in general, is similarly the continuation of a strategy of permanent desperation. The love and attention that Butch gives Philip pierce the boy (and the viewer); but they cannot be separated from a constant crisis of anxiety, and ultimately from a *telos* which is violent and tragic. They are like Philip's own iconic acquisition, the Casper costume: they answer an emotional need and are genuinely touching, but are finally incongruous and impossible. This is most fully conveyed by the agonizing scene of Butch's death. Here Philip at last receives his "ride on a rocket ship" as he is taken away by the police helicopter, but the experience is entirely traumatic. He has shot his father and benefactor, and as he is lifted away back to the world at large he can only cry piteously, "Butch! Butch!"[3] Butch's intervention into his life has been nothing but painful and destructive, a source of future regret and deep feelings of loss.

That, indeed, may stand as the film's representation of fatherhood. Fatherhood is chimaera: absence and failure on the part of the father, pain and loss on the part of the son. Not only is this pattern reduplicated throughout the family histories of Butch and Philip, but it is seen in parallel fashion in the Eastwood persona of Red Barnett—and by implication in all the substitute fathers of Eastwood's other films. The elegiac tone evoked by this prospect is struck near the beginning of the film. It is Texas in 1963, and as the Eastwood character is introduced, preparations are being laid for President Kennedy's visit to Dallas. Everyone is about to lose their idealized substitute father, and thus the condition the film paints is a general one in some fashion. This configuration recalls not just Eastwood's immediately preceding film *In the Line of Fire*—in which he failed to prevent the assassination of John Kennedy and can only make up for it narratively or fictionally—but all of those Eastwood films from *Bronco Billy* to *Heartbreak Ridge* and *White Hunter, Black Heart* in which the Eastwood-father gives his children a sustaining *fiction*. In *A Perfect World* the enormous affective appeal of such a fiction is acknowledged, but the attempt to act out the fiction as a substitute, to make up the loss, fails utterly. The "perfect world" of the title is precisely the world of idealizations, of clean narrative solutions, of the effectiveness of heroic action. It is the world Butch impossibly wants to find in Alaska, wants to give Philip. But as Barnett's assistant Sally remarks about the entire predicament, "in a perfect world none of this would happen."

A Perfect World also restages on a larger scale a momentary poetic impulse found in *In the Line of Fire*: on the day of Kennedy's death, the failed agent recalls, the air was wonderfully fresh and clear and the sun shone beautifully. Throughout the less than two days of story time covered by *A Perfect World,* the world does, indeed, look perfect. The weather is bright and clear, the rural countryside verdant and fruitful. Bountiful green cornfields are everywhere — and in fact provide strong particularized settings for some of the scenes. The freshness and innocence of the world are exactly those of the child whose hopes are still intact and whose future is full of promise. The brilliant casting of Kevin Costner as Butch shows its virtues especially here. Most of Costner's best previous roles have been of upright and compassionate men, men whose commitments to family were strong. One thinks of *The Untouchables*, *Dances With Wolves* — and, in this context of beautiful cornfields and ideal aspirations towards absent fathers, above all *Field of Dreams.* The heartbreaking beauty and hope of this idealized vision is pressed, then, from every angle, only to be finally denied and its impossibility to be exhaustively and inescapably demonstrated. We may note one more symbolic detail of the bright, open landscape: it is full of roads whose construction was begun in optimism decades ago but which have subsequently been abandoned and now lead nowhere.

This Eastwood film deconstructs the idealism from which the very conception of the Eastwood-father is formulated. There is no ideal father. Butch's wish to have one has been derisively denied and has left him an emotional cripple and a sociopath. His attempt to be one for Philip, and for Cleve, results in nothing but terror and loss. There is no doubt that Philip would have been far better off with an absent father than he will be after Butch's intervention — and the damage done by that intervention has been through not only the violence and the disruption but, equally harmful, the profound stirring-up of ideal-father desires and their most brutal severance. Ideal fathers, insofar as they have even a projected and partial existence, are unattainable; they leave or die, and they can only cause pain which will in turn produce emotional pathology in the sons.

There is no Good Father. There may be good fathers, but they are rather of the order of the *paterfamilias* (his name is Bob) whose station wagon Butch hijacks. Harassed, inconsistent, banal, timid, clumsily reassuring his children after their mother yells at them, worried about damage to his new car even after the hijack, Bob offers no recognizable ideal of masculine strength and protectiveness. Apart from his concern for his vehicle, he is a gender-neutral parent. He bears no resemblance to the authoritative and heroic Eastwood Good Father, but rather the reverse. Philip, seeing with what ease Butch dominates and controls this man, recognizes the disparity at once and correctly remarks to Butch that Bob "looked silly." It is left to Butch to intone with moral assurance:

> No, he did the right thing. What if he'd put up a fight? I might have had to shoot him. Where'd that family be now? Bob's a fine family man—that's the best thing a fellow could hope to be.

The homiletic blandness of these words makes a strong contrast with the heroic lawlessness of Butch's own behaviour. Power and self-assurance are the tokens of masculinity, especially in the realm of the ideal (and in the cultural-ideological realm in which the movie is positioned). The viewer, and particularly the Eastwood viewer, recognizes that charismatic masculine power as the one which trumps all others: Butch is the hero of the picture in this sense, exactly as the Eastwood persona is of so many others. His "natural" dominance over the "bad" escapee Pugh, and in particular the scene of contemptuous, didactic power-demonstration in which he breaks Pugh's nose while lecturing him on the difference between "a threat" and "a fact," is exactly in the tradition of Eastwood's strong masculine heroes. Being "a fine family man" carries no force in this world of masculine power; the culture pays it lip-service but, like motherhood, this kind of fatherhood is essentially a meaningless cliché here. When earlier Eastwood heroes (such as those in *Josey Wales*, *Bronco Billy*, or *Heartbreak Ridge*) occupied the role of

Good Father, they did so from a position of power. Their power was what enabled them to be Good Fathers. Even the shadows and doubts of *Honkytonk Man* and *Tightrope* left the Good Father essentially a functional persona—his net worth as a Good Father was a positive one. In *Unforgiven,* the issue is joined more complexly and deconstructively, in the following way: 1) the good father is a clumsy pig-farmer who, though "a fine family man," absolutely "looks silly"; 2) he is rehabilitated as a powerful masculine agent, but only at the price of making him a monster; and 3) he can finally, after the end of the movie, revert to goodness and truly occupy the role of Good Father, but can only be established in this security through the horrific operation of a violence that is anything but "good."

In *A Perfect World*, the Good Father is seen as a contradiction in terms. The very qualities of love and nurturing, when combined with masculine power, produce the schizophrenic, dysfunctional person of Butch. He is a charismatic masculine hero; moreover, in him can be clearly discerned the outlines of the warm and protective Good Father. But the combination is in fact a self-cancelling, impossible one. Actual good fathers are "silly," unheroic, un-ideal, un-perfect. Butch's strength and assurance are movie qualities, qualities of "a perfect world." This is Eastwood's world, and in this film Eastwood pretty much destroys it. If we are left with an agonizing regret for the impossibility (the death) of Butch, if we share something of Philip's terrible sense of loss, these are testimonies to the continuing power of ideal yearnings. But the film leaves nothing good standing from this escapade—or rather, makes it retrospectively clear that there never was anything good in it. The legacy to Philip from these events can only be a destructive and emotionally disabling one. Even Barnett can take from them only a detailed spectacle of his own failure. All that remains is an elegiac sadness, an awareness of the waste and loss of Butch's life, perhaps of Philip's life, and a piercing sense of the impossibility of the Good Father.

The film's retrospective self-judgement seems most articulate in its handling of the Eastwood persona. Now completely marginalized, it cannot save Butch at any stage: neither from his father in the past nor from the federal "suit" sharpshooter in the present. When the FBI sniper shoots Butch, the Eastwood cop is finally defeated by the hated bureaucracy, and his trademark all-American retort, the punch to the jaw, is delivered only when it is too late and will put nothing right.[4] The Geritol and the other comic devices which gently satirize Eastwood's decline as strong masculine body are far less damaging to the stature of the persona than his failure of judgement, of wisdom. The decision to have Butch put in prison for a minor offence was a deliberate attempt to intervene in a positive way in the boy's life. Even on a *prima facie* level this decision is questionable: one of Barnett's deputies clearly sees the prison term as having made Butch a criminal and says, in a way that pointedly, if unintentionally, embarrasses his boss, "we've seen that lots of times, haven't we, Red?" And of course subsequent events suggest powerfully that the decision was the wrong one. More than that, it is hinted that the Eastwood character was operating in an outmoded paradigm. In defence of his action he says: "Gatesville's not so bad; I've known kids get turned around—one even became a priest." This latter remark sounds like something out of a 1930s Warner Brothers social-message picture, the plot of an old movie. The film clearly articulates the responsibility the Eastwood character bears. He himself, in a speech to Sally, emphasizes that when things go wrong, he bears the weight. And as the film reveals, behind Butch's whole narrative stands Eastwood, with a historical and institutional responsibility to make right the local failures of institutions such as families and courts as he has (metanarratively) done so often in the past. Now he fails. He confesses his responsibility and bears the weight; he is also old and tired and discouraged. Eastwood cannot win the war any more, says the film.

———

After more than two decades of moviemaking in which the Eastwood persona's heroic masculinity has increasingly carried a shadow of its negation, a few of his most recent films have gone right through deconstruction to actual demolition. *White Hunter, Black Heart* is an astonishingly negative film when you think about it in this context. *Unforgiven* retains massive shards of the violent transcendental persona, but so hedged round with horror that it is difficult for the viewer even to think about that persona without an accompanying nausea. *In the Line of Fire* seems to revert to the dominant Eastwood cinematic model in which, notwithstanding elements that undermine and inspire doubt, the heroic persona is allowed to triumph in the end. Yet the feeling of loss and regret in the film is very strong, and the movie finds it harder than ever to repress the knowledge that the president who was actually killed was John Kennedy and the one whom Eastwood is allowed to save in the replay is purely fictional. The drama of restitution of the father through masculine heroic action is weakened and deflated to a painful degree. But in *A Perfect World* that project cannot be described merely as weakened and deflated: rather, it is massively defeated. In this film, masculinity and power themselves are empty shells, and the beneficent, nurturing, empowering fatherhood that is rooted in them is elaborately revealed as a cultural and ideological fiction.

In all four of these films, *fictions*—which in earlier Eastwood films were first presented as mysterious and uncanny (e.g., *High Plains Drifter*, *The Gauntlet*), then clearly as fictions but also as positive necessities for effectiveness and vitality (e.g., *Bronco Billy*, *Heartbreak Ridge*)—are now presented rather as distortions, as lies. If characters attempt to act them out or use them as a basis for self-inventing empowerment, they lead to the deaths of innocent participants (*White Hunter*, *Unforgiven*, *In the Line of Fire*), to ugly and unredeemable violence practised by the hero (*Unforgiven*, *A Perfect World*), and to false and twisted assumptions and traumatic disillusionment (*White Hunter*, *A Perfect World*). *Unforgiven* and *A Perfect World* are a remarkable pair of self-critiques and myth-renunciations for Eastwood: the former of the violent hero, the latter of the Good Father, between them of the whole Eastwoodian institution of heroic masculinity. (One might then note that *The Bridges of Madison County* contains no vestige of either the violent hero or the Good Father, but finally cedes the central role to a woman and is in every respect a "women's movie." And if the Eastwood character in this film still retains a suggestion of the mysteriously arriving and departing perfect male, he is in the end marginalized and banished to the world of memory and non-presence by the decision of the dominant, female, subject.)

A Perfect World, almost empty of women characters, is certainly in that respect a "men's movie," but nothing could be further from the validations of male agency and power we associate with that genre than this film. It is a men's movie whose work is to diminish and even extinguish the notion of heroic male action. Its greatest strength, I believe, is its simultaneous depiction in extremely vivid and affective terms of *both* the fierce tug of longing for ideal masculinity and ideal fatherhood *and* its impossibility and the completely destructive effects of acting to realize that longing. The film does not denounce the fiction of the Good Father; instead, it points to its overpowering emotional seductiveness and to the dire consequences of listening to that siren song, while seeing clearly how impossible it is to block one's ears in the cultural environment we all occupy. And it is another late stop in the progress of Clint Eastwood's cinema which has along its journey modified a rock-like and impassive image of heroic maleness into an image of suffering and loss.

6

Absolute Power and True Crime

Postscripts of Disavowal

After the symphonic explorations of fatherhood

in *A Perfect World*, Eastwood's next film as director/star, *Absolute Power*, regresses to a far less complex perspective. Its tale of master burglar Luther Whitney, who, while robbing a mansion, accidentally witnesses appalling crimes committed by the President and the Secret Service, reinstalls Eastwood as the quasi-transcendental lone hero who outwits all institutional forces—now conceived as automatically corrupt to the point of nausea or at best incompetent. Politicians and bureaucrats (and, even more regressively, the "power" career woman) arc once again the enemy, as unproblematically evil as any of their predecessors in the Dirty Harry movies. The tarring of President and Secret Service is a particularly striking reversal of position from *In the Line of Fire*. And Eastwood's restoration of moral order from a position of individual heroic separateness with respect to society is accompanied by a similar restoration of his authority as a father. For *Absolute Power* also thematizes Eastwood as father—moreover, as an absentee criminal father whose actions disconcertingly resemble the paradigm of *A Perfect World*.

In *A Perfect World*, Butch Haynes' criminality is qualified by our knowledge of his dreadful childhood. It is worth pointing out how liberal an interpretation this is of crime and the criminal, for Butch is a career criminal and, as the narrative proceeds, a killer as well. Socially conservative philosophies are profoundly uninterested in facts about disadvantaged childhoods, dysfunctional families, or any other explanations for criminal behaviour which might lead to mitigation of punishment. *A Perfect World*, in identifying Butch's criminality as determined to an important degree by just such a history, is a narrative of almost textbook social liberalism. One of the noteworthy things about *Absolute Power*, considering the strong narrative-structural similarities between it and *A Perfect World*, is the way in which that entire political landscape is re-imagined—or perhaps *de*-imagined.

Like Butch Haynes, Luther Whitney is a career criminal who kills before the story is over, but his criminality is sentimentalized and mythologized. He is a cat burglar, a second-storey man who only commits crimes against property when people are absent from the premises; he never even has to wave a gun at anybody. His criminality is presented simply as superior professionalism, indeed even as art. His avocation as a connoisseur of painting and a painter himself is entirely in keeping with his dazzling perform-ance as a criminal, where his feats are so elegant that they, too, have an important aesthetic dimension. He bears the name of a museum of American art, and is seen at the beginning of the film sitting in the National Gallery in Washington, DC sketching an El Greco (most appropriate, when the lanky Eastwood looks like an El Greco himself)—thus taking his place as another Eastwood character who is an artist-performer.[1]

The film is breathless with admiration for Whitney's skill, his intelligence, his virtuosity. He is such a master of disguise and strategy that he never gets caught.[2] His victims are all so rich that any robbery of their goods will not cause them serious hardship. Indeed, if the particular example we see in this film is any guide, they are people with far too much money, and in taking some of it away, Whitney is actually restoring some kind of moral balance. In this way his thefts—wholly motivated by a desire to acquire mate-rial wealth—can be "covered" by a Robin-Hood-like alibi of rough social justice, in a manner entirely representative of the main-stream Hollywood habit of keeping things untroubling. (How different in effect this is from the similar scenario of *Unforgiven*, where the Eastwood character also cloaks a mercenary project in a moralistic covering.) Burglarizing the mansion of the obscenely wealthy plutocrat played by E.G. Marshall, Whitney doesn't touch paintings or *objets d'art*, possibly because he is an artist himself—another move in the strategy to make the character a spiritually sensitive, indeed almost an anti-materialist, thief. At the end of the film, he actually gives back everything he stole in the opening scene (performing yet another virtuoso break-in to replace the stuff). He finishes as a thief who isn't a thief.

Moreover, Whitney is a Korean War hero with medals (as in *Heartbreak Ridge*). He also has a disability pension from the army, no doubt as the result of a gloriously suffered war wound. But he has made this sacrifice for his country without actually having any perceptible disability (just as he is a criminal who doesn't commit crimes). There are also jokes about his age and decrepitude (as in *In the Line of Fire* and *A Perfect World*), but these do not prevent him from shinnying down the outsides of three-storey buildings and outrunning posses of Secret Service agents half his age. When everything is finished, he doesn't go to jail, doesn't get charged, miraculously decriminalizes himself, and lives happily ever after.

Whitney's role as a father is presented in an equally "easy" way. His daughter Kate starts out hating him because he was "never there" during her childhood. He has really no answer for this accusation, but we are led to understand that it was somehow not his fault that he had to spend all those years in prison or on the run, that these are simply the penalties of male professional life which women and children must bear the consequences of and which the absent or derelict husbands and fathers may redeem through a display of penitence and regret. Whitney always speaks of his saintly departed wife (Kate's mother) with reverence and tenderness, notwithstanding the fact that they were separated for years before her death, and it would seem that her judgement of him was one of forgiveness and acceptance. So Whitney also has a broken marriage that isn't a broken marriage. Having introduced Whitney as a derelict parent, the film's aim is then to show that he isn't, and it strains every sinew to accomplish this. We (and eventually Kate) see Whitney's apartment covered in surreptitiously taken photographs of his daughter at various points of her childhood (another both/and move: he was absent, but he wasn't *really* absent). He routinely (invisibly, silently) breaks into her apartment to see how she is doing, sometimes restocking the refrigerator. In the end he saves her life from the creepy Secret Service agents who are trying to kill her, and cold-bloodedly executes one of the perpetrators who begs him for mercy ("Sorry, all out of that," he says, just like Dirty Harry).

Whitney is guilty of very serious family and parental sins: he is absent and derelict, he brings shame to his daughter. But in the end, all negative consequences of these sins are dismissed. Indeed, his original position as absentee criminal husband and father has been magically translated into its opposite: he is now exactly the powerfully protective Good Father whose very existence had been denied by *A Perfect World*. He only *appears* as negligent, selfish, criminal, absent: he was *really* deeply caring, selfless, creatively entrepreneurial, and invisibly present. This is, of course, a massive act of disavowal, since the character's factual status as lawbreaking, imprisoned, and effectively absent is never challenged. Everything that was laboriously, painfully deconstructed in *A Perfect World* is here reconstructed with dismaying ease.

One aspect of the configuration in *Absolute Power* is particularly striking, though, and this is especially the case in the hindsight of Eastwood's subsequent film, *True Crime*. Whitney is able to compensate for his ordinary, everyday failures as a father—absence, divorce, imprisonment—through the exercise of his *special talents*. The skill and artistry he has acquired as a criminal, which are textually and metatextually the characteristics of a *star*, are the means whereby he counterbalances and reverses his "real" failures. His astonishing abilities to be invisible and omnipresent, to outsmart and outmaneuver everybody, are a kind of faint, transmuted echo of the quasi-supernatural abilities of the transcendental persona all the way back to Leone. Now, with the addition of a specifically artistic and creative orientation, the situation becomes potentially rather reflexive, as Whitney doubly represents Eastwood as star performer and as director/creator. Given the aggressively virtuosic nature of this figure of mastery, it is also appropriate to invoke again the idea of fictionality. Whitney the idealized magical father and fixer-of-everything is a fictional character who makes up the deficits of a real dysfunctional father and career criminal. Once again, the lessons of *A Perfect World* are disavowed, and the sustaining fiction reinstalled—but in a context where quite a few of the strings are left showing.

The antitheses in the Eastwood character of the heroic (master burglar) and the humanized (husband and father) are evident again, too. Earlier films (*The Outlaw Josey Wales*, *Heartbreak Ridge*, *Unforgiven*) presented the movement towards human relationships and away from solitude as a necessary revision of the heroic persona, and *A Perfect World* went so far as to attack the whole notion of an ideal/heroic fatherly masculinity as chimerical, leading only to family pathology. But in *Absolute Power*, the solitary, heroic, quasi-transcendental figure is reconstituted, and if his daughter is literally the personage whom he rescues and protects with these powers, one might say that at a deeper metaphorical level the one being rescued is the humanized, social—and now inadequate and failed—version of his own character. In fact, even the heroic (or fictional) "star" Whitney persona has his shadow of doubt and negation, albeit in a marginal and temporary way. In the early scenes, for example, he is actually reduced to watching passively as predatory men assault and murder a young woman. This is a scenario which has always been Eastwood's cue to intervene violently, but here his status of *in flagrante* criminal prevents him from acting. It is from this failure too that the subsequent hero-pyrotechnics are required to redeem the Eastwood persona. Once again in an Eastwood film, doubling and contradiction or disavowal are primary tools of a complex working, but in *Absolute Power* the strange synthesis of opposites is a new one—though not a better one.

●TRUE CRIME (1999)

Absolute Power is a regression, politically and artistically, from *Unforgiven* and *A Perfect World*. So is *True Crime*, but its attempts to heal up or compensate for the cracks in the Eastwood persona are more interesting and perhaps more confessional than in the earlier film. For in this film at least some of what is disavowed in *Absolute Power* is allowed to remain openly visible. Here the Eastwood character, Steve Everett, is an ex-alcoholic womanizing newspaper reporter who is assigned to do a death-row interview and execution-watch as a last-minute replacement when a female fellow-reporter is killed in an auto crash. Everett is explicitly represented as a dysfunctional person in a number of ways: he is a compulsive skirt-chaser (currently having an affair with the wife of his immediate superior), with an extensive series of social messes left in his wake, preceded by an even more extensive series of alcoholic ones. Although not exactly a bad person, he is clearly a systematically selfish and irresponsible one. In fact, the only thing this character has going for him is his famous reporter's instinct, his infallible "nose" for a story: he is a great, natural newspaperman. He doesn't have feelings, he doesn't care about right and wrong (he makes this amazing admission rather blankly fairly early into the film), he just has a fabulous talent for sensing a story. He has a wife and a little daughter (Eastwood's own daughter Francesca Ruth—another extratextual doubling like the ones in *Honkytonk Man* and *Tightrope*), and this nuclear family has been put under intolerable strain by Everett's self-indulgent behaviour. Indeed, the family disintegrates before our eyes almost immediately, in an intense and piercing scene in which his wife, weeping tears more of sorrow than anger, tells him to leave and details, crushingly, why the marriage is beyond repair, and how Everett can never be trusted to change. Everett responds to this powerful speech unhappily, but with a recognition of its truth. At the office, things are going equally badly, as the cuckolded superior has flatly announced to the editor-in-chief that he will not work with such a slack-ass and treacherous colleague and that if Everett isn't fired, he will resign. All of this adds up to a picture of the Eastwood character's life as something resembling a train wreck.

But as he is fulfilling what will very likely be his last assignment for the paper, interviewing this condemned murderer twelve hours before his execution, his famous "nose" twitches. The prisoner, a black man named Frank Beachum, is seen spending his last day with his family—his wife Bonnie and little daughter Gail. Here we find a picture of enormous family dignity under extreme pressure, of a sort that recalls the family of black sharecroppers in *A Perfect World*. The uncomprehending Gail draws pictures for her daddy, while he attempts to remain calm and rational and to help his loving wife bear the blow which is coming. The first priority of both the parents is to shield their daughter as much as possible from the horrific circumstances. The whole family is religious, and trying to lean on the staff of faith and the justice of the next world. Meanwhile the viewer is being mercilessly informed about the protocols of the execution process and the technical details of lethal injection.[3]

When Everett conducts his interview with Frank, his "nose" tells him something is not right about the circumstances. A whirlwind inquiry into the history of the crime (the shooting of a pregnant convenience-store clerk) leads him to the conclusion that the man is innocent. Suspensefully fighting the clock in a series of fantastic investigative coups, he intuitively figures out who the murderer must have been (a black youth seen leaving the store), tracks down the now-deceased man's surviving mother, comes up with a piece of hard evidence proving his guilt and the innocence of Beachum, and saves the day by getting his editor to call his old buddy the governor and get the execution stopped actually after the first tranquilizing injection has taken place but before the second, fatal, one has. The whole narrative mechanism of the instinctive disbelief, the inspired surmise, the successful discovery of proof (all this years after the event, and after an exhaustive police investigation), and finally the protracted last-minute rescue sequence complete with frustrating traffic-jam and Griffithian crosscutting between rescuer and execution-chamber, is as hokily conventional as anything imaginable. ("Aesthetically bad" might be another appropriate term.) A brief epilogue shows Everett, a solitary wanderer who has, however, won a Pulitzer Prize for his journalistic intervention, one day seeing Frank with his wife and daughter in the street, now reunited into a free and ideal nuclear family. They wave to each other. End of movie.

What is certainly most striking about this narrative is its "duplicate" structure. You might be able to argue about whether Steve Everett is an all-around jerk and inadequate human being. But what is beyond argument is that he is a bad husband and no bargain as a father (he horseplays affectionately with his little daughter, but clearly isn't around very much) and is guilty of producing a poisonous atmosphere in the home. In other words, he is a failed family man. But this failed family man is able, because of his extraordinary special talent, to rescue and restore another family—as it were to *produce* and *enable* a perfect family even when he is lamentably unable to achieve one himself. Through his human failings, he effectively *subtracts* himself as husband and father from his own family; meanwhile, through his special talent, he *adds* (restores) another husband and father—this time a worthy one—to another family. Moreover, Everett's fabulous reporter's gift is so instinctive and mysteriously inexplicable that it becomes another example of Eastwood's transcendental power, and also (as in *Absolute Power*) another *fictional* character. In this respect, indeed, the more hokey and exaggerated his feats are, the more visibly transcendental-artificial they become; so that moderating the film's structure into something a little more plausible (e.g., having Everett on the case for months or at least weeks instead of half a day) would actually diminish the quasi-miraculous nature of his intervention and thus his "Eastwoodian" transcendent specialness.

In any case, the result is to produce an amazing schizophrenia of affirmation and doubt—another one of the already-how-many in Eastwood's cinema. On the one hand, the protagonist is unmistakably the hero: he divines the truth, makes the moves, conquers the difficulties, and saves the day, all in dashing style. On the other hand, he is a pathetic loser in human relations: selfish, impervious, damaging to others, full of lame excuses and ineradicable habitual lapses. The combination is not any less challenging to viewers because of its resemblances to the traits of the familiar male movie hero, whose rebel individuality (unwillingness to conform, offences to "good taste" and conventional rules of behaviour) are merely the extra signs of his charismatic independence. Steve Everett may look like this stereotype, but it would take an extraordinarily blind viewer to actually *mistake* him for it. His womanizing has a compulsive and even miserable quality right from the beginning. An early scene shows him in bed with his colleague's wife (at least twenty-five years younger than he is) engaging in postcoital banter. The sixty-seven- or sixty-eight-year-old Eastwood hardbody is ostentatiously displayed for all to see, and it is a disturbing sight: on the one hand grey, wrinkled, sagging like any old man's; on the other hand still heroic in outline and musculature, definitely not the typical old-age-pensioner's body. Here the tension between incompatible thoughts is extreme: on the one hand, "how could anybody think this body is a sexually-attractive sight, what was Eastwood thinking?"; on the other, "gee, Eastwood still looks pretty good, he can still do it." (The woman is also characterized as indulging in the relation mainly to get her husband's attention.) This double-think is in fact characteristic of the really contradictory nature of the character as a whole: on the one hand a sorry spectacle of self-indulgence, self-deception and human incapacity; on the other hand not just a guy with a particular talent, but a hero who can through brilliant intuition and courageous action reverse tragic errors and institute justice. Somebody, in other words, who can't do it in life but who can do it in narrative, in myth.

The similarities between this thematic configuration and that in *Absolute Power* are very strong. The comparison certainly emphasizes the far more unreflective and even cowardly stance of *Absolute Power*, and concomitantly shows the relative complexity and self-insight of *True Crime*. In the specific context of fatherhood, where *Absolute Power* totally absolves the Eastwood character of his parental dereliction and reinstates him as the Good Father whose special talents enable him to *be* the ideal protector, *True Crime* separates those two functions utterly: the special talent enables another family to be ideal, but the character himself is marooned in self-made family dysfunction. It is rather wrenching to see Eastwood in his one early scene with his daughter (again, his daughter both fictionally and extra-fictionally), tumble her about affectionately and lavish her with endearments, and then to see him at the end of the film watching the ideal family he has enabled while standing alone, exiled from any such family of his own and accompanied only by the cold comfort of his public fame—wrenching and self-deconstructive.

At the same time, *True Crime* is scarcely a fully realized film, nowhere close to the mature confrontation of contradiction of *A Perfect World*. In *True Crime*, rather, we are back once more to that curious and highly characteristic quality of Eastwood the filmmaker of simply setting contradictory facts side by side, with no attempt to blend or disguise their jarring mutual negation—back to the aesthetically jumbled but *ipso facto* provocative and interesting world of films like *Pale Rider* and *Heartbreak Ridge*. The corny conventionalisms of Everett's amazing intuition and last-minute ride to the rescue are hardly less trashily conventional than the recruit-humour inanities of *Heartbreak Ridge*, and probably somewhat more off-putting than the numbing incongruities of *Pale Rider*. But the effect in all three films is once again to proclaim the artifice of the Eastwood persona and denaturalize it—and in the context of a narrative like *True Crime*'s, which is much less oriented towards the larger-than-life than those of the other two, the persona's split is more painful and visible.

7
The Beguiled
and
Play Misty
for Me

He Who Lives by the Sword

The Beguiled and *Play Misty for Me* form a fascinating little pocket near the beginning of Eastwood's career as a star. They were made in direct succession, both in 1971; the former directed by Eastwood's American mentor Don Siegel and the first production to be released by Eastwood's Malpaso company, the latter Eastwood's first film as a director. From the standpoint of screen authorship, it would probably be wise to consider both of these movies as collaborations between Eastwood and Siegel, since Eastwood was clearly a crucial presence as star and (more or less) executive producer of *The Beguiled*, and Siegel watched the proceedings of *Play Misty for Me* closely from behind the camera and had a supporting role in front of it. But I am not concerned here to sort out who was responsible for what—or more exactly, to estimate just what Siegel's (undoubtedly very important) contribution was to either film. Rather, I am interested primarily in the way these films present the Eastwood protagonist in a guise which is on the one hand very similar in both movies and on the other instructively different from the ways in which his surrounding movies present him.

Here we find an Eastwood persona whose primary characteristic is the fact that he is attractive to women. Now the persona has to a degree shaken off the transcendent hero's unknowableness and untouchableness—and also his violent mastery. Or it might be better to say that the charismatic distance and self-possession which are coexistent with the transcendent hero's violent power over men is now translated into a different variety.

This charisma and self-sufficiency takes the form of an overpowering appeal to women: Eastwood cannot be successfully resisted
by men in his transcendent-killer mode, and he cannot be
successfully resisted by women in his (one might almost say) tran-
scendent-lover mode. But whereas the Eastwood of the early
westerns and the Dirty Harry films and all the relations of both
types essentially establishes his mastery totally and invincibly, he
finds himself in *The Beguiled* and *Play Misty for Me* in real trouble.
In these films, the Eastwood character finds himself at different
points and to different degrees off-balance, outmaneuvered,
embarrassed, figuratively or literally disabled, and *unmanned* in his
relationships with women—relationships which seem to take the
form of battles, which he is now losing instead of winning. In *The
Beguiled*, as a wounded Union soldier during the Civil War, he
gains first the affections and then the animosity of a Southern
ladies' seminary, eventually has his leg amputated and at last is
fatally poisoned. In *Play Misty for Me,* he is a cool West Coast disc
jockey with a seductive manner, whose one-night stand with a fan
turns into a nightmare as she refuses to be casually shucked off,
turns herself into a giant nuisance, and finally starts attacking
people with a knife.

Perhaps the persona suffers these reverses because any relationship with a woman, even (or as sometimes happens here,
especially) a casual sexual encounter, requires a degree of intimacy
and openness, and this surrender of distance becomes a crucial
weakness for the transcendent persona whose distance is essential to his mastery. At the same time, the power-masculinity of the
transcendent hero might seem to require some reassurance that
its mastery extends into the realm of heterosexuality, that the
hero has power over women as he has over men. We have seen
how in subsequent films (for example, *The Outlaw Josey Wales*,
Tightrope, *Heartbreak Ridge*, *Unforgiven*, *True Crime*) Eastwood
tries, or else pointedly fails, to negotiate some meeting point
between the transcendent killer and a more human-sized persona
with emotional connections to women and/or children. But in
these two films it is as though Eastwood is momentarily trying
another option, the option (again) to transport the heroic persona's
power more or less directly from violent mastery to sexual power.
And it is quite illuminating to see how this transference works
out—or rather, fails to work out.

Both *The Beguiled* and *Play Misty for Me* have a reputation for misogyny.[1] Certainly the forms of female empowerment they depict are potentially or actually murderous, and the spectacle presented of women bending or subduing the elsewhere-invincible Eastwood persona is the occasion for an atmosphere of hysteria in both films. It is easy, therefore, to see how these films can be misinterpreted simply as misogynist representations of the female sex as dangerous, not to be empowered. But this is to look at the picture only from one angle—an angle which excludes the behaviour of the male "victim." For here the Eastwood persona's limitless self-confidence and self-sufficiency becomes a kind of sexual arrogance, a cold manipulativeness which now looks not only morally unattractive but also blind and reckless. In other words, the sexually desiring women in these narratives may—or may not—be monstrous and dangerous, but the sexually manipulating hero is certainly a full collaborator in the production of the bad situations he finds himself in; not to notice his primary culpability is a gross oversight. Looked at from this perspective, these films are early examples of Eastwoodian self-deconstruction.

The one element that seems to be present and operative in the persona's relationships here with women, and that does not seem to be present in his relationships with men, is the dimension of ethics. In the Leone films, in *High Plains Drifter* and *Dirty Harry*, the villainous male adversary is so low that no ethics are required; indeed, an absence of scruples is a definite advantage and constitutes one of the empowering strengths of the Eastwood persona. But in *The Beguiled* and *Play Misty for Me*, the arrival of women as the primary opposite-numbers changes the rules. Both films ground the hero's difficulties in infringements of sexual ethics. It is not that men and women are not allowed to have sex without warfare in these films; but it *is* the case that the male protagonist is not allowed to have casual, throwaway sex, or to play manipulatively upon a woman's feelings, without suffering a severe punishment. Women become homicidal in these films, but they do so as the result of torrents of emotion the Eastwood character has stirred up and tried to control to his advantage. If the films are sexist, it is because they assume that women's emotions (especially sexual jealousy and possessiveness) are different from men's, perhaps of a different order, and that they are strong enough and heedless enough to dare anything. At the same time, to see women assuming the power in narratives where Clint Eastwood is the central figure is certainly a disconcerting and potentially productive spectacle in patriarchal culture.

———

The Beguiled is for the most part an intelligent and subtle film and also, when everything is finished, a chilly and almost cynical one. It takes a stance of merciless detachment towards the voluminous array of human disorders it observes. On a social and national level, the country is tearing itself apart, men are killing each other without pity and laying waste to the landscape, the white race has enslaved the black, the sexes are ready to prey on one another. On a personal level, individuals are either unscrupulous and powerful, or ignorant and deluded, or simply helpless. The law which governs all is that of a Machiavellian calculation, a Nietzschean contest of strengths and weaknesses. Where tenderer feelings of compassion or love sprout momentarily, they are ruthlessly trodden out, almost as if in punishment. The fears and desires of the characters are strong and often raw; but the victor will be the one who plays his, or her, hand the most effectively. If the solitary male in the little female kingdom of the school seems, despite the handicap of his wounds and enemy-soldier status, to have enough cards to prosper in the game, he misplays some of them and turns out in the end not to have had enough to win—and he loses badly. And despite the force of the emotions whirling through the personages of the film, the final tableau—Eastwood's burial—is such a formal completion of the action, so neatly folds all the turbulence back into invisibility, that it once again enforces the detachment of a dark satire. The picture, complete with the corpse of the crow whose arrival at the school had symbolized the Union soldier's, and Eastwood's own keening vibratoless voice over the end-credits softly singing again the opening ballad,[2] is so perfectly appalling that it is almost delicious.

Really none of the characters escape this horizon. All of them are capable at some point or another of the serpent's sting that puts whatever virtues they have in a rather different perspective and places a limitation not so much on their humanity as on all of humanity. For this reason alone the term "misogynist" is ill-advised: the correct term is "misanthropic." Certainly the demonstration-male, Corporal John McBurney, is not a very pleasant prospect as a human being. In his first appearance, he staggers out of the underbrush, singed and bloody, towering over little pig-tailed Amy exactly like a monster. But McBurney's monstrosity is not essentially violent or coercive. Rather it is seductive, wheedling, manipulating. As a Confederate patrol comes past the fallen tree where McBurney and Amy are crouching, he instantly and instinctively turns to sexual manipulation to prevent his discovery:

> MCBURNEY: How old are you, Amy?
> AMY: Twelve. But I'll be thirteen in September.
> MCBURNEY: Sshh. Old enough for kisses.

Then he bends and kisses her as the patrol rides by, leaving her astonished face blackened by his powder-burns. The next scene has the pupil's in Miss Edwina's French class distracted by thoughts that "if the Yankees win, they'll rape every one of us." Cut directly to another low angle shot of McBurney lurching towards the school. Other portents attend his coming: birds fly from the bushes, a raven appears (as in the ballad), and the hens unaccountably begin laying eggs once he has gotten installed as an invalid (as the slave-woman Hallie says to him, "you must got some rooster blood in you"). He is a sexual threat, then, to the eight women in the school.

His seductive manipulations are constant and virtuosic. Every scene with every one of the women who will come near him (and this does not include among the five pupils three who want to turn him over to the Confederate troops immediately and think that harbouring him is treasonous) reveals a new stratagem of emotional manipulation, quickly fashioned from a lightning appraisal of the peculiarities of the woman he is talking to. With the pre-adolescent Amy it is the overpowering charm accompanied by indications that they are special friends — and of course the premature sexuality. With the virginal idealist Edwina it is high romance ("I wonder if you don't sometimes think of yourself as Sleeping Beauty in a castle waiting for a prince to free you with a kiss," and "I've never felt this way about anyone before"). With Hallie it is instant promises to try to find her man, who ran away when he was about to be sold, in return for her help in McBurney's escape. With the pouting, sexually eager Carol it is cool, sexually knowing compliments on *her* sexual knowingness. And with the harder and cannier proprietess Martha Farnsworth, once he recognizes that blanket sexual flattery is not going to work, it is a barrage of different kinds of lies and promises cut to her profile as a Southern lady: he is a non-violent Quaker and his wound was suffered in an attempt to succour a fallen Confederate officer; he has always had "a great respect for the land." A set of brief flashbacks derisorily contradicts these latter assertions by showing him burning crops and acting as a sniper at the moment he was wounded; and these flashbacks simply confirm in bold, unmistakable terms the fact that this man will say anything to get what he wants, that he is quite without honour and scruple. As he plays on Edwina's emotional vulnerability and professes his love, she says desperately, "Oh, don't say things like that if you don't mean them!" McBurney, not meaning a syllable, presses on regardless and damns himself in the eyes of the viewer.

Of course, much may be forgiven a man who is in desperate circumstances, as McBurney is. He is wounded and separated from his army. If he is given over to the Confederates, he will rot in their notorious POW camp, certain to die there if he arrives wounded, and quite likely to do so even in good health. But there is something so easy and practised especially about this sexual manipulation of women that his behaviour seems to go well beyond what is required. The hypocritical poses he is able to don and shuck at a moment's notice suggest a deep, instinctive dishonesty—of such dimensions, indeed, that they entirely exceed the pragmatic requirements of the situation. Eventually, when his position has become more secure and settled, when Martha and Edwina have become committed to him and Martha has even lied to Confederate troops about his presence, he begins to enjoy his condition and indulge himself—and certainly his actions at this point no longer have the alibi of necessity. His mistake is also in a sexual sphere: he starts to behave exactly like the rooster in the henhouse, trying to manipulate all the women simultaneously instead of seeing clearly where his interest is and not complicating things for himself.[3]

It is important to emphasize that it is the *Eastwood* of 1971 occupying this unsavoury role, and that it is the Eastwood charisma that makes it so interesting. He is certainly a powerful seductive presence—again a kind of equivalent of the powerful violent presence he is in the "man's man" films; he is just *beautiful*. And what the film does with this beauty is fascinating. It unites it, on the one hand, with the manipulativeness and dishonesty we have been discussing, emphasizing its power and self-serving detachment. But simultaneously, it places it in a strange position of weakness and limitation and physical passivity, and configures it as a kind of fetish-object of female sexual desire. Again the double nature of the persona is present, though now in a different form than usual: this Eastwood is (physically) beautiful but (morally) ugly, (sexually) powerful but (physically) weak, all-conquering but ultimately killed by an aggregation of "helpless" women. The ideal of power and beauty is present but so—and much more explicitly than usual—is the negating shadow, now to the extent that it encompasses the total defeat and eclipse of the hero.

The film's peculiar hysteria arises from a kind of muted frenzy of (female) sexual excitements which arises as a man is brought into the male-deprived all-female colony. And not just a man, but the perfect man. He is perfect in physical form, perfect in his knowledge of the female heart (he knows just where to press), and perfect in his condition of dependency and forced attention—really a kind of fantasy-object. His maleness is deliciously arousing, but of course dangerous. This fact is emphasized in many ways, including his initial monstrosity of appearance, his belligerent status, the portents accompanying him, and the isolation of the girl's school from other, potentially protective, males. At the same time, this danger is almost entirely allayed, at least temporarily, by his prostrate condition. He is in their power; he can do nothing for himself. They may extinguish him in a moment by turning him over to the Confederate army or they may keep him awhile, dress and feed and bathe him as a fetish-object, a kind of super-Ken-doll of the greatest possible interest.[4] As he becomes more capable and active, their play and fantasies become more extensive and complex, and they discover they are getting in probably over their heads. (Of course, so is he.)

In any event, the character is really *constituted* in this two-edged way: on the one hand, wonderfully attractive (from the feminine standpoint) and powerful (from the male standpoint); on the other, always crippled, limited, and kept on a leash.

The situation is perpetuated as a response to every development which threatens to alter the balance. When things have progressed so far that McBurney can more or less agree with three separate women (Martha, Edwina, and Carol) that he will visit their bedrooms on the same night, his assumption of control is too strong; and Edwina, discovering his infidelity with Carol, whacks at him so that he falls down the stairs and badly injures his leg. Martha determines that the break is too severe and will become gangrenous, so she amputates the leg. McBurney is, as it were, set down a peg. And when he recovers physically enough to steal the school's pistol, rummage through Martha's old letters, and institute a real male tyranny by taking over the operation of everything and drunkenly throwing Amy's beloved pet turtle to its death, all the women but Edwina collaborate in poisoning him. At no time, from the beginning of the film to the end, does Eastwood appear as anything other than physically crippled. It is, again, an extraordinary thing for Eastwood to be doing at this stage of his career.

The women certainly have their inner lives messed with during this process, especially Edwina, Martha, and Amy. All of them hold McBurney dear at one point or another, and all collaborate in destroying him (Edwina pushes him down the stairs, Martha cuts off his leg, and Amy picks poisoned mushrooms "especially" for him). For Edwina he represents True Love; for Amy a charismatic friend triangulated somewhere between her dead father, her pet turtle, and her barely awakening sexuality; and for Martha a kind of practical solution to all of her managerial and sexual problems. If Edwina and of course Amy are virginal, the middle-aged Martha seems like a compendium of outrageous Southern Gothic hothouse perversities: she has conducted an incestuous relationship with her now-fled brother and has lesbian designs on Edwina as well as "regular" heterosexual ones on McBurney. The frank eroticism of McBurney and Carol seems like an isolated outpost of sexual straightforwardness — though Carol too is capable of throwing McBurney in the deep end by alerting Confederate troops that he is on the premises when she overhears him professing love to Edwina, and later asserting to everyone that he forced his attentions upon her. It is true that all of the women are shown in the end to be capable of murder — whether in quasi-homicidal rage or in sneaking, simpering, poisoning premeditation. But morally and humanly speaking they are certainly no more pathological than McBurney is. They saved this man's life, no matter for what variety of motives, and he has repaid them by trying to put them under his thumb.

After the amputation of his leg, McBurney becomes more sexually hysterical than any of the women ever do. His immediate assumption is that Edwina and especially Martha have done this to him purely out of jealousy, as a punishment for the fact that he preferred another woman. He considers himself definitively unmanned by the amputation and in a delirium of rage cries, "Why didn't you just—*castrate* me?" Commentators have regularly accepted McBurney's interpretation of these events, and have talked about the recompense of symbolic castration which the character receives at the hands of women whose sexual desire he has too imprudently aroused; from here it is a short step to the charge of misogyny. But Edwina simply lashed out at her betrayer in the traumatic moment of discovering his awful treachery. She clearly had no intention of pushing him down the stairs; and when she screams at his fallen form, "You lying son of a bitch! I hope you're dead!", the impartial viewer can accept her lack of remorse without suspecting her of intention to injure and moreover can clearly see her behaviour as justified. As for the amputation, Martha is quite possibly capable of cutting off McBurney's leg as a way of punishing him, but there is really no indication that she does so. Her spoken rationale for her action before the fact is quite persuasive, and Hallie—not a member of anyone's camp in this war—expresses her conviction of its necessity after it. Even the murder is as reasonable an action as any murder can be. McBurney has shown himself capable of tyrannical abuse and is furthermore viciously threatening to blow the lid off every explosive secret in the place. To somehow expel him from the school would be to invite him to come back with a troop of marauding Yankee soldiers. They have given him his life; now they will take it back. (At this point the film does pull a fast one by sobering McBurney up and apparently converting him into an honourable man who is going to marry Edwina and protect the school—but this not-very-convincing transformation comes deliberately too late to avert his fate and seems to emanate more from the film's will to a formally perfect dénouement than from any inherent qualities of the character.)

The Beguiled stages two reversals in the heroic masculinity of the Eastwood persona. One is to transfer charismatic power away from the dimension of violent mastery and into that of heterosexual attraction. The other is to bring with that transference a dramatic disabling of the physical strength of the figure and to subject him to a process of lingering negotiation and final *Untergang*. Like Hercules with Omphale, or Samson with Delilah, the Eastwood persona is unmanned by women; but unlike those figures, he seems to produce his own destruction through his invention and pursuit of the power-game of seduction. But ultimately the moral is the same as with Hercules: to dally with women is to risk *becoming* a woman. It is almost shocking to see Eastwood in this film. He is crippled, bedridden or hopping about on crutches, amputated, poisoned, and buried in a sack with his eyes open—the most complete defeat of an Eastwood hero depicted in any of his films, even *Honkytonk Man*. This is not just a moderation of his heroic masculinity, it is its cancellation. But then, McBurney's whole cajoling, flattering, sweet-talking, *beguiling* strategy is already "feminine"—certainly in contrast to the majestic indifference of the power-masculine transcendent hero. For this (in this sense) feminized figure then to occupy the position of physical passivity and powerlessness seems simply like a further enforcement of the condition of femininity. From this perspective, the character's acute sense that he has been deprived of masculine power, concentrated finally in his terrible cry that he has been castrated, seems to emanate from the heroic persona rather than simply from John McBurney. It is a striking counterpoint to the very basis of Eastwood's star-construction at the time, and an equally striking demonstration of the complications and contradictions which Eastwood the creator is interested in exploring as he begins the process of commanding his own films.

———

Play Misty for Me, the film that marks Eastwood's debut as a director, is another such demonstration. Here the persona's crippling is not so explicit and his defeat not so total. Moreover, the ending of the film at least to some extent recuperates the Eastwood character's power-masculinity in a way *The Beguiled* never does. But in a more "realist" modern setting than *The Beguiled* and without that film's narrative formalism and fabular qualities, *Play Misty for Me* presents a picture not so starkly negating but, if anything, even more profoundly disconcerting than its predecessor. The plot—often cited as an inspiration for the film *Fatal Attraction* (1987)—features Eastwood as David Garvey, a Bay-Area night-show DJ who plays soft jazz and reads poetry and who is a little local star with a little cult of followers, many of them female. The sexual revolution is at high tide, and David has an extensive and ongoing string of brief sexual encounters, notwithstanding the fact that they interfere with his relationship with the one woman he is serious about (her name is Tobie). One of these encounters begins when he picks up Evelyn Draper in a bar and takes her rather perfunctorily to bed. But instead of simply fading away like all his other conquests, Evelyn becomes more and more insistent and bothersome, then panic-inducing, and finally mortally threatening. Now the sexually attracted and threatening female is concentrated in a single personage, rather than spread out among an all-female community as in *The Beguiled*. But the metamorphosis of Evelyn from a compliant one-night-stand groupie into a murderous harpy is accompanied geometrically by the metamorphosis of the hero David from a cool, smooth womanizer who picks up and discards females with complete control into a disconcerted, humiliated, and ultimately frightened figure of weakness.

There is no defence for Evelyn, whose subtly, then stridently, increasing demands move into registers of shrieking psychosis well before the end of the narrative and who may be described with no exaggeration, finally, as a monster. (The film indeed resembles a horror movie in a number of ways, with its gradual revelation of an "unnatural" and dislocated world underneath the "normal" one, its representation of its antagonistic force as more and more uncanny and unrestrained, and of course its escalating violence.) But whose monster is Evelyn? She is the protagonist's monster: it is only as his nightmare, and that of the patriarchal ideologies he embodies, that this character really has meaning. One must interpret Evelyn as a *product* of David's repressed fears rather than as any naturalistically observed phenomenon, however exaggerated. The character Eastwood plays here is in even stronger contrast to the primary persona of the transcendent killer. John McBurney was at least a soldier, if a disabled one. But as proto-New Age DJ David Garver, Eastwood is very far indeed from that figure of violence and raw power. Iconographically, the soothing voice quoting poetry and talking about feelings, the flowered shirts and long hair, the seaside house with indoor grotto, the whole relaxed hedonistic Californianism of the character diametrically opposes to the flint-like hardness, taciturnity, and violence of the Man With No Name or Harry Callahan. David's personal style and career-choice have not only softened this persona beyond recognition, they have actually deliberately gravitated to a more feminized character, where McBurney has one to some extent thrust upon him. Certainly David's profession, his star status as a sexy, beguiling voice in the night, makes him an object of female desire. As in *The Beguiled*, this Eastwood character is self-consciously selling his sex-appeal in a way that is more characteristic of the female gender than the male, rather than regarding it with indifference or contempt as the "man's man" Eastwood of the westerns and cop movies does.

The persona's strength is at first maintained through the assumption of dominance in this realm of offered sexuality: David has power over women, he picks them up and discards them, he sets the rules. The iron distance and impersonality of the transcendent Eastwood hero is here recast as boundless self-confidence and "cool." But it is characteristic that even from the beginning this self-confidence should hint rather at self-regard, and the cool at a certain preening fatuity. It is worth emphasizing that from a power-masculinist point of view, devoting so much time and energy to attracting women is at best undignified, at worst dishonourable. The truly masculine hero will, "naturally," be attractive to women; but if there is one thing he ought never to be, it is a quasi-gigolo. The "boys will be boys" games of sexual manipulation David plays especially in collaboration with his bartender friend—first to pick up Evelyn and then to get rid of her—carry something very close to the stigma of prevarication and dishonour. These are, in the eyes equally of gender consciousness and of traditional chivalrous patriarchal ideology, transgressions against honesty and honour, and they create a muffled sense of unease which, in Hitchcockian fashion, comes home to roost with a vengeance later in the film. In this context, the desirable female Evelyn becomes a disconcerting "conquest" because she refuses to be controlled and disposed of by the supposedly all-powerful male. As in the field of masculine warfare the violent man's nightmare is the antagonist who refuses to stay killed (a role Eastwood himself has played repeatedly from *A Fistful of Dollars* to *High Plains Drifter* to *The Gauntlet* to *Pale*

Rider), so in this "battle of the sexes" the hero's nightmare is the female sexual conquest who refuses to go away after she has been bedded, but keeps returning so persistently that she begins to seem uncanny and monstrous to the baffled David, just as the heroic Eastwood has so often been for the villainous antagonists trying to dispose of him.

This doubling reversal of patterns in Eastwood's work reminds us of another perspective: Eastwood is here playing a performer, a star—something that he himself, metatextually, is.[5] The narrative becomes not just David's nightmare of the horrific "off-air" consequences of wielding charismatic attraction but (as it were) Eastwood's. Thus when, under the relentless pressure of Evelyn's emotional and physical demands, Eastwood is again and again disconcerted, humiliated, shown as weak and powerless, there is something reflexively self-critical (or at least unnerving) about the spectacle. David has his bartender-friend lie to Evelyn that he is not at the bar—and she catches him in the lie. As he tries to drive off, she snatches his car keys away and he has to chase her and wrest them back in a most undignified fashion. While he, weakly, *sleeps,* she steals his house keys and copies them. As he is pitching his radio show to a powerful woman producer at a restaurant, Evelyn barges in and creates the most embarrassing scene imaginable. And in the end she wields the knife, which is both the castrating tool and the phallus itself, and wounds him repeatedly.[6] These humiliations, these weaknesses, are simply not supposed to happen to Clint Eastwood no matter what the context. When they *do* happen, the result produces unease in the audience—an unease (again) reminiscent of Hitchcock in that it is buried in a *hubris* and a transgression which the viewer has collaborated in—and this unease gives rise to a subliminal consciousness of the potential fallibility of the Eastwood heroic persona itself, of the fact that Eastwood's invincibility is not immutable and transcendent but conventional and artificial, as contingent as David's smooth charisma.

Much of Evelyn's power to unman David, to affect the heroic Eastwood in the way kryptonite affects Superman, derives from her mastery of the conventions ruling male-female relations. Paul Smith speaks of this character as embodying the new sexual freedom accorded to women in the late '60s, and says that *Play Misty* is a message to women who would empower themselves with such freedom that, in embracing sexual autonomy, they will forsake any more lasting claims on male affections.[7] But although Evelyn certainly feels at liberty to sleep "casually" with David in a sexually free way, to describe her as an emblem of this type is shortsighted. Not only does it overlook the way in which Evelyn in her first scene disguises herself as a pickup and allows David to think that he has wielded the sexual initiative, but it quite neglects the chameleon quality of transformation that makes Evelyn (again, like the monster in a horror movie) uncontainable and undisposable. Having indeed presented herself in the light of a "liberated" — and thus disposable — woman, and having stood still for David's disclaimer speech in which he explains to her that their sexual encounter will have no consequences in emotional attachment or subsequent obligation, Evelyn begins her horrifying metamorphosis precisely into a consequence and an attachment which uses every weapon of sexual convention, traditional and new, to maintain a limpet-like grip on the protagonist. When, for example, she begins to visit his house uninvited or to import bags of groceries to cook them a meal without forewarning, she is acting out a degree of domestic consequence which under a more traditional rubric would "naturally" have followed from an event as serious as sexual intimacy. And in behaving like a traditional woman, for whom the act of sexual union must of course imply a commitment, a relationship of some substance, Evelyn puts *David* in the extremely uncomfortable position of acting with respect to that traditional woman like a traditional cad. In vain does he protest that they had a deal, that she is not supposed to press any claims which her social predecessors might have been justified in pressing. Notwithstanding the fact that Evelyn has blatantly changed the "rules" literally overnight, David still finds himself inescapably trying to scrape off a woman as if she were something he had stepped in, and there is simply no way in which he can do this without looking selfish, mean-spirited, and above all like every man who has ever "had his way with" a woman and then cravenly tried to evade the consequences.

In this configuration, it really doesn't matter how unfair Evelyn is, or for that matter how invasive, shrill, or even violent: all that matters is that the protagonist's posture of moral rectitude, of cool sexual control, of male dominance, is continually and fatally compromised. Evelyn has essentially nothing to lose.

At best she is a trivial event in the life of the protagonist. But David—or rather Eastwood—has a position to maintain, above all in the eyes of the audience. (Nor should we forget that Evelyn is, for the Eastwood fan, a kind of stand-in for that audience.) Evelyn moves from merely assuming too much about the continuation of their relationship into more extreme but clearly related gambits of "female" warfare in the battle to keep a man who has no interest in her: temporary self-abnegating compliance, histrionic suicidal suffering, and violent maniacal possessiveness. Again, in sacrificing her "credibility," or indeed in becoming completely hateful in this campaign, she loses nothing in the estimation of the audience: it is David who loses dignity, control, the facade of gentleness, sensitivity and concern with which he had wished to cloak his behaviour as "the old Adam." It is of the greatest interest that David sleeps with Evelyn at least twice more *after* the first announcement that their relationship is at an end. Moreover, there are constant indications from the other characters that David's womanizing is neither "sexual liberation" nor a "natural" outgrowth of his sensitivity, gentleness, and poetic soul, but rather a quasi-pathological obsession which is nothing less than the quieter masculine counterpart of Evelyn's murderous feminine one. That is, while Evelyn cunningly, desperately, obsessively tries to cling to the man she desires, David tries to "use up" as many women as he possibly can with a persistence whose cunning, desperation, and obsessiveness may not be visible itself but is suggested precisely by the visibility of Evelyn's. (McBurney in *The Beguiled* has the excuse that he exercises his wiles because his very life is in danger, but what is David's excuse?) We might also be note that in this context, David's continuing attempts to regain the idealist shore of a committed relationship with a perfect woman—the doll-like, "artistic" Tobie (Donna Mills) who proclaims that the thing she hates most in the world is a jealous woman—look more and more unreal.

Evelyn is, then, exactly the punishment best suited for David's promiscuity. Far from representing the liberated woman's unwillingness to accept that men will now be liberated too (as Smith has it), Evelyn represents instead the always-already-unencumbered single male's fear that even the new sexual freedom will not enable him to skate blithely from one woman to another without the slightest consequence—or rather, that perhaps a day of reckoning will come for the manipulativeness and instrumentality which have characterized his relations with women, in which all the accumulated debt will have to be paid at once. In this light, Evelyn represents not the woman's frightening id, but the man's frightening superego. And the effect of this menace is not (or at least not simply) to depict the female as potentially evil and dangerous, but rather to present a spectacle of female power and male impotence.

But as we have seen, David is an Eastwood who has forsaken the harsh world of male combat for the perfumed one of poetry, soft music, and women; who has displaced conflict and mastery from the rocklike masculine world of violence into the soft, feminine one of sexual relationships. Of course, *Play Misty for Me* is not, from the standpoint of genre, primarily a melodrama or "relationship" movie: it is a thriller, defined by its violence and threat of violence. Even Eastwood here has not left the narrative environment in which characters kill one another. And in the end, of course, it must be Eastwood who does the final killing. So at the very end of the narrative, after scene upon scene of Eastwood furiously backpedalling, horribly embarrassed, outmaneuvered, and finally terrified, the character does indeed rediscover his violent masculinity. Ambushed by a knife-wielding Evelyn, he is stabbed and slashed repeatedly (and in one awful shot grasps the blade with his bare hand, cutting it horribly). Finally he resorts to the traditional American male's most characteristic movie weapon: the punch. The essence of Evelyn's hold upon David is that it relies continually upon the fact that he (and especially the Eastwood persona) would never take anything like this from a *male* character: a male character would have been violently obliterated at the first affront. But against a woman, the heroic male cannot exercise violence so easily; it is unchivalrous, brutal in a distinctly unheroic fashion. In the end, though, Evelyn's female transgressions are so extreme that he must treat her like a man. He uncorks one powerful punch to the jaw which sends her crashing through the railing and plummeting down onto the rocks by the seashore to her death. And while when this long-awaited punch is delivered there are often (male) cheers in the audience at the employment of brute masculine strength too long restrained by misplaced delicacy, David's (and Eastwood's) dignity and mastery have been far too gravely compromised for everything to be "put right" by any final victory.

The reflexivity of Eastwood the performer and artist in *Play Misty for Me* is the foundational example of a strand that has run right through Eastwood the creator's cinema—the clearest examples occurring in *Bronco Billy*, *Honkytonk Man*, and *White Hunter, Black Heart*. *Play Misty* dramatizes both the temptations of ego and the vulnerability of that distant and charismatic figure, the star. As we have seen, the film picks out for staging the quality of sex-appeal—or to put it another way, the appeal of the Eastwood persona for the "female" viewer rather than for the "male." His fetishized status is underlined from the beginning, with the film's first important image being that of Tobie's oil-painted portrait of David, an icon of romantic charisma. It is just this quality which becomes the centre of Evelyn's mad fetish-production (and it is noteworthy that her homicidal rampage at the end of the film takes time out to viciously slash to ribbons the idealized image of that portrait). The heroicization of the Eastwood character at the hands of sexually and romantically desiring women forms the bedrock of the action; and the protagonist is shown first enjoying the benefits of that process, then very much suffering the punishments. The whole movement is such as to cast into doubt specifically the sexual power Eastwood wields over women, and by extension the charismatic performer's power he wields over all fans. The film thus begins in the "natural"—David is "naturally" a star, a seductive male presence, the magnet of female attention—and proceeds to "denaturalize" that state—as it gives rise to Evelyn's crazed worship/need-to-own. The film might be seen perhaps as an anxiety that any star (including Eastwood) might have about the possible actions of a deranged fan. But *Play Misty for Me* (like *The Beguiled*), in bringing in questions of sexual guilt, gender roles and conventions, and especially the contrast of the supposed dominant mastery of the male star and the actual weakness and powerlessness of the character, enlarges itself far beyond that narrow scope, or indeed the narrow scope of any film content to be simply and only a thriller.

———

The double vision of *The Beguiled* and *Play Misty for Me*, then, is exercised in the realm of the relationship between the Eastwood persona and female characters with whom he has some kind of sexual connection beginning in seduction and ending in antagonism. On the one hand, these films show an anxiety, sometimes even a panic or hysteria, about the loss of masculine power in such a relation—a loss quite at odds with the stability and invincibility of the transcendent killer's power in the surrounding films. On the other hand, they depict, sometimes subtextually but nonetheless very clearly, the female antagonist's point of view, and demonstrate that the antagonistic aspects of the connection are rooted primarily in just that self-serving and self-sufficient masculine imperviousness which is inseparable from the transcendent killer and helps to give him his power. In a way that is admittedly indirect and sometimes neurotic, this latter perspective is nonetheless a way of giving the woman her viewpoint and her due; it is at least the opposite of simply ignoring her or disposing of her, which is mostly her fate in the arena of power-masculinity. If Eastwood is not yet comfortable with this activity, it is noteworthy that he is attempting it already at the beginning of his creative career, and doing so in ways which are detrimental in every sense to the mythic power of his primary persona.

These films are thus the starting point for Eastwood's more widely noticed accommodation to women characters and women's concerns in later films.[8] As we have noted, the project— not attempted at all in *The Beguiled* and *Play Misty for Me*—to negotiate a meeting place between the transcendental hero and the humanized lover is carried on in different ways throughout *The Outlaw Josey Wales*, *Bronco Billy*, *Tightrope*, *Heartbreak Ridge*, and *In the Line of Fire*. Meanwhile, in another part of the forest, *Honkytonk Man*, *Unforgiven*, and (in its incoherent way) *True Crime* eventually deconstruct both sides of the dialectic. And in *The Bridges of Madison County* Eastwood completely deserts masculinity as a set of values defined by men and moves entirely into the "woman's man" sphere. Here the Eastwood character is the fantasy-object of a woman, just as in *The Beguiled* and *Play Misty for Me*, but instead of trying to use this attraction for his own selfish ends, he selflessly devotes himself simply to being that object as satisfactorily as he can. He puts himself into the hands of the woman almost as totally as he is put into them in *The Beguiled*, but now this is what he wants; he accepts his passivity and his secondariness. The "femininity" which in the two earlier films is hysterically equated with castration is now actually savoured for its own subtle taste. To be sure, the most extended exercises of this kind, *Heartbreak Ridge*, *In the Line of Fire*, and *Bridges*, all conflate Eastwood the sensitive charmer with Eastwood the aging man—and thus in a sense make these romantic pleasures a consolation for the *loss* of power masculinity. But, as we have seen, the priorities were never as clear as that statement implies, and Eastwood's forays into the realm of femininity have always been as interestingly complicated as his other activities.

8
Eastwood, Auteur and Metteur-en-scène

To conclude these meditations, I would like to devote some space to a potpourri of authorial traits in Eastwood's work which deserve a closer look than they have so far received here — especially traits that have a strictly cinematic basis. I start with the premise that Eastwood is a film author, even an *auteur* (to bring in the full baggage of the old French and then Anglo-Saxon discourse regarding film authorship). The films he has directed have a highly personal set of themes and tropes, even if they are formed also by the cultural and ideological environment of which they are a part. The preceding essays detail many of the recurring topics of Eastwood's cinema: heroic masculinity (embodied in the Eastwood screen presence) as a self-consciously transcendent project; the place of violence in narratives of mastery; the "impossible," wish-fulfilling, or fictional nature of the heroic persona; pro- or anti-sociality as a characteristic of this figure; the enabling or nurturing features of masculinity and their relation to violent transcendence; a simultaneity of heroic and deconstructive perspectives; a quasi-reflexive interest in creators, artists and performers. Although individual films directed by Eastwood do not fit comfortably into this framework of themes and subjects (e.g., *Breezy*, *The Eiger Sanction*, *Foxfire*) and although in his role as producer/demiurge there have been several Malpaso films starring Eastwood but not directed by him which *do* fit quite comfortably (e.g., *Dirty Harry*, *Tightrope*, *In the Line of Fire*), a standard auteurist analysis of the films of Eastwood the director will yield more than ample evidence for the proposition that he has "something to say" in excess of the relatively anonymous commercial norm.

Similarly he constantly and even obsessively repeats a multitude of smaller tropes in the form of narrative moments or scenes, objects, situations, iconic vistas, or details. The face, body, and voice of Eastwood the actor are of course the most obvious examples of an iconic continuity, and this is seen in the metatextually meaningful variations on themes of costume and setting, posture and angle of vision, squints and glares, and hoarse utterances. I would assert that Eastwood's manipulation of these features is, once again, more pointed and self-conscious than is the case with most other star presences, even those who are most narrowly focused in a strongly similar set of roles. Apart from this field, which is shared to some degree with all other stars, there is also a distinct collection of other repetitions and variations, large and small: armour-plating and bullets in the torso, demonic torchlit scenes of violence, questions about the technique of gunfighting, characters nicknamed "Red," references to the assassination of John Kennedy, etc., etc. Taken in the aggregate, these form a network of interconnective tissue which further asserts the family resemblance of Eastwood's films, the presence in them of a distinct personality, seen now in the micro-world of detail as clearly as in the macro-world of theme and subject. Such a collection of similarities in themes and motifs has served by itself as the basis for auteur analysis in the work of Hollywood filmmakers without any very *visible* cinematic style, such as Hawks and Capra.

But in many cases, Hollywood auteurs have also yielded a distinct "signature" in the realm of visual style: *mise en scène*, camera movement, frame composition, editing and *découpage*, textures and rhythms, and general visual environment. These range from such relatively subtle signatures as the long takes and deep focus of a Preminger or the tortuous landscapes of an Anthony Mann to styles so rigorous and unique that (in the most characteristic work) only a few shots are necessary to identify the filmmaker, as in the case of a Sternberg or a Hitchcock. So we may pose the question: does Clint Eastwood's cinema have a distinctive visual style? And if it does, how extensive and fully developed is it? I would suggest that Eastwood's work does have such a signature, although it is not visible all of the time and is most clearly seen in a number of distinct intermittent features which are not present in every film or in every scene of any film.

●WIDESCREEN

One may point in a preliminary way to Eastwood's fondness for a widescreen ratio. In certain films, notably the westerns, this privileges a kind of horizontality and openness in exterior shots, and a kind of epic space everywhere. This ratio and its attendant qualities is present in all the westerns (*Bronco Billy* excepted), and in the Harry movies and other action films as well. Sometimes it gives rise to striking widescreen photographic composition—but again it must be said that this trait never really dominates even individual works in the way it does, for example, in much Japanese cinema or indeed in any film which constantly uses the widescreen frame for dynamic composition. Here one can say, as with much of the visual realm in Eastwood's cinema, that there is evidence of a distinctive choice of format or style, but that the individuality is not such as to call constant attention to itself.

In many instances the importance of Eastwood's widescreen frame becomes most visible on cropped, panned-and-scanned video formats (including virtually all television showings), where the sense of claustrophobia and too-close-ness is distinctly stronger than usual. Unlike many Hollywood productions of the past fifteen years, widescreen Eastwood films such as *Pale Rider*, *Unforgiven*, and *A Perfect World* seem not to have been shot with one eye on the Academy-ratio television screen, just as the low-light scenes described below do not transfer at all well from the photographic to the video medium. I conclude from these data that Eastwood is concerned more with the aesthetic factors of the cinematic medium than with the commercial factors of portability across media.

●DARKNESS AND LIGHT

Among the most notable visual characteristics of Eastwood's cinema, perhaps the most widespread is a generally dark photographic palette in interior or nighttime scenes. Of course interior and nighttime scenes have a lower light level as a matter of course, but the decision to render many of these in a darkness so profound that the viewer must peer to make out details or even central actions is certainly unusual. Reviewers have been complaining about this quality ever since the mid-1970s, and that Eastwood has persisted in this path in the teeth of objections is a clear indication that it is deliberate and meaningful.[1] Nighttime scenes are often illuminated by firelight (e.g., *High Plains Drifter*, *Sudden Impact*, *Unforgiven*) or by in-shot light sources which create a *chiaroscuro* effect (e.g., *Sudden Impact*, *The Rookie*), both of which create dramatic contrasts that are almost expressionist at times. Interior scenes are frequently shot with what looks like little or no auxiliary lighting at all, with small areas of bright light coming from windows and doors, and objects and persons reduced to dark silhouettes or shadowy presences in pools of darkness. There are many, many examples of this styling, some of the most striking occurring in the western contexts of *The Outlaw Josey Wales*, *Pale Rider*, and *Unforgiven*. In one case, that of *Bird*, a whole film is dark, being set almost entirely at night or in low-lit interiors, and moreover mostly with a cast of black characters.[2] (However, the two most "Eastwoodian" films *not* directed by Eastwood, namely *Tightrope* and *In the Line of Fire*, both manifest these tendencies to a marked degree—though to what extent this is evidence against the authorship of the directors or for the authorship of the demiurge producer/star is difficult to estimate. Obviously the presence of a common director of photography, Jack N. Green, on all these projects is of considerable importance as well.)

This darkness seems to me to be partly simply an aesthetic taste—one which runs counter to the utilitarian philosophy of most mainstream Hollywood photography, particularly of the 1980s—and partly a complement to the qualities of mystery and dark power which so many Eastwood protagonists have manifested in the narrative/thematic context. The quasi-supernaturalism in particular of three of Eastwood's western heroes seems entirely harmonious with the scenes of firelit demonic carnage in *High Plains Drifter* and *Unforgiven* and the stygian interiors of *Pale Rider*. In general, too, I think we can say broadly that darkness equals seriousness, either dramatic (*High Plains Drifter*, *Absolute Power*) or psychological (*Bird*) or both (*Sudden Impact*, *Unforgiven*). *Bronco Billy*, a film which thematizes artifice and artificial optimism, is perhaps precisely the exception that proves the rule.

In most of the films (*Bird* is an exception), this world of darkness and garish expressionist light is juxtaposed with an entirely opposite visual realm: that of brightness, openness, and clarity. In films such as *High Plains Drifter*, *The Outlaw Josey Wales*, *The*

Gauntlet, *Pale Rider*, *Heartbreak Ridge*, *Unforgiven* and *A Perfect World*, there is an almost schematic contrast between these two antithetical regimes.[3] A flat horizon, a cloudless azure sky, crisp sunshine, and (often) a rippling breeze create a climate of airy freshness, whose visual contrast to those other scenes of darkness is energizing and helps to create a sense that the films bear a distinctive visual signature. As always with Eastwood, the style is most marked in the westerns. In *High Plains Drifter* the nightmarish world of darkness, flames, and violence that dominates the flashbacks and the climactic scenes is counterpoised with a flat, bright environment that is clearly descended from Leone but even more stylized. The town of Lago is perched on a flat patch of barren desert scrubland, set surreally next to an even flatter lake, so that the sensation of an empty tabletop landscape without vertical features is doubly emphasized. True, there are hills in the distance around the town (from which the Eastwood character descends, as he will do again in *Pale Rider*), but they only serve further to dramatize the flatness which they surround. The town itself, built almost entirely of new unpainted wood, has a bare and unfinished, again almost a featureless, look. Then the sun shines down unblinkingly from a cloudless sky, replicating simplicity and emptiness above as well as below. Altogether, the impression is one of a bareness so extreme as to be an aggressive statement of style — an impression not exactly diminished by the stark contrast with the equally aggressive scenes of darkness.

In *Pale Rider*, the openness of the town perched on a snow-covered, muddy patch of emptiness (and again featuring unpainted buildings) is similarly set into a natural environment, and this one is even harsher. As the Eastwood character emerges from a desert heat-haze in *High Plains Drifter*, so here the mysterious and lethal Preacher seems to materialize in longshot into a flinty and colourless background of rock and snow, and his supernaturally mandated violence is associated throughout with a threatening sky or a sunlit brightness that is as cold as death. The film's visual regime is as strong and confident as its thematic development is disordered and contradictory. And so individual scenes and individual stagings bear a powerful iconic force even as any coherent meaning escapes them: the Preacher's first appearance, his severe costume and face and his dirty-grey horse a precise answer to his environment and allegorical significance; his axe-handle fight in low angles against a lowering sky; the dark interior scenes of his exposure of his bullet scars or his retrieval of his gun; the daring near-absurdity of Stockburn's myrmidon-marshals in their identical long coats; and above all the intensely ritualized final showdown in bright cold daylight which completes a series of restaging of pieces of *High Plains Drifter* through an almost didactic narrative repetition but iconic reversal of the final scene of that film. *Unforgiven* returns to some of these scenes (not so much scenes, really, as gestures of style). Munny's horrific campfire recollections and especially the hellish final scenes recall *High Plains Drifter*. But there is also a repetition of the counterpoint of brilliant daylight and dark interiors: in the streets, saloons, and jail cells of Big Whiskey during Little Bill's punishment of English Bob, and during the scenes of Munny's recovery from fever and beating, in the intensely bright, thin-aired mountain landscape and its obscure and backlit interiors.

●HYPERTROPHY

Another very distinctive aspect of Eastwood's visual style, this perhaps the one that most clearly demonstrates his genuine interest in and grasp of the possibilities of the cinema as a medium, is what I will call a hypertrophic quality of *mise en scène*. Certain scenes, and sometimes global approaches within whole films, almost leap out at the viewer in their daring grandness and simplicity of utterance. A few examples will illustrate what I mean. I have already remarked on the stylization and simplification of the settings of *High Plains Drifter*. But the most astonishing stroke of all comes when the unpainted wood buildings of Lago are painted at last, and in the most artificial, stylized, and symbolic way. The vengeful protagonist, now holding despotic sway over the town, decrees that, as a kind of anti-salutation for the three returning criminals, the entire town be painted bright red, and a welcome sign be hung at the outskirts. In this hellish stage-set we may find the beginning of Eastwood's obsessive association of his lethal western protagonist with the forces of divine or demonic retribution — echoed (as we have seen) with great precision in *Pale Rider* and *Unforgiven*. And we may find also what will become a familiar reflexivity in the presentation of the Eastwood figure as artistic creator *inside* the movie: for the protagonist of *High Plains Drifter* stages and directs the climactic scenes of the narrative with as conscious an eye to dramatic effect as Bronco Billy or the John Huston figure in *White Hunter, Black Heart*. The self-consciousness of this "artistic stroke," which is both Eastwood the protagonist's and Eastwood the director's, is heightened by the visual boldness and vividness of the gesture. There is nothing subtle about a decision to paint the entire landscape bright red. Then, of course, that landscape is put to the torch in another breathtakingly literal realization of the metaphor of hellfire.

A similar moment occurs at the end of *Bronco Billy*, where, as a climactic celebration of Billy's ideological victory in persuading everyone of the virtue and necessity of cowboy mythology, the troupe's final performance is staged in a tent stitched out of scores or perhaps hundreds of American flags. Narratively, this tent is a replacement cobbled together to overcome the disaster of the troupe's loss of their usual tent in a calamitous fire. Thematically, however, it is as stunningly clear a visualization of the film's central metaphor as can be imagined. Out of the ashes of catastrophe springs a hopeful new construction. Out of the ashes of the loss of faith which is the crisis of American ideology in 1980 comes a new ideological habitation, purposely built from the mythic materials which are the innate components of American ideology. That the tent of flags has been fabricated by the inmates of a mental asylum is, furthermore, an echo of the incongruity (akin to a delusion) of Billy's adoption of cowboy values whose literal assertions are ludicrous. As in *High Plains Drifter*, what is most striking about this visual metaphor is that it is audacious and direct, that it draws on a kind of simple or fundamental association in the cultural experience of its viewers, and that it overwhelms the visual environment in a hypertrophic way. It may indeed be appropriate to classify these strokes as the aesthetic language of a "primitive" artist: for if they have the populist naïveté of "primitive" iconography, they have also its freshness and boldness. And we see in this style yet another configuration of the Eastwood who is simultaneously naïve and self-conscious, mythic and reflexive, classical and postmodern. For both of these scenes carry the simplicity and directness of their metaphors to such a hypertrophic extreme that their existence *as* metaphors (i.e., as fiction) once more intrudes on the unself-conscious space of the underlying classical-realist forms they inhabit.

Other, perhaps (understandably) less extremely visible, examples of this authorial trait may be seen in the three big action set-pieces of *The Gauntlet* and in the staging of the climactic scenes of *Unforgiven*. In *The Gauntlet*, the hypertrophy and the stark self-consciousness of the "gauntlet" itself come closest to the daring formula of primitiveness and reflexivity seen in *High Plains Drifter* and *Bronco Billy* (note that in all of these films Eastwood saves his grandiose visual metaphors for the big final climaxes). *The Gauntlet* has, moreover, the same constructive/ deconstructive quality in its simultaneous comprehensive staging and comprehensive undermining of the conventional violent spectacle of the action genre through a hypertrophic exaggeration. In *Unforgiven,* it is perhaps "classically" easy to miss the rigorous connections between nighttime firelight and the hyper-violent side of Munny's nature, or the utterly anthropomorphic quality of a storm which arrives in exact relation to the re-emergence and ultimate arrival of that frightening persona; and viewers cannot perhaps be counted on to catch the significantly varied returns to *High Plains Drifter* and *Pale Rider*—so that the operation of these iconic carriers of meaning is perhaps mostly invisible. But their resemblance to the visual strategy I have been describing is, I think, clear upon examination.

Elsewhere, this kind of visual daring and articulation is not so ambitious and focussed. But I would say the visual schema of *Pale Rider*, with its pervasive qualities of the harsh mineral world and the frighteningly dour colouring of both the Eastwood persona and so much of the environment he moves through—all of which are especially forceful as a cruel restaging of the organic and verdant natural world of *Shane*—represents the most extensive application of a characteristic visual regime. And the climactic combat with Stockburn and his deputies is staged with a powerful, ritualized certainty which recalls in different facets the received generic conventions of the western showdown, the conclusion very specifically of *High Plains Drifter*, and Eastwood's whole onscreen history as a ritual killer. *Sudden Impact* also furnishes some points of interest. For example the moments of private trauma suffered by the Sondra Locke character, with the Munch-like expressionist anguish of her paintings and the equally expressionist lighting of many of these scenes altogether; the use of the merry-go-round horses as similarly expressive icons (culminating in their transformation into rearing figures of terror in the climactic scene and ultimately in the iconic foregrounding of the unicorn, defender of solitary females, as the skewering bringer of death to the principal rapist); and above all the extremely self-conscious and hypertrophic staging of Harry's arrival on the nighttime boardwalk to assume his position as transcendental avenger. Then there are the Carmel coastline and living-room grotto of *Play Misty for Me*, the ghost town full of unemployed gamblers in *The Outlaw Josey Wales*, the cornfields and open roads of *A Perfect World*, and the awesome, darkly opulent viewing-room from which Eastwood is compelled to watch atrocities impotently in *Absolute Power*—all of them striking settings which add something to the thematic concerns of their films. *Heartbreak Ridge* has strong flashes of visual acuity, as for example in Eastwood's wonderful green-and-black face camouflage (operating luridly and self-consciously as the character's stage makeup for a staged battle) and above all the final return home of the victorious dress-uniformed troops to dazzling sunlight and brass bands, Stars-and-Stripes flying cleanly and proudly in the breeze, and Marsha Mason in 1950s-style formal costume complete with little white gloves waving a tiny flag and smiling complicitously in the most sophisticated moment of the film.

●THE TROPE OF THE FLAG

This scene from *Heartbreak Ridge* exemplifies Eastwood's pointed and sometimes highly reverberant use of the US flag, one representative example of his recurring use of tropes. The flag enters Eastwood's world meaningfully—and it is not a coincidence—just at the point when the Eastwood persona is beginning to occupy the position of hero of ideology. *Bronco Billy* is a signal moment in this transition, as Eastwood takes up, with a maximum of self-consciousness and his inimitable combination of naïve avowal and ironic disavowal, the role of mythic saviour of the community of his companions and his viewers. The Stars-and-Stripes conclusion of this film is the first, and remains the most powerful, adoption in his work of the flag as symbol of American ideology. In *Heartbreak Ridge*, a film which also manipulates myth and artifice as necessities of American ideological health (though with far less elegance than *Bronco Billy*), the flag is trotted out in a much more straightforward fashion, very close to jingoistic patriotism in fact. But its positioning in the ritual final scene as just described maintains an iconic force whose very sharpness edges towards self-consciousness. And Marsha Mason's *toy* flag, in conjunction with her period costume and her smile whose irony sweetly acknowledges the conventionality of her image and her gesture, offers a momentary vista of ideological health as something produced by quotation and prosthetic manipulation—a vision which is essentially identical to that of *Bronco Billy* (as well as to the virtual-neoclassical Reaganite project whose most articulate cinematic equivalent these films arguably are). In this context the toy flag is like the toy war; it is happily waved in celebration of a tiny model conflict, the awareness of whose artificiality is not going to interfere with the party.[4]

A more elegiac use of the flag is seen in *In the Line of Fire* (directed, however, by Wolfgang Petersen), where its crisp display in clean, radiant surroundings amidst Washington monuments and especially presidential cavalcades now recalls Dallas in 1963, and produces the realization that the strength and beauty of the image (and what is promised by the image) is no guarantee of its triumph or even its survival. There are further echoes in *A Perfect World*, where the optimism of this iconography is massively defeated, and Kennedy's assassination waits in the wings to perform the same dire operation on the national psyche. Generally speaking, this image of the Stars-and-Stripes against a bright-blue sky in the midst of some communal celebration recalls the cinematic *locus classicus* of this moment, in the church-commencement /hoe-down scene of Ford's western *My Darling Clementine* (1946), where it is an intensely poetic sign for the entire project of American social idealism. Sometimes in Eastwood this scene and its attendant values and beliefs are produced for positive ideological effect (as in *Bronco Billy* and *Heartbreak Ridge*, albeit in both cases with markers of its artificiality), and sometimes in an elegiac or deconstructive way (as in *In the Line of Fire*, *A Perfect World* and, as outlined below, *Unforgiven*). In any case, it is another example of Eastwood's ability to manipulate strong, simple visual motifs with flair and compressed meaning.

Eastwood's most complex staging of the flag occurs in *Unforgiven*. The Stars-and-Stripes is prominently visible (again in a fresh, sunlit environment) on the streets of Big Whisky on Independence Day and is a feature of many of the shots that show

Little Bill's brutal humiliation of English Bob. It is an uncomfortable juxtaposition, for although American viewers may well be as disgusted as Little Bill is by Bob's fatuous royalist anti-American snobbery ("You been talking about the Queen again, Bob? on Independence Day?"), they are probably not so pleased that the spectacle of vicious battery which follows is being justified by the rationales of patriotic indignation and the rule of law. Here the metaphoric and generic reverberations of the flag are meaningfully redirected by the film in the same way as it redirects those attaching to Little Bill's house—indeed, as part of the same project to contextualize Bill's symbolic prosocial function. But this same flag makes a truly startling reappearance at the end of the film. As Munny emerges from the saloon after the massacre, he shouts out to any townspeople who may be outside:

> All right I'm coming out. Any man I see out there I'm gonna kill him. If he takes a shot at me not only am I gonna kill him I'm gonna kill his wife and all his friends, burn his damn house down. Nobody better shoot. You better bury Ned right. You better not cut up nor otherwise harm no whores. Or I'll come back and kill every one of you sons of bitches!

As this chilling speech is enunciated, a series of low-angle closeups of Eastwood reveals the Stars-and-Stripes fluttering behind his head at the back of the shot, both Eastwood and flag magnified and flattened into the same transcendental plane by the telephoto lens. The flag is obscured, of course, by the darkness and the rain, seen only dimly by firelight (and, indeed, it can be missed entirely by an inattentive viewer). But its presence once more as an iconic guarantor of Eastwood's heroism—here, in this hellish homicidal context—creates a thrill of horror. The moment takes its place among the many other deconstructions of Eastwood's heroic violence which the film offers. But its repetition of that iconic connection whereby Eastwood's heroic strength and the heroic strength of America as embodied in the flag are mutually reinforcing and mutually guaranteeing now contains an especially deadly and corrosive irony, for the heroic power of America itself is now presented as being rooted in a pure, indiscriminate killing power.[5]

●THE TROPE OF TORCHLIGHT AND TRAUMA

While travelling in zigzag fashion through Eastwood's filmography, we have encountered one particular, powerful trope on a number of isolated occasions: torchlit scenes of violence. This visual landscape is grandly powerful and horrific wherever it occurs, and seems to have almost a primal-scene status for Eastwood as a filmmaker. Its first appearance is in *High Plains Drifter*, where its most extended staging forms the grand finale to that film's epic project of supernatural vengeance. But darkness and firelight are also the condition of the flashback—shared, it seems, by the protagonist and the dwarf Mordecai—depicting the sheriff's death by bullwhip. Thus, the torchlight and darkness are essential parts of the protagonist's very deliberate plan to recreate as the setting of his revenge exactly the same scene of traumatic humiliation and horror (just as the painting of the town represents a similarly dramatic-didactic emblem of the community's moral obliquity and infernal fate). The eventual enactment of the revenge is grand in scale, with Eastwood's dark figure silhouetted in ritualized fashion against the firelight, and the town itself finally put to the torch.

High Plains Drifter's impressive climax would be striking enough in isolation. But this hellish scene makes two further appearances in Eastwood's cinema—and on both occasions it is used in exactly the same way. In *Sudden Impact,* the flashback sequence showing the atrocious rape of Jennifer Spencer and her sister, a deed which would send the sister into a state of permanent catatonia and create obsessive homicide-inducing memories in Jennifer, is staged again at night, by firelight. The traumatic scene has exactly the same vengeance-producing function as in the previous film, as Jennifer suffers from obsessive memories of it which her haunted paintings cannot exorcise and which can only be answered by implacable acts of homicide.[6] In *Sudden Impact*, the expressionist nature of this visual landscape is emphasized further by the woman's paintings and by the atmosphere of darkness and pain which so often follow her. But the grand finale of vengeance-taking, though it occurs at night, lacks torches and is illuminated instead (garishly enough) by the carnival lights of the midway in which the action occurs. The most elaborate restaging of the scene is its final occurrence, in *Unforgiven*—an aspect of the film which has been extensively commented upon above. Here the trope is almost musically elaborated, with its thematic previsions in the light of Munny's and Ned's campfires, its thunder-and-lightning overture, and its majestic and awe-inspiring climactic arrival, clogged with a murky darkness surpassing anything in *Bird* or *Tightrope* and inundated in a torrential downpour which however cannot extinguish the hellish firelight.

●THE TROPE OF ARMOUR PLATING

Another tic which Eastwood the filmmaker has shown is a recurring fondness for scenes in which his heroic persona protects himself against bullets with armour plating. It is tempting to see this as deriving from that scene in *A Fistful of Dollars* in which he survives Gian Maria Volonté's rifle shots by concealing a thick piece of iron under his poncho. In Leone's film, the idea is to create in the mind of your enemy the idea that you are supernaturally protected and invincible—whereas in fact all you are is smart. But Eastwood has recycled the idea in contexts quite different from that of *A Fistful of Dollars*. In *The Gauntlet*, for example, he hypertrophically stages a real extravaganza of bullets hitting armour plating that protects the Eastwood character. But here there is no cleverness; rather the opposite as Eastwood's somewhat lunkish protagonist sets up the whole scene by inviting the entire Phoenix Police Department to fire broadsides at him along a predetermined route. In the stupefying literalness and material excess of this staging, Eastwood is perhaps satirizing the cop movie's spectacle of violence, or perhaps pointing in a different way to the qualities of stubbornness and even stupidity that characterize Detective Shockley. In any case, it is an amazing conceit and an amazing spectacle, and, as with many of Eastwood the filmmaker's most striking moments, one is hard put to say whether the idea is naïve or sophisticated.

Pale Rider refers back to that scene in *A Fistful of Dollars* when it presents the Preacher's torso being riddled with bullets which penetrated it in an anatomical location very close to that of the Leone film—obviously, however, *without* the benefit of armour on this occasion. The uncanniness of this Eastwood hero then derives not from his ability to withstand bullets and continue to live, but rather to die from them and then return from death.

Finally, *In the Line of Fire* thrusts the Man With No Name's hidden chest protecter incongruously into a modern Secret Service thriller. It is doubly incongruous when this character's most heartfelt scene has ended with the tearful statement that if as a young man he had been able to "take a bullet for the President," that would have been all right with him. Horrigan does take a bullet for his new President, diving into the assassin's line of fire just as the film's title suggests; but his Kevlar vest absorbs the shot, and Horrigan is not hurt. It is a replay of the original Leone scene, and Horrigan's opponent Leary later actually accuses him of "cheating," just as the Gian Maria Volonté character might have done in *A Fistful of Dollars*.

●SINGLE-FILM STYLES

The visual phenomena I have been discussing so far are, I would say, different manifestations of a diverse but fairly consistent visual style. That is, these characteristics can be seen across the body of Eastwood's work as a filmmaker, even if inconsistently. But in a few cases, Eastwood has adopted a focussed and consistent approach in a single film only—an approach which differs from most of what can be called his "usual" visual style.

The clearest case in point is *Bird*, a film which in so many ways is marked as different and special in Eastwood's canon. Of all Eastwood's films, it has been presented most strongly as an art film, a creator's film. The dichotomy in Eastwood's work between potboilers and personal projects has been a truism of the discourse surrounding him in the popular press ever since reviewers noticed the unusual, and specifically the non-generic, qualities of films such as *Bronco Billy* and *Honkytonk Man*. *Bird* is the biggest, longest, most ambitious, and artiest of all the personal projects. It features a 160-minute running time; a temporally scrambled modernist narrative full of flashbacks and disorienting skips; a protagonist whose agonized destruction occurs through a conjunction of social oppression, physiological addiction, and tragic personal flaw; a milieu (jazz) far removed from the commodified mainstream musical culture of 1988 (although well known as a personal enthusiasm of Eastwood himself); and, not least, the absence of Eastwood the actor. To this list one might also add the film's distinct visual style. The muddy darkness of so many of the scenes, the sense of a palpable environment of darkness and chaos in which it is scarcely possible to make out details, a visual surrounding whose clotted obscurity has an effect far removed from any sharply stylish *noir* qualities—these characteristics are, through their very difficulty and even ugliness, a testament to the film's earnestness and desire to be painfully truthful rather than pleasing. Certainly they are the visual equivalent of the traits of suffering, mess, and confusion which the film holds out as Charlie Parker's psychological condition (along with creative genius), and which are also to be seen in Forest Whitaker's agonized and pointedly inarticulate Method performance and even the muffled sounds of Parker's own saxophone on the soundtrack.[7]

There were and are divergent opinions on the artistic success of *Bird*, which did its duty by failing at the box office after receiving more negative reviews than might have been expected, although it has not turned into any kind of a cult film. The point I wish to make, though, is that part of the film's statement of its seriousness is to be seen in the aggressively unfriendly visual style, which is both "artistic" (in the sense of being uncommercial) and unlike Eastwood's usual visual style except insofar as it takes up the principle of visual darkness (but then uses it in an exaggerated and finally uncharacteristic way).

The Eastwood film that looks most like *Bird* is *Tightrope*, which extends the rule of visual obscurity to an extent that surpasses anything in the other action films and is a veritable sea of murky browns and blacks. The film seems to be applying a self-consciously dark palette to a self-consciously dark scenario, whose representations of the protagonist's "dark side" are so relentlessly articulated as to become overinsistent. It is tempting to put this simplicity and homogeneity down to the fact that the film was directed not by Eastwood but by Richard Tuggle; but another perspective is offered by *The Village Voice*'s J. Hoberman (something of an Eastwood skeptic): "I would like to think *Tightrope* is so personal Eastwood couldn't sign it."[8] And one recalls the way in which this brown murk will return momentarily but powerfully during the climax of *Unforgiven*.

Another of Eastwood's other "personal" projects is *Honkytonk Man*, and this too looks different from most Eastwood films, although not in as concentrated or unusual a way as *Bird*. It is a period film, and its dustbowl landscapes are purposefully reminiscent of documentary sources such as Walker Evans and *The*

Plow That Broke the Plains. Colour cinematography provides a degree of gloss and comfort which runs counter to that principle of austerity and poverty, however, and the film is not in any way stylized or "arty" in its appearance. Taken in itself it has perhaps nothing extraordinary to offer in the visual realm, but it indicates the degree to which Eastwood is willing to alter the look of his films in response to their artistic ambitions. *The Bridges of Madison County* has a beautifully soft and painterly (or perhaps we should say "photographerly") look, the expression of its hero's artistic profession and, by extension, his whole beautifying way of looking at the world psychologically as well as visually. Again, there is no exact equivalent for this look in any of Eastwood's other films; and again, it is a visual world called up in accordance with a distinct and (for Eastwood) unusual project.

One further film with its own look is Eastwood's first directorial effort, *Play Misty for Me.* Perhaps anxious to show his creative abilities, Eastwood here adopts a particularly aggressive and stylized form of the Hollywood-arty visual conventions of the day. In 1971, Hollywood was in a period of stylistic turbulence created when the serious breakdown of traditional classical narrative extended to its visual apparatus. The influence of the French New Wave (considerably muffled and delayed) and of British "pop" cinema in the form of Richard Lester, Karel Reisz, John Schlesinger, and others, and a general institutional sense that Hollywood had grown out of touch with the increasingly powerful youth audience in the 1960s, led to an adjustment of the Hollywood visual apparatus away from classical stability and in the direction of modernist fragmentation, discontinuity, and visible interventions of narration into narrative. It was a phase which was already on the retreat by the mid 1970s. But *Play Misty for Me* falls within this relatively narrow window. It shows many of the most characteristic devices of this adjustment: jarring camera angles and composition, garish alternations of wide-angle and telephoto lenses, showy montage, self-conscious lyricism, spectacularly gorgeous locations. All of these factors, together with the film's narrativization of such very up-to-date social phenomena as the sexual revolution and some of the styles of California pop culture, give the film a highly visible and indeed often distracting "arty" look. Other Eastwood films of the period share some of these qualities (one thinks in particular of the very dated "modernisms" of movies like *Magnum Force* and *The*

Enforcer and even to an extent of the Siegel-directed *The Beguiled*), but *Play Misty for Me* finds a very distinctive vein of the style by virtue of its setting and subject.

●SERGIO AND DON

Eastwood's two great mentors as a director are of course Sergio Leone and Don Siegel—a fact which Eastwood has always been at pains to point out and which is deliberately acknowledged in the dedication of *Unforgiven* "to Sergio and Don." Somewhat overlooked in the common acceptance of this debt is the giant stylistic gulf between Leone and Siegel.[9] Examining Eastwood the filmmaker to determine traces of a Siegel influence and a Leone influence, while it draws us to a degree away from questions of specifically visual style and towards more global authorial characteristics, is nevertheless a productive exercise, especially as it throws some further light on the general subject of Eastwood the filmmaker's dualism.

Don Siegel toiled for most of his career in the lower reaches of genre cinema, and his style is straightforward, lean, and hard-hitting—really a kind of paradigm of the classical virtues of mainstream Hollywood action cinema as described and celebrated by French cinephiles in the postwar period. It has also had a kind of populist/outsider quality of looking at the world from the underside, or from street level, and celebrating maverick individuals who have resisted conformity of any kind. This is, of course, a feature of American individualist ideology as a whole; but one can recognize a common outlook which combines ground-level heroism with a certain stoicism and even pessimism running through Siegel films as different in period and circumstances as *Riot in Cell Block 11* (prison movie, 1954), *Invasion of the Body Snatchers* (science fiction, 1956), *Hell Is for Heroes* (war movie, 1962), *Madigan* (cop movie, 1968), and *Charley Varrick* (crime thriller 1973)—to name only projects not involving Eastwood. In addition to being a defining moment in Eastwood's career, *Dirty Harry* is a typically swift and violent Siegel movie, complete with outsider-hero, while *Coogan's Bluff* has an almost textbook Siegel scenario. The not-inconsiderable artistic heights these two could scale together are indicated by *The Beguiled* and by *Escape from Alcatraz*, an action movie so methodical and stripped down that it had cinematically literate reviewers comparing it to Bresson's

Un condamné à mort s'est échappé. And of course many commentators, following Eastwood's own remarks, have pointed to Siegel as a model for the kind of rational and efficient (as opposed to bloated and wasteful) film production which has become the organizing principle of Eastwood's Malpaso production company.

Sergio Leone, by contrast, is one of the most deliriously stylized filmmakers ever to have extended success in the commercial marketplace. Eastwood the future producer may have drawn the same kinds of lessons of efficiency as he later drew from Siegel from the fact that Leone's were shoestring productions by Hollywood standards and needed to be staged and shot with a minimum of fuss and expense. But, in whatever financial context, it is the eye-popping visual exaggerations of the spaghetti westerns that compel attention. Radical simplification, exaggeration, temporal and spatial distention, overt practices of anti-realist abstraction, metaphor and metonymy—all of these qualities which might be expected in the realm of art cinema are now found in commercial genre films whose other characteristics include extreme cynicism and violence.

Between them, Siegel and Leone are virtual polar opposites of style and outlook within the bounds of commercial cinema.

Siegel	Leone
prose	poetry
artisanship	art
invisible apparatus	self-consciousness
editing	*mise en scène*
reportage	opera
sobriety	delirium
efficiency	excess
kinesis	stasis
sincerity	pastiche
stoicism	irony
pessimism	cynicism
survival	gamesmanship
struggle	narcissism
pragmatism	charisma
craftsmanship	transcendence
heroism	hyperheroism

And one could go on almost indefinitely in a similar vein.

If Eastwood the filmmaker is indeed formed in part from these two influences, a certain schizophrenia seems inevitable. And if one looks at that recurrent quality of double vision to which I have called attention in different contexts throughout this study, one can see its equivalent in these two distinct and polarized spheres of influence. Eastwood's cinema is, at different moments or even simultaneously, descended from both Siegel and Leone.

Eastwood

Siegel	Leone
classicism	modernism/postmodernism
authenticity	fantasy
construction	deconstruction
realism	metaphor
action	spectacle
technique	mystery
superiority	impossibility
masculinity	hypermasculinity
justice	revenge
the personal	the divine/the demonic
history	myth
tidiness	expressionism

The "undecidableness," the "both/and," characteristics of so much of his work may well stem in part from this dualism of heritage — although there is no doubt that Eastwood is neither Leone nor Siegel nor Leone + Siegel, but rather a completely unique creative presence formed in part from the mixture of two unmixable elements.

———

In the end, Eastwood's cinematic style is a various and inconsistent thing, but it is *there*. There is a certain sharpness of look that runs through his work and encompasses even such narratively and thematically shallow projects as *The Eiger Sanction*, *Foxfire*, *The Rookie*, and *Absolute Power*. At no point in the 1980s or '90s has an Eastwood film ever emulated the dominant big-action-movie visual style of the day: the redi-whip stedicam editing-processor approach that has taken MTV/advertising kineticism and put it through a smoothing blender. Eastwood's visual world retains a degree of classical stability, with its static shots and cuts, compositional values, unobtrusive camera movement.

To offer an estimate of Eastwood's "artistic importance" in this era of film-studies-as-science and aesthetics-as-politics would be, perhaps, to strike a discordant and pathetic note. Perhaps one can say, with as much objectivity as possible, that the era of the individual masterpiece or the masterful film author has been on the wane, certainly in Hollywood and Europe, for the past quarter-century. As all kinds of boundaries disappear (between high culture and low culture, narrative and commerce, film and television, individual style and the museum-of-all-styles), the search for—in particular—Hollywood films and Hollywood authors with a specific voice and something to say with it has yielded increasingly meagre results. It is, simply, culturally more and more difficult to perform this operation in the field of cinema, both as a viewer and as a filmmaker. Postmodernity itself rules out any philosophy of the individually distinctive or important text, also of anything individually substantial or authoritative.

It is in this environment—a Hollywood environment in which the dominant creative personalities with any history are virtual-classical figures like Spielberg and Lucas; where once-powerful creative personalities like Coppola and even Scorsese are marooned in postmodernity with little or nothing to say; where the "hottest" recent creative personalities have been figures like Tim Burton and Quentin Tarantino for whom style is an end in itself; and where the overpowering technical sophistication of an arty-modernist visual *lingua franca* has permeated everything from Oliver Stone to Disney—it is in this environment that Clint Eastwood the filmmaker stands out. The list of his interesting (i.e., interestingly conflicted, stylistically confident, provocative) films is simply longer than almost anyone else's. Who else in Hollywood since 1988 can match for emotional and even intellectual complexity Eastwood's lineup of *Bird*, *White Hunter, Black Heart*, *Unforgiven* and *A Perfect World* (and this is omitting *In the Line of Fire*)? As an actor-director—that is, as a director and wholesale creator of his own onscreen persona—he already belongs on the short list with the comedian-directors Chaplin, Keaton, Sacha Guitry, Jacques Tati, and Jerry Lewis; and since Eastwood has played in drama and across genres, he is historically unique. Nor has he simply presided over that persona, but has constantly striven to offer it in different lights, to visibly construct and deconstruct it, throughout an extended period in which he never relinquished a place near the top of the box-office polls.

The way in which *Absolute Power* and *True Crime* regress from the peaks of *Unforgiven* and *A Perfect World*—and even from the lesser heights of *White Hunter, Black Heart* and from the still-lower ones of *In the Line of Fire*—tells us something about Eastwood's status as a creative filmmaker. It was one thing to oscillate regularly, as Eastwood did during the late 1970s and '80s, from interesting personal projects to relatively witless conventional ones and back again: from *The Outlaw Josey Wales* to *The Enforcer* to *The Gauntlet* to *Every Which Way But Loose* to *Bronco Billy* to *Firefox* to *Honkytonk Man*. Even as late as the 1989-1992 sequence *Pink Cadillac – White Hunter, Black Heart – The Rookie – Unforgiven* one could see the alternation of "commercial" and "artistic" projects as a canny survival tool necessary for any Hollywood filmmaker who wanted to take some chances but also wanted to work regularly and freely. But *Unforgiven* and *A Perfect World* seemed so much (as I have said) *summations* of Eastwood the filmmaker's concerns, so superior in awareness and intelligent self-examination, that it is painful to see the director relapsing into the unaware, unintelligent posturings of, in particular, *Absolute Power*. In the glow of *Unforgiven* and *A Perfect World*—and even *The Bridges of Madison County*—Eastwood's artistic career could in a sense be seen as a gradual and intermittent but nonetheless inexorable growth of sensitivity and reflectiveness.

But *Absolute Power* reminds us of the fact that Eastwood has never owned a really articulate or even an entirely conscious self-analysis for any length of time. In *Unforgiven* and *A Perfect World,* he had the benefit of superbly complex screenplays, whose balance, depth, and intelligence went far beyond those of most of even Eastwood's best films. Of course Eastwood found each of those projects and made them (in the case of *Unforgiven* after sitting on it for a very long time until he judged the conditions exactly right), and undoubtedly their appeal for him had a lot to do with their complex and analytical treatments of subjects which had been close to him for decades, with the opportunities they offered to exercise an evolving persona and thematic landscape. But Eastwood is not a Renoir or a Rossellini — not, that is, a filmmaker with a probing consciousness of his subject in every dimension. He is not a *thinker* at all, in fact. He gropes his way towards themes, he finds himself in positions, rather than setting out to realize them in a conscious way. It is not a bad stance for a creator; in fact, it is probably a highly desirable one for a creator who is operating within the aggressively anti-intellectual atmosphere of Hollywood cinema and who is himself a popular-culture artist who has graduated from a popular-culture school. I so often have the sense of Eastwood stubbornly insisting on the rather strange configurations of his work in ways which are destructive of conventional good craftsmanship but also authentically original and thought-provoking despite their awkwardness. Again, his authorial presence has much of the stamp of primitivism. In any event, this creative method is susceptible to blind spots and backslidings, to suffer the disadvantages of semi-consciousness just as it receives the benefits. A teleological procession towards self-awareness and fully conscious mastery, then, is not on the cards — even though it appeared to be so for a few years in the mid 1990s. Instead, as his most recent films demonstrate, there will be the same creative thrashing around, the same series of glancing blows, solid hits, and almost complete misses that have, in retrospect, characterized Eastwood's cinema always.

Perhaps only in two films, *Unforgiven* and *A Perfect World*, has he reached the kind of intensity and depth that characterizes the very best Hollywood movies of the past thirty years (e.g., *Godfather II*, *Chinatown*, *Raging Bull*, *Fire Walk With Me*), and nowhere has he shown the total immersion in and control of the medium seen in Scorsese and Lynch (or for that matter in a very large number of style merchants such as Ridley Scott, the Coen brothers, Sam Raimi, Burton, Tarantino, etc., etc.) But he has been an authorial presence offering both substance *and* style, and moreover the interest and depth in his films sprang from just that ground where Hollywood films have traditionally found complexity — namely in the conflict (often unearthed in the arena of genre-cinema) between superficial ideological certainties and deep unacknowledged doubts. In this respect, it is even possible to claim Eastwood as an *auteur* in the tradition of Douglas Sirk and Nicholas Ray, Penn and Peckinpah — except that none of them had Eastwood the powerful, culturally central screen persona at their disposal. And Eastwood survived the transition from late classicism to postmodernism without losing his viability on either side of that divide — that in itself is remarkable.

It is when all of these factors are added together that Eastwood emerges as (perhaps one can just say it after all) an artistic presence second to none in the American cinema of the past three decades. It is a contradictory, uneven combination of factors: difficult to assimilate and identify, difficult to describe, difficult finally to evaluate — impossible to do any of these simply. But taken as a whole, Eastwood's cinema is unlike anything else in the history of Hollywood; and at its best, it is fully worthy of the best traditions of American filmmaking.

Appendix

Eastwood Filmography

This list includes only theatrical feature films either directed by Eastwood or in which Eastwood plays a major role. Films marked with an asterisk are directed by Eastwood.

●1964

A Fistful of Dollars (Per un pugno di dollari)

Italy/West Germany/Spain. 100 min. Widescreen.

Production: Jolly (Italy)/Constantin (West Germany)/Ocean (Spain). *Distribution:* United Artists [USA, 1967]

Dir: Sergio Leone. *Scr:* Sergio Leone, Duccio Tessari. *Prod:* Arrigo Colombo, Giorgio Papi. *Phot:* Massimo Dallamano (Techniscope, Technicolor). *Mus:* Ennio Morricone. *Des:* Caro Simi. *Ed:* Roberto Cinquini.

Cast: Clint Eastwood (*Joe* [*The Man With No Name*]), Gian Maria Volonté (*Ramón Rojo*), Marianne Koch (*Marisol*), Pepe Calvo (*Silvanito*), Wolfgang Lukschy (*John Baxter*), Sieghardt Rupp (*Esteban Rojo*), Joseph Egger (*Piripero*), Antonio Prieto (*Benito Rojo*), Margherita Lozano (*Consuela Baxter*), Daniel Martin (*Julián*).

●1965

For a Few Dollars More (Per qualche dollaro in più)

Italy/Spain/West Germany. 130 min. Widescreen.

Production: P.E.A. (Rome)/Arturo Gonzales (Spain)/Constantin (West Germany). *Distribution:* United Artists [USA, 1967]

Dir: Sergio Leone. *Scr:* Sergio Leone, Luciano Vincenzoni. *Prod:* Alberto Grimaldi. *Phot:* Massimo Dallamano (Techniscope, Technicolor). *Mus:* Enrico Morricone. *Des:* Carlo Simi. *Ed:* Alabiso Serralonga, Giorgio Serralonga.

Cast: Clint Eastwood (*Manko* [*The Man With No Name*]), Lee Van Cleef (*Col. Douglas Mortimer*), Gian Maria Volonté (*Indio*), Mara Krup (*Hotel Manager's Wife*), Luigi Pistilli (*Groggy*), Klaus Kinski (*Hunchback*), Josef Egger (*Old Man over Railway*), Rosemary Dexter (*Mortimer's sister*).

●1966
The Good, the Bad and the Ugly (Il Buono, il brutto, il cattivo)

Italy. 180 min. Widescreen.

Production: Produzioni Europee Associate. *Distribution*: United Artists [USA, 1968]

Dir: Sergio Leone. *Scr*: Agenore Incrocci, Furio Scarpelli, Luciano Vincenzoni, Sergio Leone. *Prod*: Alberto Grimaldi. *Phot*: Tonino Delli Colli (Techniscope, Technicolor). *Mus*: Ennio Morricone. *Des*: Carlo Simi. *Ed*: Eugenio Alabiso, Nino Baragli.

Cast: Clint Eastwood (*Blondie* [*The Man With No Name*]), Lee Van Cleef (*Angel Eyes*), Eli Wallach (*Tuco*), Aldo Giuffrè (*Northern officer*), Luigi Pastilli (*Padre Ramirez*), Rada Rassimov (*Maria, the prostitute*).

●1967
Hang 'em High

USA. 114 min.

Production: Leonard Freeman Productions/The Malpaso Company. *Distribution*: Universal.

Dir: Ted Post. *Scr*: Leonard Freeman, Mel Goldberg. *Prod*: Leonard Freeman. *Phot*: Leonard South, Richard Kline (DeLuxe). *Mus*: Dominic Frontiere. *Des*: John B. Goodman. *Ed*: Gene Fowler Jr.

Cast: Clint Eastwood (*Jed Cooper*), Inger Stevens (*Rachel*), Ed Begley (*Cap'n Wilson*), Pat Hingle (*Judge Adam Fenton*), Ben Johnson (*Sheriff Dave Bliss*), Arlene Golonka (*Jennifer*), James MacArthur (*Priest*), Charles McGraw, Bruce Dern, Dennis Hopper, L.Q. Jones, Alan Hale Jr.

●1968
Coogan's Bluff

USA. 94 min.

Production: Universal/Malpaso. *Distribution*: Universal.

Dir: Don Siegel. *Scr*: Herman Miller, Dean Riesner, Howard Rodner. *Prod*: Don Siegel. *Phot*: Bud Thackery (Technicolor). *Mus*: Lalo Schifrin. *Des*: Alexander Golitzen, Robert MacKichan. *Ed*: Sam E. Waxman.

Cast: Clint Eastwood (*Walt Coogan*), Lee J. Cobb (*McElroy*), Susan Clark (*Julie*), Tisha Sterling (*Linny Raven*), Don Stroud (*Ringerman*), Betty

Field (*Mrs Ringerman*), Tom Tully (*Sheriff McCrea*), Melodie Johnson (*Millie*), James Edward (*Jackson*), Rudy Diaz (*Running Bear*).

●1969

Two Mules for Sister Sara

USA. 116 min. Widescreen.

Production: Sanen Pictures/Universal/Malpaso. *Distribution*: Universal.

Dir: Don Siegel. *Scr*: Albert Maltz (*story* Budd Boetticher). *Prod*: Martin Rackin, Carroll Case. *Phot*: Gabriel Figueroa (Panavision, Technicolor). *Mus*: Ennio Morricone. *Des*: José Rodríguez Granada.

Cast: Shirley MacLaine (*Sara*), Clint Eastwood (*Hogan*), Manolo Fabregas (*Col. Beltran*), Alberto Morin (*Gen. LeClaire*), Armando Silverstre (*1st American*), John Kelly (*2nd American*), Enrique Lucero (*3rd American*), David Estuardo (*Juan*).

Where Eagles Dare

UK. 148 min. Widescreen.

Production: Winkast Films. *Distribution*: MGM.

Dir: Brian G. Hutton. *Scr*: Alistair MacLean, based on his novel *Prod*: Elliot Kastner. *Phot*: Peter Ibbetson (Panavision 70, Metrocolor). *Mus*: Ron Goodwin. *Des*: Peter Mullins. *Ed*: John

Cast: Richard Burton (*John Smith*), Clint Eastwood (*Lt. Morris Schaffer*), Mary Ure (*Mary Ellison*), Patrick Wymark (*Col. Turner*), Michael Hordern (*Vice-Admiral Rolland*), Donald Houston (*Christiansen*), Peter Barkworth (*Berkeley*), Robert Beatty (*Cartwright Jones*).

Paint Your Wagon

USA. 164 min. Widescreen.

Production: Paramount/Alan J. Lerner Productions. *Distribution*: Paramount.

Dir: Joshua Logan. *Scr*: Paddy Chayefsky, based on the Lerner and Loewe musical. *Prod*: Alan J. Lerner. *Phot*: William A. Fraker (Panavision 70, Technicolor). *Mus*: Frederick Loewe, André Previn. *Des*: John Truscott. *Ed*: Robert Jones.

Cast: Lee Marvin (*Ben Rumson*), Clint Eastwood (*Pardner*), Jean Seberg (*Elizabeth*), Harve Presnell (*Rotten Luck Willie*), Ray Walston (*Mad Jack Duncan*), Tom Ligon (*Horton Fenty*), Alan Dexter (*Parson*), William O'Connell (*Horace Tabor*), Ben Baker (*Haywood Holbrook*).

●1970

Kelly's Heroes

USA/Yugoslavia. 143 min. Widescreen.

Production: The Warriors Company (USA)/Avala Films (Belgrade).
  Distribution: MGM-EMI.

Dir: Brian G. Hutton. *Scr*: Troy Kennedy-Martin. *Prod*: Gabriel Katzka,
  Sidney Beckerman. *Phot*: Gabriel Figueroa (Panavision, Metrocolor).
  Mus: Lalo Schifrin. *Des*: John Barry. *Ed*: John Jympson.

Cast: Clint Eastwood (*Kelly*), Telly Savalas (*Big Joe*), Don Rickles
  (*Crapgame*), Carroll O'Connor (*Gen. Colt*), Donald Sutherland
  (*Oddball*), Gavin MacLeod (*Moriarty*), Hal Buckley (*Maitland*), Stuart
  Margolin (*Little Joe*), Jeff Morris (*Cowboy*), Richard Davalos
  (*Gutowski*), Perry Lopez (*Petruko*), Tom Troupe (*Job*), Harry Dean
  Stanton (*Willard*).

●1971

The Beguiled

USA. 105 min.

Production: Universal/Malpaso. *Distribution*: Universal.

Dir: Don Siegel. *Scr*: John B. Sherry, Grimes Grice, based on the novel by
  Thomas Cullinan. *Prod*: Don Siegel. *Phot*: Bruce Surtees
  (Technicolor). *Mus*: Lalo Schifrin. *Des*: Ted Haworth. *Ed*: Carl
  Pingitore.

Cast: Clint Eastwood (*John McBurney*), Geraldine Page (*Martha
  Farnsworth*), Elizabeth Hartman (*Edwina Dabney*), Jo Anne Harris
  (*Carol*), Darleen Carr (*Doris*), Mae Mercer (*Hallie*), Pamelyn Ferdin
  (*Amy*), Melody Thomas (*Abigail*), Peggy Drier (*Lizzie*), Pattye Mattick
  (*Janie*).

*Play Misty for Me

USA. 102 min.

Production: Universal/Malpaso. *Distribution*: Universal.

Dir: Clint Eastwood. *Scr*: Jo Heims, Dean Riesner. *Prod*: Robert Daley.
  Phot: Bruce Surtees (Technicolor). *Mus*: Dee Barton. *Des*: Alexander
  Golitzen. *Ed*: Carl Pingitore.

Cast: Clint Eastwood (*Dave Garland*), Jessica Walter (*Evelyn Draper*),
  Donna Mills (*Tobie Williams*), John Larch (*Sgt. McCallum*), Jack Ging
  (*Frank Dewan*), Irene Hervey (*Madge Brenner*), James McEachin (*Al
  Monte*), Clarice Taylor (*Birdie*), Don Siegel (*Murphy*), the Johnny Otis
  Show, the Cannonball Adderley Quintet..

Dirty Harry

USA. 101 min. Widescreen.

Production: Warner Bros./Malpaso. *Distribution*: Columbia/Warner.

Dir: Don Siegel. *Scr*: Harry Julian Fink, Rita M. Fink, Dean Riesner.
Prod: Don Siegel. *Phot*: Bruce Surtees (Panavision, Technicolor).
Mus: Lalo Schifrin. *Des*: Dale Hennesy. *Ed*: Carl Pingitore.

Cast: Clint Eastwood (*Harry Callahan*), Andy Robinson (*Scorpio*), Harry
Guardino (*Lt. Bressler*), Reni Santoni (*Chico*), John Vernon (*The
Mayor*), John Larch (*Chief*), John Mitchum (*De Georgio*), Mae Mercer
(*Mrs Russell*), Lyn Edgington (*Norma*), Ruth Kobart (*Bus driver*).

●1972

Joe Kidd

USA. 87 min. Widescreen.

Production: Universal/Malpaso. *Distribution*: Universal.

Dir: John Sturges. *Scr*: Elmore Leonard. *Prod*: Sidney Beckerman. *Phot*:
Bruce Surtees (Panavision, Technicolor). *Mus*: Lalo Schifrin. *Des*:
Alexander Golitzen, Henry Bumstead. *Ed*: Ferris Webster.

Cast: Clint Eastwood (*Joe Kidd*), Robert Duvall (*Frank Harlan*), John
Saxon (*Luis Chama*), Don Stroud (*Lamarr*), Stella Garcia (*Helen
Sanchez*), James Wainwright (*Mango*), Paul Koslo (*Roy*), Gregory
Walcott (*Mitchell*), Dick Van Patten (*Hotel Manager*).

*High Plains Drifter

USA. 105 min. Widescreen.

Production: Malpaso/Universal. *Distribution*: Universal.

Dir: Clint Eastwood. *Scr*: Ernest Tidyman. *Prod*: Robert Daley. *Phot*:
Bruce Surtees (Panavision, Technicolor). *Mus*: Dee Barton. *Des*:
Henry Bumstead. *Ed*: Ferris Webster.

Cast: Clint Eastwood (*The Stranger*), Verna Bloom (*Sarah Belding*),
Mariana Hill (*Callie Travers*), Mitch Ryan (*Dave Drake*), Jack Ging
(*Morgan Allen*), Stefan Gierasch (*Mayor Jason Hobart*), Ted Hartley
(*Lewis Belding*), Billy Curtis (*Mordecai*), Geoffrey Lewis (*Stacey
Bridges*), Walter Barnes (*Sheriff Dan Shaw*), Scott Walker (*Bill
Borders*), Paul Brinegar (*Lutie Naylor*), Richard Bull (*Asa Goodwin*),
Robert Donner (*Preacher*).

●1973
*Breezy

USA. 107 min.

Production: Malpaso. *Distribution*: Universal.

Dir: Clint Eastwood. *Scr*: Jo Heims. *Prod*: Robert Daley. *Phot*: Frank
 Stanley (Technicolor). *Mus*: Michel Legrand. *Des*: Alexander Golitzen.
 Ed: Ferris Webster.

Cast: William Holden (*Frank Harmon*), Kay Lenz (*Breezy*), Roger C.
 Carmel (*Bob Henderson*), Marj Dusay (*Betty Tobin*), Joan Hotchkis
 (*Paula Harmon*), Jamie Smith Jackson (*Marcy*).

Magnum Force

USA. 122 min. Widescreen.

Production: Malpaso/Warner Bros. *Distribution*: Columbia-Warner.

Dir: Ted Post. *Scr*: John Milius, Michael Cimino (*story* John Milius). *Prod*:
 Robert Daley. *Phot*: Frank Stanley (Panavision, Technicolor). *Mus*:
 Lalo Schifrin. *Des*: Jack Collis. *Ed*: Ferris Webster.

Cast: Clint Eastwood (*Harry Callahan*), Hal Holbrook (*Lt. Neil Briggs*),
 Mitchell Ryan (*Charlie McCoy*), David Soul (*Ben Davis*), Felton Perry
 (*Early Smith*), Robert Urich (*John Grimes*), Kip Niven (*Red Astrachan*),
 Tim Matheson (*Phil Sweet*), Christine White (*Carol McCoy*).

●1974
Thunderbolt and Lightfoot

USA. 115 min. Widescreen.

Production: Malpaso/United Artists. *Distribution*: United Artists.

Dir: Michael Cimino. *Scr*: Michael Cimino. *Prod*: Robert Daley. *Phot*:
 Frank Stanley (Panavision, DeLuxe). *Mus*: Dee Barton. *Des*: Tambi
 Larsen. *Ed*: Ferris Webster.

Cast: Clint Eastwood (*John "Thunderbolt" Doherty*), Jeff Bridges (*Lightfoot*),
 George Kennedy (*Red Leary*), Geoffrey Lewis (*Goody*), Catherine
 Bach (*Melody*), Gary Busey (*Curly*).

●1975
*The Eiger Sanction

USA. 125 min. Widescreen.

Production: Universal/Jennings Lang/Malpaso. *Distribution*: Universal.

Dir: Clint Eastwood. *Scr*: Warren B. Murphy, Hal Dresner, Rod Whitaker
 (based on the novel by Trevanian). *Prod*: Robert Daley. *Mus*: Frank
 Stanley (Panavision, Technicolor). *Des*: George Webb, Aurelio
 Crugnola. *Ed*: Ferris Webster.

Cast: Clint Eastwood (*Jonathan Hemlock*), George Kennedy (*Ben Bowman*), Vonetta McGee (*Jemima Brown*), Jack Cassidy (*Miles McHough*), Heidi Bruhl (*Anna Montaigne*), Thayer David (*Dragon*), Reiner Schoene (*Freytag*), Michael Grimm (*Meyer*).

●1976
*The Outlaw Josey Wales

USA. 134 min. Widescreen.
Production: Malpaso/Warner Bros. *Distribution*: Warner Bros.
Dir: Clint Eastwood. *Scr*: Phil Kaufman, Sonia Chernus (based on the novel *Gone to Texas* by Forrest Carter). *Prod*: Robert Daley. *Phot*: Bruce Surtees (Panavision, DeLuxe). *Mus*: Jerry Fielding. *Des*: Tambi Larsen. *Ed*: Ferris Webster.
Cast: Clint Eastwood (*Josey Wales*), Chief Dan George (*Lone Watie*), Sondra Locke (*Laura Lee*), Bill McKinney (*Terrill*), John Vernon (*Fletcher*), Paula Trueman (*Grandma Sarah*), Sam Bottoms (*Jamie*), Geraldine Keams (*Little Moonlight*), Woodrow Parfrey (*Carpetbagger*), Will Sampson (*Ten Bears*), Joyce Jameson (*Rose*), Sheb Wooley (*Travis Cobb*), Royal Dano (*Ten Spot*), Matt Clarke (*Kelly*), John Verro (*Chato*), John Russell (*Bloody Bill Anderson*).

The Enforcer

USA. 96 min. Widescreen.
Production: Malpaso/Warner Bros. *Distribution*: Warner Bros.
Dir: James Fargo. *Scr*: Stirling Silliphant, Dean Reisner. *Prod*: Robert Daley. *Phot*: Charles W. Short (Panavision, DeLuxe). *Mus*: Jerry Fielding. *Des*: Allen E. Smith. *Ed*: Ferris Webster.
Cast: Clint Eastwood (*Harry Callahan*), Tyne Daly (*Kate Moore*), Harry Guardino (*Lt. Bressler*), Bradford Dillman (*Capt. McKay*), John Mitchum (*DiGeorgio*), DeVeren Bookwalter (*Bobby Maxwell*), John Crawford (*The Mayor*), Samantha Doane (*Wanda*), Robert F. Hoy (*Buchinski*).

●1977
*The Gauntlet

USA. 112 min. Widescreen.
Production: Malpaso/Warner Bros. *Distribution*: Warner Bros.
Dir: Clint Eastwood. *Scr*: Michael Butler, Dennis Shyrack. *Prod*: Robert Daly. *Phot*: Rexford Metz (Panavision, DeLuxe). *Mus*: Jerry Fielding (jazz soloists Art Pepper, Jon Faddis). *Des*: Allen E. Smith. *Ed*: Ferris Webster, Joel Cox.
Cast: Clint Eastwood (*Ben Shockley*), Sondra Locke (*Gus Mally*), Pat Hingle (*Josephson*), William Prince (*Blakelock*), Bill McKinney

(*Constable*), Michael Cavanaugh (*Feyderspiel*), Carole Cook (*Waitress*), Mara Corday (*Jail Matron*), Doug McGrath (*Bookie*), Samantha Doane, Roy Jenson, Dan Vadis (*Bikers*).

●1978
Every Which Way But Loose

USA. 114 min.

Production: Malpaso/Warner Bros. *Distribution*: Warner Bros.

Dir: James Fargo. *Scr*: Jeremy Joe Kronsberg. *Prod*: Robert Daley. *Phot*: Rexford Metz (DeLuxe). *Mus*: Steve Dorff. *Des*: Elayne Ceder. *Ed*: Ferris Webster.

Cast: Clint Eastwood (*Philo Beddoe*), Sondra Locke (*Lynn Halsey-Taylor*), Ruth Gordon (*Ma Boggs*), Geoffrey Lewis (*Orville Boggs*), Beverly D'Angelo (*Echo*), Walter Barnes (*Tank McMurdock*), George Chandler (*Clerk at DMV*), Roy Jenson (*Woody*), James McEachin (*Herb*), Bill McKinney (*Dallas*). William O'Connell (*Elmo*).

●1979
Escape from Alcatraz

USA. 112 min.

Production: Malpaso/Paramount. *Distribution*: Paramount.

Dir: Don Siegel. *Scr*: Richard Tuggle (based on the book by J. Campbell Bruce). *Prod*: Robert Daley. *Phot*: Bruce Surtees (DeLuxe). *Mus*: Jerry Fielding. *Des*: Allen Smith. *Ed*: Ferris Webster.

Cast: Clint Eastwood (*Frank Morris*), Patrick McGoohan (*Warden*), Roberts Blossom (*Doc*), Jack Thibeau (*John Anglin*), Paul Benjamin (*English*), Larry Hankin (*Charley Butts*), Bruce M. Fischer (*Wolf*), Frank Ronzio (*Litmus*).

●1980
*Bronco Billy

USA. 116 min.

Production: Warner Bros./Second Street. *Distribution*: Warner Bros.

Dir: Clint Eastwood. *Scr*: Dennis Hackin. *Prod*: Robert Daley. *Phot*: David Worth (DeLuxe). *Mus*: Steve Dorff (songs performed by Merle Haggard, Ronnie Milsap, Penny De Haven, Clint Eastwood and others). *Des*: Gene Lourie. *Ed*: Ferris Webster, Joel Cox.

Cast: Clint Eastwood (*Bronco Billy McCoy*), Sondra Locke (*Antoinette Lily*), Geoffrey Lewis (*John Arlington*), Scatman Crothers (*Doc Lynch*), Bill McKinney (*Lefty LeBow*), Sam Bottoms (*Leonard James*), Dan Vadis (*Chief Big Eagle*), Sierra Pecheur (*Lorrain Running Water*), Walter Barnes (*Sheriff Dix*).

Any Which Way You Can

USA. 115 min.

Production: Malpaso/Warner Bros. *Distribution*: Warner Bros.

Dir: Buddy Van Horn. *Scr*: Stanford Sherman. *Prod*: Fritz Manes. *Phot*:
    David Worth (DeLuxe). *Mus*: Steve Dorff. *Des*: William J. Creber.
    Ed: Ferris Webster, Ron Spang.

Cast: Clint Eastwood (*Philo Beddoe*), Sondra Locke (*Lynn Halsey-Taylor*),
    Geoffrey Lewis (*Orville Boggs*), William Smith (*Jack Wilson*), Harry
    Guardino (*James Beekman*), Ruth Gordon (*Ma Boggs*), Michael
    Cavanaugh (*Patrick Scarfe*), Barry Corbin (*Fat Zack*), Roy Jenson
    (*Moody*), Bill McKinney (*Dallas*), William O'Connell (*Elmo*), John
    Quade (*Cholla*).

●1982

*Honkytonk Man

USA. 123 min.

Production: Malpaso/Warner Bros. *Distribution*: Warner Bros.

Dir: Clint Eastwood. *Scr*: Clancy Carlile (based on his novel). *Prod*:
    Clint Eastwood. *Phot*: Bruce Surtees (Technicolor). *Mus*: Steve
    Dorff. *Des*: Edward Carfagno. *Ed*: Ferris Webster, Michael Kelly, Joel
    Cox.

Cast: Clint Eastwood (*Red Stovall*), Kyle Eastwood (*Whit*), John
    McIntyre (*Grandpa*), Alexa Kenin (*Marlene*), Verna Bloom (*Emmy*),
    Matt Clark (*Virgil*), Barry Corbin (*Arnspringer*), Jerry Hardin
    (*Snuffy*), Tim Thomerson (*Highway Patrolman*), Macon McCalman
    (*Dr. Hines*), Johnny Gimble (*Bob Wills*), Linda Hopkins (*Blues singer*),
    Marty Robbins (*Smoky*), Ray Price, Shelly West, David Frizzell
    (*singers*).

*Firefox

USA. 136 min. Widescreen.

Production: Malpaso/Warner Bros. *Distribution*: Warner Bros.

Dir: Clint Eastwood. *Scr*: Alex Lasker, Wendell Wellman (based on the
    novel by Craig Thomas). *Prod*: Clint Eastwood. *Phot*: Bruce Surtees
    (Panavision, DeLuxe). *Mus*: Maurice Jarre. *Des*: John Graysmark,
    Elayne Ceder. *Ed*: Ferris Webster, Ron Spang.

Cast: Clint Eastwood (*Mitchell Grant*), Freddie Jones (*Kenneth Aubrey*),
    David Huffman (*Buckholz*), Warren Clarke (*Pavel Upenskoy*), Ronald
    Lacey (*Semelovsky*), Kenneth Colley (*Col. Kontarsky*), Klaus Löwitsch
    (*Gen. Vladimirov*), Nigel Hawthorne (*Piotr Baranovich*).

●1983
*Sudden Impact

USA. 117 min. Widescreen.

Production: Malpaso/Warner Bros. *Distribution*: Warner Bros.

Dir: Clint Eastwood. *Scr*: Joseph C. Stinson. *Prod*: Clint Eastwood. *Phot*:
Bruce Surtees (Panavision, Technicolor). *Mus*: Lalo Schifrin. *Des*:
Edward Carfagno. *Ed*: Joel Cox.

Cast: Clint Eastwood (*Harry Callahan*), Sondra Locke (*Jennifer Spencer*),
Pat Hingle (*Chief Jannings*), Bradford Dillman (*Capt. Briggs*), Paul
Drake (*Mick*), Audrie J. Neenan (*Ray Parkins*), Jack Thibeau (*Kruger*),
Michael Currie (*Lt. Donnelly*), Albert Popwell (*Horace King*).

●1984
City Heat

USA. 97 min.

Production: Deliverance/Malpaso/Warner Bros. *Distribution*: Warner Bros.

Dir: Richard Benjamin. *Scr*: Blake Edwards [as Sam O. Brown], Joseph C.
Stinson. *Prod*: Fritz Manes. *Phot*: Nick McLean (Technicolor). *Mus*:
Lennie Niehaus. *Des*: Edward Carfagno. *Ed*: Jacqueline Cambas.

Cast: Clint Eastwood (*Lt. Speer*), Burt Reynolds (*Mike Murphy*), Jane
Alexander (*Addy*), Madeline Kahn (*Caroline Howley*), Rip Torn (*Primo
Pitt*), Irene Cara (*Ginny Lee*), Richard Roundtree (*Dehl Swift*), Tony Lo
Bianco (*Leon Coll*).

Tightrope

USA. 115 min.

Production: Warner Bros./Malpaso. *Distribution*: Warner Bros.

Dir: Richard Tuggle. *Scr*: Richard Tuggle. *Prod*: Clint Eastwood, Fritz
Manes. *Phot*: Bruce Surtees (Technicolor). *Mus*: Lennie Niehaus. *Des*:
Edward Carfagno. *Ed*: Joel Cox.

Cast: Clint Eastwood (*Wes Block*), Geneviève Bujold (*Beryl Thibodeaux*),
Dan Hedaya (*Det. Molinari*), Alison Eastwood (*Amanda Block*), Jenny
Beck (*Penny Block*), Marco St. John (*Leander Rolfe*), Rebecca Perle
(*Becky Jacklin*), Regina Richardson (*Sarita*), Randi Brooks (*Jamie Cory*),
Jamie Rose (*Melanie Silber*), Margaret Howell (*Judy Harper*).

●1985
*Pale Rider

USA. 116 min. Widescreen.

Production: Malpaso. *Distribution*: Warner Bros.

Dir: Clint Eastwood. *Scr*: Michael Butler, Dennis Shryack. *Prod*: Clint
Eastwood. *Phot*: Bruce Surtees (Panavision, Technicolor). *Mus*: Lennie
Niehaus. *Des*: Edward Carfagno. *Ed*: Joel Cox.

Cast: Clint Eastwood (*The Preacher*), Michael Moriarty (*Hull Barret*), Carrie Snodgress (*Sarah Wheeler*), Sydney Penny (*Megan Wheeler*), Chris Penn (*Josh LaHood*), Richard A. Dysart (*Coy LaHood*), Richard Kiel (*Club*), Doug McGrath (*Spider Conway*), John Russell (*Stockburn*).

●1986
*Heartbreak Ridge

USA. 130 min.

Production: Malpaso/Warner Bros. *Distribution*: Warner Bros.

Dir: Clint Eastwood. *Scr*: James Carabatsos. *Prod*: Clint Eastwood. *Phot*: Jack N. Green (Technicolor). *Mus*: Lennie Niehaus. *Des*: Edward Carfagno. *Ed*: Joel Cox.

Cast: Clint Eastwood (*Gunnery Sgt. Tom Highway*), Marsha Mason (*Aggie*), Mario Van Peebles (*Stitch*), Everett McGill (*Maj. Powers*), Moses Gunn (*Sgt. Webster*), Eileen Heckart (*Little Mary*), Boyd Gaines (*Lt. Ring*), Arlen Dean Snyder (*Choozoo*), Vincent Irizarry (*Fragetti*), Ramón Franco (*Aponte*), Tom Villard (*Profile*), Mike Gomez (*Quinones*), Rodney Hill (*Collins*), Peter Koch (*Swede Johanson*), Richard Venture (*Col. Meyers*).

●1988
The Dead Pool

USA. 91 min.

Production: Warner Bros./Malpaso. *Distribution*: Warner Bros.

Dir: Buddy Van Horn. *Scr*: Steve Sharon. *Prod*: David Valdes. *Phot*: Jack N. Green (Technicolor). *Mus*: Lalo Schifrin. *Des*: Edward Carfagno. *Ed*: Ron Spang.

Cast: Clint Eastwood (*Harry Callahan*), Patricia Clarkson (*Samantha Walker*), Liam Neeson (*Peter Swan*), Evan C. Kim (*Al Quan*), David Hunt (*Harlan Rook*), Michael Currie (*Capt. Donnelly*), Michael Goodwin (*Lt. Ackerman*), Darwin Gillett (*Patrick Snow*), Anthony Charnota (*Lou Jannero*).

*Bird

USA. 160 min.

Production: Malpaso/Warner Bros. *Distribution*: Warner Bros.

Dir: Clint Eastwood. *Scr*: Joel Oliansky. *Prod*: Clint Eastwood. *Phot*: Jack N. Green (Technicolor). *Mus*: Lennie Niehaus (with original recordings of Charlie Parker). *Des*: Edward Carfagno. *Ed*: Joel Cox.

Cast: Forest Whitaker (*Charlie "Yardbird" Parker*), Diane Venora (*Chan Parker*), Michael Zelnicker (*Red Rodney*), Samuel E. Wright (*Dizzie Gillespie*), Keith David (*Buster Franklin*), Michael McGuire

(*Brewster*), James Handy (*Esteves*), Damon Whitaker (*young Charlie Parker*), Morgan Nagler (*Kim*), Arlen Dean Snyder (*Dr Heath*), Sam Robards (*Moscowitz*)., Diane Salinger (*Baroness Nica*).

●1989
Pink Cadillac

USA. 122 min.

Production: Malpaso/Warner Bros. *Distribution*: Warner Bros.

Dir: Buddy Van Horn. *Scr*: John Eskow. *Prod*: David Valdes. *Phot*: Jack N. Green (Technicolor). *Mus*: Steve Dorff. *Des*: Edward Carfagno. *Ed*: Joel Cox.

Cast: Clint Eastwood (*Tommy Nowak*), Bernadette Peters (*Lou Ann McGuinn*), Timothy Carhart (*Roy McGuinn*), John Dennis Johnston (*Waycross*), Michael Des Barres (*Alex*), Jimmie F. Skaggs (*Billy Dunston*), Bill Moseley (*Darrell*), Michael Champion (*Ken Lee*), William Hickey (*Mr. Barton*), Geoffrey Lewis (*Ricky Z*).

●1990
*White Hunter, Black Heart

USA. 110 min.

Production: Malpaso/Rastar/Warner Bros. *Distribution*: Warner Bros.

Dir: Clint Eastwood. *Scr*: Peter Viertel, James Bridges, Burt Kennedy (based on the novel by Peter Viertel). *Prod*: Clint Eastwood. *Phot*: Jack N. Green (Technicolor). *Mus*: Lennie Niehaus. *Des*: John Graysmark. *Ed*: Joel Cox.

Cast: Clint Eastwood (*John Wilson*), Jeff Fahey (*Pete Verrill*), Charlotte Cornwell (*Miss Wilding*), Norman Lumsden (*Butler George*), George Dzundza (*Paul Landers*), Edward Tudor- Pole (*Reissar*), Roddy Maude-Roxby (*Thompson*), Richard Warwick (*Basil Fields*), Catherine Neilson (*Irene Saunders*), Marisa Berenson (*Kay Gibson*), Richard Vanstone (*Phil Duncan*), Boy Mathias Chuma (*Kivu*).

*The Rookie

USA. 121 min. Widescreen.

Production: Kazanjian-Siebert/Malpaso/Warner Bros. *Distribution*: Warner Bros.

Dir: Clint Eastwood. *Scr*: Scott Spiegel, Boaz Yakin. *Prod*: Howard G. Kazanjian, Steven Siebert, David Valdes. *Phot*: Jack N. Green (Panavision, Technicolor). *Mus*: Lennie Niehaus. *Des*: Judy Cammer. *Ed*: Joel Cox.

Cast: Clint Eastwood (*Nick Pulovski*), Charlie Sheen (*David Ackerman*), Raul Julia (*Strom*), Sonia Braga (*Liesl*), Tom Skerritt (*Eugene Ackerman*), Lara Flynn Boyle (*Sarah),* Pepe Serna (*Lt. Ray Garcia*), Marco

Rodríguez (*Loco*), Pete Randall (*Cruz*), Donna Mitchell (*Laura Ackerman*).

●1992
*Unforgiven

USA. 131 min. Widescreen.
Production and distribution: Warner Bros.
Dir: Clint Eastwood. *Scr*: David Webb Peoples. *Prod*: Clint Eastwood.
Phot: Jack N. Green (Panavision, Technicolor). *Mus*: Lennie
Niehaus. *Des*: Henry Bumstead. *Ed*: Joel Cox.
Cast: Clint Eastwood (*William Munny*), Gene Hackman (*Little Bill
Daggett*), Morgan Freeman (*Ned Logan*), Richard Harris (*English Bob*),
Jaimz Woolvett (*The Schofield Kid*), Saul Rubinek (*W.W. Beauchamp*),
Frances Fisher (*Strawberry Alice*), Anna Thomson (*Delilah Fitzgerald*),
David Mucci (*Quick Mike*), Rob Campbell (*Davey Bunting*), Anthony
James (*Skinny Dubois*), Tara Dawn Frederick (*Little Sue*), Beverley
Elliott (*Silky*), Liisa Repo-Martell (*Faith*), Josie Smith (*Cross Creek
Kate*), Shane Meier (*Will Munny*), Aline Levasseur (*Penny Munny*),
Cherrilene Cardinal (*Sally Two Trees*), Robert Koons (*Crocker*), Ron
White (*Clyde Ledbetter*), Mina E. Mina (*Muddy Chandler*), Henry
Kope (*German Joe Schulz*), Jeremy Ratchford (*Deputy Andy Russell*),
John Pyper-Ferguson (*Charley Hecker*).

●1993
In the Line of Fire

USA. 128 min. Widescreen.
Production: Castle Rock/Columbia. *Distribution*: Columbia.
Dir: Wolfgang Petersen. *Scr*: Jeff Maguire. *Prod*: Jeff Apple. *Phot*: John
Bailey (Panavision, Technicolor). *Des*: Lilly Kilvert. *Ed*: Anne V.
Coates
Cast: Clint Eastwood (*Frank Horrigan*), John Malkovich (*Mitch Leary*),
Rene Russo (*Lilly Raines*), Dylan McDermott (*Al D'Andrea*), Gary
Cole (*Bill Watts*), Fred Dalton Thompson (*Harry Sargent*), John
Mahoney (*Sam Campagna*), Gregory Alan Williams (*Matt Wilder*),
Jim Curley (*President*), Clyde Kusatsu (*Jack Okura*), Steve Hytner
(*Tony Carducci*), Tobin Bell (*Mendoza*), Mary Van Arsdel (*Sally*).

*A Perfect World

USA. 137 min. Widescreen.
Production: Malpaso/Warner Bros. *Distribution*: Warner Bros.
Dir: Clint Eastwood. *Scr*: John Lee Hancock. *Prod*: Clint Eastwood,
Mark Johnson, David Valdes. *Phot*: Jack N. Green (Panavision,

Technicolor). *Mus*: Lennie Niehaus. *Des*: Henry Bumstead. *Ed*: Joel
Cox, Ron Spang.

Cast: Kevin Costner (*Butch Haynes*), T.J. Lowther (*Phillip Perry*), Clint
Eastwood (*Red Garnett*), Laura Dern (*Sally Gerber*), Keith Szarabajka
(*Terry Pugh*), Jennifer Griffin (*Gladys Perry*), Wayne Dehart (*Mack*),
Mary Alice (*Lottie*), Kevin Jamal Woods (*Cleveland*), Ed Geldart (*Fred
Cummings*), Bruce McGill (*Paul Sanders*), Margaret Bowman (*Trick or
Treat Lady*), John M. Jackson (*Bob Fielder*), Connie Cooper (*Bob's wife*),
Lucy Lee Flippin (*Lucy*), Elizabeth Ruscio (*Paula*).

●1995
*The Bridges of Madison County

USA. 135 min. Widescreen.
Production: Amblin/Malpaso/Warner Bros. *Distribution*: Warner Bros.
Dir: Clint Eastwood. *Scr*: Robert James Waller, Richard LaGravenese
(based on the novel by Robert James Waller). *Prod*: Clint Eastwood,
Kathleen Kennedy. *Phot*: Jack N. Green (Panavision, Technicolor).
Mus: Lennie Niehaus. *Des*: Jeannine Claudia Oppewall. *Ed*: Joel Cox.

Cast: Meryl Streep (*Francesca Johnson*), Clint Eastwood (*Robert Kincaid*),
Annie Corley (*Caroline*), Victor Slezak (*Michael Johnson*), Jim Haynie
(*Richard Johnson*), Phyllis Lyons (*Betty*), Debra Monk (*Madge*), Richard
Lage (*Lawyer*), Michelle Benes (*Lucy Redfield*).

1997
*Absolute Power

USA. 121 min. Widescreen.
Production: Castle Rock/Columbia/Malpaso. *Distribution*: Columbia.
Dir: Clint Eastwood. *Scr*: David Baldacci, William Goldman (based on
the novel by David Baldacci). *Prod*: Clint Eastwood, Karen Spiegel.
Phot: Jack N. Green (Panavision, Technicolor). *Mus*: Clint Eastwood,
Lennie Niehaus. *Des*: Henry Bumstead. *Ed*: Joel Cox.

Cast: Clint Eastwood (*Luther Whitney*), Gene Hackman (*President
Richmond*), Ed Harris (*Seth Frank*), Laura Linney (*Kate Whitney*), Scott
Glenn (*Bill Burton*), Dennis Haysbert (*Tim Collin*), Judy Davis (*Gloria
Russell*), E.G. Marshall (*Walter Sullivan*), Melora Hardin (*Christy
Sullivan*), Kenneth Welsh (*Sandy Lord*), Penny Johnson (*Laura Simon*),
Richard Jenkins (*Michael McCarty*), Mark Margolis (*Red*).

*Midnight in the Garden of Good and Evil

USA. 155 min. Widescreen.
Production: Silver/Warner Bros./Malpaso. *Distribution*: Warner Bros.
Dir: Clint Eastwood. *Scr*: John Berendt, John Hancock (based on the
book by John Berendt). *Prod*: Clint Eastwood, Arnold Stiefel. *Phot*:

Jack N. Green (Panavision, Technicolor). *Mus*: Lennie Niehaus. *Des*: Henry Bumstead. *Ed*: Joel Cox.

Cast: John Cusack (*John Kelso*), Kevin Spacey (*Jim Williams*), Jack Thompson (*Sonny Seiler*), Irma P. Hall (*Minerva*), Jude Law (*Billy Carl Hanson*), Alison Eastwood (*Mandy Nichols*), Paul Hipp (*Joe Odom*), Lady Chablis (*Frank "Chablis" Devau*), Dorothy Loudoun (*Serena Dawes*), Anne Hancy (*Margaret Williams*), Geoffrey Lewis (*Luther Driggers*), Richard Herd (*Henry Skerridge*), Leon Rippy (*Det. Boone*), Bob Gunton (*Finley Largent*).

●1999

*True Crime

USA. 127 min. Widescreen.

Production: Malpaso/Zanuck. *Distribution*: Warner Bros.

Dir: Clint Eastwood. *Scr*: Andrew Klavan, Larry Gross, Paul Brickman, Stephen Schiff (based on the novel by Andrew Klavan). *Prod*: Clint Eastwood, Lili Fini Zanuck, Richard D. Zanuck. *Phot*: Jack N. Green (Panavision, Technicolor). *Mus*: Lennie Niehaus. *Des*: Henry Bumstead. *Ed*: Joel Cox.

Cast: Clint Eastwood (*Steve Everett*), Isaiah Washington (*Frank Beachum*), Denis Leary (*Bob Findley*), Lisa Gay Hamilton (*Bonnie Beachum*), Diane Venora (*Barbara Everett*), Bernard Hill (*Warden Luther Plunkitt*), James Woods (*Alan Mann*), Michael McKean (*Reverend Shillerman*), Michael Jeter (*Dale Porterhouse*), Mary McCormack (*Michelle Ziegler*), Hattie Winston (*Mrs Russell*), Penny Bae Bridges (*Gail Beachum*), Francesca Fisher-Eastwood (*Kate Everett*).

Chapter 1: Between Classical and Postmodern

1   The definitive historical account of this model of filmmaking is in
    Bordwell, Staiger, and Thompson, *The Classical Hollywood Cinema*,
    which traces the evolution during the 1910s and '20s of the tech-
    niques of story construction, continuity editing, and other formal
    devices through which the model proceeds. Whether the form is *in
    itself* ideologically complicit—that is, whether narrative closure,
    shot dispositions, and continuity editing (or "suture") are innately a
    brainwashing device to sustain dominant social and psychological
    structures—is of course the central topic of one branch of film
    theory over the past three decades. Some variants of this "apparatus
    theory" have the disadvantage of making all classical Hollywood
    films the same film and foreclosing debate on most of the internal
    complexities of individual works.

2   A good and thought-provoking (though in my view somewhat over-
    stated) analysis of the troubled state of the classical model during
    the 1940s is Dana Polan's *Power and Paranoia*. For a lively and pene-
    trating account of how Hollywood was working through some of
    the social issues of the 1950s, see Peter Biskind, *Seeing Is Believing*.
    There is also an extensive literature on the complex ideological
    operation of melodrama and so-called "women's pictures" during
    this period, notably in Christine Gledhill, ed., *Home Is Where the
    Heart Is* (British Film Institute, 1987), Robert Lang, *American Film
    Melodrama* (Princeton, 1989), Jacki Byars, *All That Hollywood Allows*
    (North Carolina, 1991), and Marcia Landy, ed., *Imitations of Life*
    (Wayne State, 1991).

3   Data from the annual Quigley poll of film exhibitors. Wayne also
    placed in the top four for nineteen of these years, and Eastwood in
    the top four fifteen times. No other performer approaches this kind
    of dominance. See Wills, 12.

4   Wills, 11-12.

5   Of course this pattern applies not just to Wayne but to all heroes of
ideology of the period. Wayne is special (different from, say, Gable,
Bogart, or even Cooper) because he is the largest and most visible
iteration of the warrior hero, whose dramatic field is stylized through
an equation between ideological conflict and the violent conflicts
depicted in his films, and where ideological victory is equated with
victory in battle. This simplified, almost primitive symbolic field
allows its principal protagonists to reach a quasi-Homeric stature.

6   I feel that this crucial decade in Hollywood movie history has never
been adequately dealt with in scholarly literature. The best treatments are in the latter sections of Robert Ray's *A Certain Tendency of
the Hollywood Cinema, 1930-1980*, which talks very usefully about "left
and right cycles" and is aware of the dimensions of this period's challenges to classical optimism; Robin Wood's *Hollywood from Vietnam to
Reagan*, which conveys a geological sense of the period's aura of crisis,
although it is basically a collection of separate pieces; and Ryan and
Kellner's *Camera Politica*, which is the only systematic analysis of most
of the important films of the decade but which views all of them
strongly through the filter of their relevance to left/countercultural
projects and issues. Most commentaries on the decade of the 1970s
emphasize its industrial changes and attribute its transformations of
classical narrative to the arrival of a new generation of "Hollywood
auteurs" such as Coppola, Altman, Scorsese, Spielberg, and Lucas. For
some very recent examples of this longstanding view, see David
Cook's essay "Auteur Cinema and the 'Film Generation' in 1970s
Cinema," and Timothy Corrigan's "Auteurs and the New Hollywood,"
both in Jon Lewis, ed., *New American Cinema* (1998). My own eschato-
logical view of the era's importance is, as far as I know, unique. See
also my article "The Crisis of Classicism in Hollywood, 1967-77." Of
course these periodizations are never uniform or absolute, and classicism survives in individual films right through this decade, and
through the two following ones, too. What is important is that the
climate changed to such a degree that the classical film became more
and more widely difficult to imagine, and lost its dominance.

7   These two narrative types also correspond to Robert Ray's "left and
right cycles."

8   This is not really the case in the *Godfather* films and *Taxi Driver*—
films which, although they observe the "right-wing" structure of
individuals taking power in a chaotic society, do so in a heavily ironic
or completely derisory fashion. Ray's term for this phenomenon is the
"corrected right-wing" film.

9   "Re-arrived" would be more accurate, since Eastwood had gone from
Hollywood to work in Europe with Leone. But the first phase of his

movie career had been confined to minor roles in minor films, and
to one substantial role in a television series, *Rawhide*.

10   "Unique" may not be quite accurate. One notices a similar quality in
other Leone characters—especially the one played by Charles
Bronson in *Once Upon a Time in the West* (1968), in which Eastwood
does not appear. (This was, in fact, the character Leone developed
to succeed Eastwood's Man With No Name, and at one stage of the
scenario the Bronson character was supposed to kill the Eastwood
character at the very beginning of the movie; unsurprisingly,
Eastwood would not agree to appear in that capacity. See Frayling's
The Spaghetti Western for a full account, and for a number of script
variants for *Once Upon a Time in the West*.) Of course Bronson also
returned to Hollywood with this persona and extrapolated his later
career from it, perhaps even more markedly than Eastwood did.
One could speak of the basically one-dimensional Bronson as in
some respects a homuncular Eastwood-figure, a demonstration of
what Eastwood might have been without the irony, the contradictions, and the deliberate pushing of impermeable masculine power
all the way to transcendence and "impossibility." Significantly,
Bronson's career was very big during the ugly death-of-classicism
1970s, but faded more and more during the 1980s when Eastwood's
ironic dimension was carrying him safely across into neo-optimistic
postmodernism.

11   This fact became clear to me during a discussion with a colleague
who was performing an intelligent analysis of the Schwarzenegger
character in *Total Recall* as a scattered subject. The character's brain
has been implanted with false memories, and he is not at all "really"
who he "thinks" he is—and is thus a perfect example of the virtual,
rather than the authentic, subject. While this is an unarguable
analysis of the narrative itself, it fails to take account of the fact that
Schwarzenegger in *any* capacity is a virtual, not an authentic, subject
by reason of his cartoon-like bodily presence. From this standpoint,
any distinction between a Schwarzenegger character who is himself
and one who only thinks he is himself is, shall we say, academic.

12   It is to postmodern masculinity, as seen most exaggeratedly in the
films of Schwarzenegger and Stallone, in the frankly artificial environment of movies inspired by comic-book superheroes or set in
the elsewhere of the cybertechnoid future, that current cultural
theory has directed much of its energy. In addition to the hypermasculine Schwarzenegger and Stallone (and Jean-Claude Van Damme,
Dolph Lundgren, and Stephen Seagal), there are a number of more
"realist" icons presented by actors of not such trophy bodybuilder
dimensions—most notably Bruce Willis (the *Die Hard* series) and
Mel Gibson (the *Lethal Weapon* series). There is a forest of books and

articles on masculinity in postmodern action cinema (for example, the titles cited in the bibliography by Cohan and Hark, Jeffords, Kirkham and Thumim, Murphy, Penley and Willis, Tasker, and Willis). When these studies turn their attention to Eastwood, it is mostly to mention him as simply another manifestation of the same phenomenon as Schwarzenegger or Van Damme, or the Bruce Willis or Mel Gibson action heroes. It is my contention, of course, that Eastwood is of a different type from all of these figures, and in fact unique. Paul Smith and Dennis Bingham are the only commentators working broadly in the field of cultural theory to devote really special attention to Eastwood in book-length projects. Smith seems not entirely happy navigating through the world of popular culture and seeks to attach to the existing cultural-studies theory-set without spending much time watching action movies, while Bingham's interesting treatment has a strong psychoanalytic-theory bent.

13 And probably also James Bond, the pioneer, in the early 1960s, in the business of sealing the death of an enemy with a fatuous pun. Such style-statement heartlessness was an integral quality in a figure whose ironic impossibility started at a high level and grew throughout the 1970s and '80s into Roger Moore's amazing flatnesses, every bit as exaggerated and self-knowing as any of Schwarzenegger's. The bizarre attempts in the 1990s to bring Bond back to some kind of "believability" in relation to Moore's truly inescapable artificialities show perhaps that even the always ultra-ironic Bond films need some element of the classical.

14 Contrast, for example, Stallone's movement from his arrival as a still recognizably classical subject in *Rocky* (1976), through his recasting as agonized late-nihilist regressive hero in *First Blood* (1982), thence to cartoon action-figure in *Rambo* (1984), and on into the land of eternal flatness in *Tango and Cash*, *Cliffhanger*, *Demolition Man*, etc., etc. The character of Rocky Balboa, needless to say, was drained of its classical substance in even the first sequel (1982), and quickly assumed proportions just as unclassically caricatured as the comic-book character Stallone finally played literally in *Judge Dredd* (1995). Other charismatic actors (one thinks of Paul Newman or Robert Redford) were able to sustain or reclaim classical subjectivity throughout this period; but they are only tangential to the archetypes of heroic masculinity, and their appearance in comedies, romantic films, and realist dramas is more important than their stature within the action-movie genres like westerns and crime films. (Bruce Willis and Mel Gibson are probably their '80s and '90s equivalents as actors not confined to the types of power-masculinity.) It is true that as the Dirty Harry series proceeds, Harry becomes more a caricature and self-caricature (probably an inherent feature of sequels), and that in other projects, mostly

comedies — such as *Bronco Billy*, *Every Which Way But Loose* (1978), and above all *City Heat* (1985) — Eastwood has moved into the area of pastiche. But these projects always depended on the continued existence of a more substantial figure which could be caricatured and pastiched, and never replaced that figure. For Stallone and Schwarzenegger, this flattened field is career bedrock.

Chapter 2: Heroic Deconstruction; or, Is Clint Eastwood Possible?

1   A misinterpretation which continues into the present and even into the high-academic ground of theory-based interpretation. See for example Paul Smith's claim that Leone's westerns restore repressed aspects of American history (1-17).

2   Bingham, 164-179.

3   Frayling, 88.

4   There is an antecedent for Harry within the crime genre. When the violent, at moments even psychotic, gangster persona of James Cagney migrated into cop movies in the mid 1930s, many of the qualities of his criminality marked out this first "gangster cop." Subsequently the tough cop became a standard generic feature. Only rarely, though, has this law-and-order-seeking figure taken on quite so antisocial a tinge as in the character of Harry Callahan.

5   *Magnum Force* is actually incoherent on the subject of vigilante cops — as it necessarily must be if it is to preserve the oxymoronic institution of the cowboy cop whose most dominant embodiment Harry is. The film in effect has Harry saying that cops must abide by the letter of the law rather than by self-derived principles of natural justice; but to bind Harry himself to that stricture would be to abolish him. This "undecidableness," however, does nothing to diminish the mythic reflexivity of the film. See also Eric Patterson, "Every Which Way But Lucid: The Critique of Authority in Clint Eastwood's Police Movies."

6   This kind of cartoon-like hyperstylization, with attendant self-consciousness and irony, is of course a constant feature of big postmodern action movies of the 1980s and '90s. It is worth noting that *The Gauntlet* preceded the general trend by several years, and that its peculiar effect here springs from its juxtaposition with the metatextual (i.e., largely offscreen) presence of the transcendental Eastwood persona. The *Batman* movies (to take the handiest example) have no dimension apart from their ironic one — except perhaps for children. At the same time, it would not be incorrect, I think, to call the big set pieces of destruction in *The Gauntlet* pioneers of postmodern Hollywood action-spectacle.

7   See for example the articles by Christine Holmlund and Robert Miklitch, and the chapter on *Tightrope* in Paul Smith's book.

8 There is some disagreement about just who the Eastwood figure in the film is. Eastwood himself has said that in his mind the character is actually the brother of the dead sheriff, but that other interpretations, including the "returned from the grave" one, are all right with him (see Knapp, 61). The film itself provides not even a wisp of a suggestion that the character might be the sheriff's brother, but a good deal of suggestion that it is the victim himself. The fact that he has a dream-flashback in which the sheriff's murder is replayed indicates that he was present, while at the end of the film, when the dwarf says to him, "I never did know your name," Eastwood replies, "Yes you do." Admittedly there are problems with this interpretation too, especially the fact that the guilty townspeople do not recognize the character, and perhaps the best thing would simply be to say that the whole affair remains wrapped in mystery. Yet the "returned from the grave" interpretation works so well in so many ways—particularly in view of the Eastwood character's transcendent omniscience, imperviousness, and godlike anger.

9 This statement refers to major studio theatrical releases. In this domain of the "A" picture, westerns had moved progressively against the "pure" cowboy hero throughout the postwar era. But the naïve classical western model survived much longer in "B" movies and serials, and then on television, where during the 1960s and even later figures ranging from Roy Rogers and Gene Autry to Matt Dillon (*Gunsmoke*) and the *Bonanza* family had a hardy grassroots life. TV western culture was so naïve, in fact, that relatively complex characters such as Paladin in *Have Gun, Will Travel* were felt to be astonishingly advanced. In this context, it is in retrospect ironic that Eastwood effectively got his start playing a relatively naïve figure in the television series *Rawhide* 1959–66.

10 Especially in the light of Eastwood's own description of *Bronco Billy* as "Capraesque," it is interesting to think of this film as a kind of updating of Frank Capra's equally semi-conscious attempts to think through what was good about American innocence, how it was threatened, and what could be done about the threat, in *Mr Deeds Goes to Town* (1936), *Mr Smith Goes to Washington* (1939), and *Meet John Doe* (1941). The need for a hero who is unusually, unrealistically innocent is common to all these films (and to *Bronco Billy*), but in the most hysterical and imperilled of the trio, *Meet John Doe*, it is especially striking that the hero is initially a wholly fictitious creation of the brassy journalist played by Barbara Stanwyck. In the light of *Bronco Billy*'s place in the development of Eastwood as a substitute or inspirational father figure, it is especially noteworthy that the inspiration for her creation is the words and beliefs of her transcendentally wise and benevolent late *father*. The hero's meaning-giving ideology in *Bronco Billy* is simi-

larly at some initial state necessarily a fiction, and then embodied in the articulate words of a benevolent patriarch. The "fatherly" aspects of the protagonist are dealt with at greater length in "Eastwood the Father."

11 Again this looks back to that evidently seminal scene in *A Fistful of Dollars* where Eastwood takes multiple gunshots to the torso. The character in *Pale Rider* was obviously not wearing armour plating and was probably (?) killed. But having shown a human mortality not manifested by Leone's hero, he then demonstrates (as in *High Plains Drifter*) an additional *super*human immortality by coming back from the dead.

12 One might also note the strong persistence of particular iconic qualities across these three characters. Each wears an angular, uncompromisingly aggressive square-cut hat; black or deep-brown clothing, a long coat, and an unshaven countenance all conspire to enfold the character in darkness, which is also emphasized in the low-key lighting of climactic scenes. Out of this literal darkness — which is also the metaphor for the character's frightening unknowableness — flashes only the menacing glint of a lethal glance. (Hat iconography is highly codified in Eastwood's films. compare the angry angles of the hats in *High Plains Drifter* and *Pale Rider* with the billowing curves of Bronco Billy's hat, or that of the aging 1960s Texas Ranger played by Eastwood in *A Perfect World*.)

13 The girl who prays for his appearance, through whose youthful eyes the Preacher is seen, asks him at one point: "Who are you, really?" His reply is itself a question which merely articulates the necessity for mystery: "Does it matter?" This question and response forms a perfect complement to the Sondra Locke character's scornful early question to Bronco Billy: "Are you for real?," and his equally laconic and illuminating reply: "I'm who I want to be." On the other hand, when Stockburn at last recognizes and identifies the Preacher at the end of the showdown ("You!"), it signals the moment of his death.

14 Wright 59-73. Wright classifies this "Vengeance Variation" as a subset of the foundational "Classical Plot," whose protagonists engage relatively straightforwardly in prosocial acts. Wright's first example of the "Classical Plot" is *Shane*.

15 The remainder of Revelations 6:8 reads as follows: "And power was given unto them over the fourth part of the earth, to kill with sword, and with hunger, and with death, and with the beasts of the earth." (The Preacher employs a sword-like axe-handle to dispose of a gang of ruffians soon after his appearance — although this is actually a reversing paraphrase of the axe-handle which the decent sodbuster Starrett wields in *Shane*.) The Preacher, then, bears a demonic countenance, but is doing God's work: he is "the wrath of God."

16 This is one of the central organizing ideas of *A Certain Tendency of the American Cinema*.

17 Other Eastwood films, most notably *Honkytonk Man*, have presented a classical narrative featuring an Eastwood persona who was *not* transcendent; but this category of films—not unproblematical to categorize in the first place—stands apart from the lines I am trying to trace here.

18 One notes the almost derisory pastiche of this quality in *Unforgiven*, where the bounty-contract Munny comes to fulfill is a punishment for an assault on a woman.

19 In two later films, *Absolute Power* (1997) and *True Crime* (1999), Eastwood has tried to some extent to resurrect the masterful hero, and these works represent a disconcerting coda to the films dealt with in the present essay. But even these films, especially *True Crime*, reveal shadowy or subtextual deconstructions of the heroic presence. See the essay "*Absolute Power* and *True Crime*: Postscripts of Disavowal," later in this volume.

Chapter 3: Unforgiven: Anatomy of a Murderer

1 Tompkins, 47-67.

2 This figure again recalls Bingham's description of the impervious and omnipotent Eastwood persona, with its lack of language, history, affect and even name, as the viewer's ego-projection (see "Heroic Deconstruction," n.2). Again I would stress that this is a useful and suggestive description, but that it overlooks the character's strong, often frightening, sense of otherness and superiority, to which even the viewer is subservient.

3 Tompkins, 72.

4 This remark is not so applicable to *The Outlaw Josey Wales*, however, as it is to *High Plains Drifter* and *Pale Rider*. Although in some crucial respects as granitic as the other protagonists, the character of Josey Wales undergoes a softening process as the narrative proceeds through its last half. But *Unforgiven* deconstructs *The Outlaw Josey Wales* too: the Outlaw William Munny of legend is exactly the fearsome mad-dog murderer that Josey is falsely reputed to be. Josey is misunderstood, betrayed, victimized, and *driven* to killing; in *Unforgiven* the instinct for homicide has no such justification.

5 Ned's character, upon examination, raises questions as to motivation and development which the film does not answer. For example, how can such a thoroughly good person have been so closely associated with the old Munny? No Claudia is presented to account for *his* change. What makes him agree to accompany Munny this time— friendship? money? the wish to get away from domesticity for a while?

But the narrative doesn't really need to answer such questions. It is enough that Ned should be the good friend, the good man.

6   My assumptions about the genre are drawing here upon Jim Kitses' powerful structuralist essay on western antinomies in *Horizons West*, especially 7-27.

7   The foundational description of this feature of the genre is in Robert Warshow, 137-8. Warshow says, "the important thing about a prostitute is her quasi-masculine independence: nobody owns her, nothing has to be explained to her, and she is not, like a virtuous woman, a 'value' that demands to be protected." Note that in *Unforgiven*, while the prostitutes (especially Alice) do display a "quasi-masculine independence," they are indeed to some degree literally owned by men; and that the film at least holds out the notion that they should be promoted to the status of "values that demand protection." The role of women in the film is a topic which deserves its own essay, but cf. Maurice Yacowar's interesting comments on this and related topics in "Re-Membering the Western," 249-253.

8   Its unpainted wooden walls and roof recall the unpainted wooden buildings of Lago in *High Plains Drifter*, and also the half-painted ones of *Pale Rider*—buildings which arguably also signify a frontier community which has not been put together right.

9   E.g., LITTLE BILL: "You've just shot an unarmed man." MUNNY: "Well, he should have armed himself...."

10 And on Josey Wales in particular. Josey's Indian fellow-traveller Lone Watie watches him gun down half a dozen men in one of the towns they move through. Fascinated as ever by the amazing killing-power of his companion, he quizzes Josey about how he knew which man to shoot first. Josey responds with a detailed breakdown of his lightning estimate of their respective powers, rather like Sherlock Holmes explaining to Watson how he deduced something. In *Josey Wales*, the explication of heroic violence in terms of technique and skill is part of that film's attempt to reclaim the heroic Eastwood for humanity and prosociality. In taking this humanized and rational-ized violence and moving it back into unconsciousness and "luck," *Unforgiven* emphasizes the eternal separateness of transcendence, and then goes on to characterize it as pure horror. In any event, for anyone who knows *The Outlaw Josey Wales*, this particular moment in *Unforgiven* acts as a really explicit self-deconstruction of the transcendent-killer Eastwood.

Chapter 4: Eastwood the Father

1   Robert Ray's book *A Certain Tendency in the American Cinema* formulates the most lucid and succinct description of this "reluctant hero" (see especially 64–65).

2   I am indebted in what follows to Paul Smith's extensive discussion of the issue of fatherhood in Eastwood's films (*passim.*, but especially 36–54 and 248–263), notwithstanding my strong disagreement with much of his argument.

3   It might be felt that the comedic and self-parodic Eastwood is equally important. I would not agree.

4   Recall the strange and entirely anti-characteristic action of the Man With No Name in *A Fistful of Dollars*, giving his money to and risking his safety for a persecuted family of peasants—a gesture of the narrative which equally seems to contradict the meticulously constructed cold self-interest of the protagonist.

5   Again, the term "official hero" is Robert Ray's. In *A Certain Tendency of the American Cinema*, Ray proposes the categories of "official hero" and "outlaw hero" to describe the contradictions of a narrative ideology where heroes must simultaneously act to save the community and keep themselves charismatically separate and individual (see especially 59–66 and 71–88). He uses the Paul Henreid and Humphrey Bogart characters in *Casablanca* as examples of "official" and "outlaw" heroes, and points out how in any contest between the two for the affections of the viewer, the "outlaw hero" always wins. The "outlaw hero" also overlaps strongly with the "reluctant hero" mentioned above. Even to suggest faintly that the Eastwood character in *High Plains Drifter* has to worry about being taken for an "official hero" is ludicrous, and I am not really using the term properly in this regard, only trying to suggest the depth of the period's bitter skepticism regarding prosocial poses of any kind.

6   That is, if you don't count its four sequels. *Death Wish* also spawned a dozen or so pretty direct imitations throughout the 1970s and '80s. But of course there are countless examples of the basic narrative structure in which there is an atrocious crime committed at the outset against a protagonist who then spends the entirety of the story in a delicious program of violent revenge, morally authorized in advance for any excess by the "suffering" he has endured. The disproportion between the protagonist's quickly-gotten-out-of-the-way pain and the pleasure experienced by viewers in his protracted "payback" (the name, incidentally, of a recent example of the type) strongly suggests that the initial crime is merely a legalism necessary to provide a minimal decent covering for the rampage-pleasure, rather than a true cause of the action. This narrative subgenre has progressed without a hitch from the regressive resentfulness of

"right-wing" films of the 1970s to the present environment of affect-less postmodern spectacle-bloodletting, as displayed in innumerable action movies where the protagonist is nominally motivated by some traumatic event in his past.

7 For other resemblances between *Bronco Billy* and some Capra films, see "Heroic Deconstruction," n.10.

8 *The Gauntlet* (a work that comes between *Josey Wales* and *Bronco Billy*) is much more dependent than either of the flanking films on the mechanism of a woman's humanizing influence, but there the topic of leadership or fatherhood is not present at all.

9 Paul Smith (36, 55) strongly emphasizes the crypto-tyrannical nature of Billy's rule.

10 The Eastwood character dies in only three of his films to date. In both *The Beguiled* and *Honkytonk Man*, his death also signals his defeat and eclipse—and not surprisingly, neither film was very successful at the box office or with Eastwood's core fans. The third film is *The Bridges of Madison County*, where the entire elegiac narrative occurs in flashback following the deaths of both protagonists, and where death is, in the tradition of a certain kind of "women's-picture" romance, simply a removal from the limitations of reality and a transportation into the limitless realm of eternity.

11 It might be held, psychoanalytically, that desire cannot actually be defeated but only repressed or that by "defeat" what is really meant is "repression." *Tightrope*, however, must ultimately put the question in the dramatic moral terms of "evil which must be resisted" rather than the psychoanalytic amoral terms of "socially inconvenient desire which must be repressed," for the film does not intend (and cannot afford) to depart *that* radically from the landscape of mainstream narrative. Nevertheless, much of *Tightrope*'s power lies in its mere acknowledgement of the presence of emotional forces which have been repressed into absence in other narratives (e.g., the Dirty Harry movies) and are to that degree unrepressed in this film.

12 A recurring configuration has Eastwood either encouraging his reluctant partners to endure the violent horrors of the job against their first instincts or else watching them lose their lives in the attempt to be as heroic as Eastwood. (*In the Line of Fire* offers a typically uncomfortable late-Eastwood reflection on this configuration wherein Eastwood begs his traumatized partner not to retire, then watches him killed on duty.) One recalls also *Josey Wales*'s fascination with techniques and strategies of violence.

Chapter 5: A Perfect World: There Is No Good Father

1   The Halloween connection persists throughout the movie and assumes the status of a central metaphor. The white-clad escapees Butch and Pugh are in effect frightening trick-or-treaters. Philip is bitter at being forbidden to trick-or-treat and commits his own first crime in stealing a Halloween costume: that of the comic-book character Casper the Friendly Ghost. Butch is anxious to provide Philip with the trick-or-treat experience, as part of what every father should do for his son (again, a variation on the initiations into pleasures which Red Stovall provides for Whit in *Honkytonk Man*). Philip incongruously wears the Casper costume for much of the ensuing action. Butch sends Philip trick-or-treating to a farmhouse, where the homespun motherly woman answering the door moves from hospitality to terror when Butch quietly shows her his gun, even while she and Butch pretend to be giving Philip his Halloween treat. As a departing "prank," Butch rips out the telephone line. In this case, Casper's visit is not such a friendly one. The Casper mask is an incongruously happy and innocent icon strongly featured during the uneasy first and tragic last sequences of the film. In general, the banal and excessively harmless nature of the Casper icon is perhaps an embodiment of the thematically central wish to find a benevolent and "magical" higher power to console and guide — a wish which is thus represented as at once touchingly childlike and too naïve for adults. In addition, Philip, and to some extent the film, strives to see the Butch as a *friendly* spectre despite his frightening and dangerous qualities. (Incidentally, two years later Eastwood put in an uncredited cameo appearance in the kids' movie *Casper*, which revived the comic-book character.)

2   Some doubt is cast on whether Butch's threat is completely in earnest. After Philip has shot him, Butch tells him: "You're a hero — probably be in all the papers tomorrow, how you saved those folks. Truth is, I don't think I'd have killed them, though. I only ever killed two people in my whole life — one hurt my momma, one hurt you [i.e., Pugh]." At the time of the shooting, however, it is impossible for Philip, or the audience for that matter, to divine that Butch might not be serious in his threat. It is not even clear that he might not kill all three of the family.

3   Particularly in view of *Pale Rider*'s relation to *Shane*, one may recall the famous conclusion of the latter film here, where the young Joey shouts "Shane! Shane!" to his departing father-substitute and masculine role model. Of course in *A Perfect World*, the situation is reversed and turned against itself: now it is the boy who is leaving, the hero has not shot the bad guys but has been shot by the boy, and the hero's removal from the scene didactically fails to reproduce the ideologically productive placement of loss so evident in *Shane*.

4   From another angle—and in another striking reversal—it is
     Eastwood who is the ineffectual restraining superior officer and the
     FBI agent who is the "cowboy cop" exercising overhasty force. This
     stands the Dirty Harry situation on its head.

Chapter 6: Absolute Power and True Crime: Postscripts of Disavowal

1   A further tic of Eastwood the filmmaker appears when we find
     Whitney hanging out at a bar called "Red's."
2   The spectacle of the gauntly "authentic" Eastwood reappearing in a
     succession of disguises may be an attempt to move into the territory
     of the John Malkovich character in *In the Line of Fire* (and thus
     perform another reversal of that film's Secret-Service-vs.-the-Man-
     of-a-Thousand-Faces conflict), but instead it prompts involuntary
     recollections of Peter Sellers as Inspector Clouseau with his farcical
     wigs and putty noses. It is, I would say, embarrassing. Eastwood can
     perhaps get away with such impersonations in the context of
     comedy (*Pink Cadillac*), but *Absolute Power* presents the character as
     every bit as virtuosic and impressive in this function as, say, the
     Count of Monte Cristo.
3   At moments, the movie is as powerful an anti-capital-punishment
     vehicle as *Dead Man Walking*—indeed a more wholehearted one,
     since it is always easier to make a strong case against the death
     penalty where the case in question involves an innocent person
     rather than a guilty one. Nevertheless, a film that depicts the
     studied and ritualized execution of a black man as a dreadful thing
     can't help but have a certain liberal tinge no matter how innocent
     the man is. Generally speaking, this is one of a number of ways in
     which *True Crime* moves back towards the left (or the centre) after
     the rightward lurch of *Absolute Power*.

Chapter 7: The Beguiled and Play Misty for Me: He Who Lives by the Sword

1   See especially Karyn Kay's "*The Beguiled*: Gothic Misogyny" and
     Paul Smith's chapter on these two films, entitled simply "Misogyny."
     The reputation is not uncontested, though: see Gina Herring's "*The
     Beguiled*: Misogynist Fable or Feminist Myth?" Adam Knee's essay
     "The Dialectic of Female Power and Male Hysteria in *Play Misty for
     Me*," whose reading of the film overlaps with my own to some
     degree, also emphasizes the movie's reversal of gender positions and
     suggests that it is simultaneously and incoherently progressive and
     regressive in its sexual politics.
2   "*For the dove she will leave you / The raven will come / And death will
     come marching / at the beat of a drum.*"
3   This point is made explicitly by Gina Herring (215).

4 This perspective is always hovering near awareness, but sometimes it pops into explicit focus, as when the lewd Carol offers to take over ministrations to the unconscious McBurney from Edwina in her Florence-Nightingale mode, with the comment, "I might sponge parts of him you wouldn't."

5 This reflexivity is only strengthened by the onscreen presence of Don Siegel in the role of the bartender—a role where he serves as the confidant and abettor of Eastwood's philandering attitudes and behaviour. The various ways in which David's situation resembles the real offscreen Eastwood's are detailed by Adam Knee (89-91).

6 Earlier, David's disc-jockey partner has called repeated attention to David's womanizing and warned, "he who lives by the sword will die by the sword." In the last scene, Evelyn wields that sword-knife-phallus against David and almost kills him.

7 Smith, 82-3.

8 The road was certainly not a direct one, though. One need only reflect that Eastwood's next project after *Play Misty for Me* was *High Plains Drifter*, where the transcendental killer reaches perhaps his all-time high-water mark, and where the hysterically desiring woman (i.e., a small equivalent of Evelyn in *Play Misty for Me*) is raped and tossed aside by *this* Eastwood persona, who is not threatened by her in any way.

Chapter 8: Eastwood, Auteur and Metteur en scène

1 Eastwood's refusal to modify this visual environment despite complaints is in contrast to his evident attempts to accommodate to criticism (at least to some extent) in other areas. For example, the different scenarios of *Magnum Force* and *The Enforcer* demonstrate a wish to counteract (in the first case) criticisms of Harry Callahan's vigilante philosophy and (in the second case) accusations of the regressive sexism of Harry and the whole genre he rode in on. That neither film is a coherent or substantial rebuttal of the criticisms is irrelevant to the fact of their efforts to respond to attacks with some kind of correction.

2 This film has given rise to the most bizarre of all commentators' complaints about an Eastwood movie being too dark, namely Paul Smith's attempt (225-241) to interpret the very striking muddiness and obscurity as a failure to represent racial difference properly.

3 Indeed, the high-contrast silhouetted gloom of many of the interior scenes is actually *created* by the bright light of the outdoors shining strongly through apertures and, in the relative or absolute absence of supplementary lighting, reducing everything which is not a light-source to underexposed darkness.

4   Incidentally, some of the resonance of this image (almost the last one in the film) may arise from its symbolic unification of the "masculine" and "feminine" sides of the movie. The Eastwood character's new (feminine) awareness of feelings in the arena of personal relationships opens the way for a reinterpretation of (masculine) American history in response to the emotional needs of Americans. Being as tender and sensitive to the American warrior spirit as he is to Mason, Eastwood can offer it the balm of Grenada. When Mason waves the tiny flag at her man during the victory celebration, all of this comes together.

5   Maurice Yacowar also comments revealingly upon this appearance of the flag, and the way it labels William Munny as a symbol of America: "...Eastwood's troubling gunman, a savage who became civilized but then recovered his savagery when needed, becomes an emblem of modern America. Munny represents America's capacity/tendency to revert to brutish violence despite its desire to conform to the higher idealism it has been taught. ...He is the bill that America continues to pay: guilt for its violent origins and its continuing tendency to violence...." (254-255).

6   If Eastwood's idea that the protagonist of *High Plains Drifter* is the victim's brother is taken into account, the parallel becomes even stronger, since the most painful of all of Jennifer's sufferings is the spectacle of her destroyed sibling.

7   Paul Smith has turned his attention to many of these features of the film (225-241), though the description is subordinated to an overarching argument which seeks to convict Eastwood of political and cultural *hubris* in the area of race. Every aspect of narrative and style becomes for Smith a new evidence of Eastwood's complicity in the white institutions of racial oppression.

8   Quoted in Smith, 133. One might also note here another example of exuberant (if not quite "hypertrophic") *mise en scène* in the concluding scenes, taking place first in a deserted parade-float warehouse full of gigantic Mardi Gras balloon characters, and then along a desolate stretch of railway tracks where Block and his *Doppelgänger* engage in a truly desperate death struggle. These are good *mise en scène*, good cinema, without being particularly unique or extraordinary. To what extent Tuggle was directing with his boss looking over his shoulder must be a matter of speculation.

9   Paul Smith makes a good deal of Eastwood's foundations in Leone (1-17) and Siegel (69-83). But I am afraid I cannot agree that Leone's westerns, in stressing the Hispanic presence in American history, are performing a progressive task which Smith links with a Deleuzian-Guattarian "subaltern" culture: the "Mexicans" in Leone's spaghetti westerns are uniformly trotted out in exactly the

same stereotypes they have always occupied in dominant western mythography—as vile "greasers" and noble peasant martyrs. To see substantial evidence of Leone's sentimental professed Marxism in these films seems to me like hallucination (one has to look to the post-Eastwood *Duck, You Sucker* and to the epic gangster movie *Once Upon a Time in America* to see any politics of this kind in a Leone movie). Smith's commentary on Siegel's influence is in his chapter mostly on *The Beguiled* and *Play Misty for Me* (69-84), which focusses pretty much exclusively on the patriarchal wickedness of those two films, and also contains an analysis of Siegel's and Eastwood's visual styles which identifies as personal traits features which are far more widespread throughout Hollywood filmmaking than he seems to realize.

Bibliography

Beard, William. "The Crisis of Classicism in Hollywood, 1967-77." *S: European Journal for Semiotic Studies*, 10:1-2; *Transscientific Semiotics I/II* (1998), 7-23.

Bingham, Dennis. *Acting Male: Masculinities in the Films of James Stewart, Jack Nicholson and Clint Eastwood*. New Brunswick, New Jersey: Rutgers University Press, 1994.

Biskind, Peter. *Seeing Is Believing: How Hollywood Taught Us To Stop Worrying and Love the Fifties*. New York: Pantheon, 1982.

Bordwell, David, Janet Staiger and Kristin Thompson. *The Classical Hollywood Cinema: Film Style and Mode of Production to 1960*. New York: Columbia University Press, 1985.

Cawelti, John G. *The Six-gun Mystique*. Bowling Green, Ohio: Bowling Green University Popular Press, 1971.

Cook, David. "Auteur Cinema and the 'Film Generation' in 1970s Hollywood." In *New American Cinema*, Lewis, ed., 11-37.

Corrigan, Timothy. "Auteurs and the New Hollywood." In *New American Cinema*, Lewis, ed., 38-63.

Cohan, Steven and Ina Rae Hark, eds. *Screening the Male: Exploring Masculinities in Hollywood Cinema*. New York: Routledge, 1993.

Frayling, Christopher. *Clint Eastwood*. London: Virgin, 1992.

———. *Spaghetti Westerns: Cowboys and Europeans from Karl May to Sergio Leone*. London: Routledge & Kegan Paul, 1981.

Gallafent, Edward. *Clint Eastwood: Filmmaker and Star*. New York: Continuum, 1994.

Grant, Barry K., ed. *Film Genre Reader*. Austin: University of Texas Press, 1986.

Herring, Gina. "*The Beguiled*: Misogynist Myth or Feminist Fable?" *Literature Film Quarterly*, 26:3 (1998), 214-220.

Holmlund, Christine. "Sexuality and Power in Male Doppelgänger Cinema: The Case of Clint Eastwood's *Tightrope*." *Cinema Journal*, 26:1 (1986), 31-42.

Jeffords, Susan. *Hard Bodies: Hollywood Masculinity in the Reagan Era*. New
    Brunswick, New Jersey: Rutgers University Press, 1994.
Johnstone, Iain. *The Man With No Name*. London: Plexus, 1981.
Kay, Karyn. "*The Beguiled*: Gothic Misogyny." *Velvet Lighttrap*, 16 (Fall
    1976), 32-33.
Kirkham, Pat and Janet Thumin, eds. *You Tarzan: Masculinity, Movies and
    Men*. New York: St. Martin's Press, 1993.
Kitses, Jim. *Horizons West*. London: Thames and Hudson, 1969.
Knapp, Laurence F. *Directed by Clint Eastwood : Eighteen Films Analyzed*.
    Jefferson North Carolina: McFarland, 1996.
Knee, Adam. "The Dialectic of Female Power and Male Hysteria in *Play
    Misty for Me*." In *Screening the Male*, Cohan and Hark, eds., 87-102.
Lewis, Jon, ed. *The New American Cinema*. Durham, North Carolina:
    Duke University Press, 1998.
Martin, Joel W. and Conrad E. Ostwalt, Jr., eds. *Screening the Sacred:
    Religion, Myth, and Ideology in Popular American Film*. Boulder:
    Westview Press, 1995.
Miklitsch, Robert. "Lust, Fantasy, Male Hysteria: Clint Eastwood (Un-)
    Bound." *Minnesota Review*, 43-44 (1995), 150-163.
Murphy, Peter F., ed. *Fictions of Masculinity: Crossing Cultures, Crossing
    Sexualities*. New York: New York University Press, 1994.
O'Brien, Daniel. *Clint Eastwood: Film-Maker*. London: B.T. Batsford,
    1996.
Ostwalt, Conrad E., Jr. "Hollywood and Armageddon: Apocalyptic
    Themes in Recent Cinematic Presentation." In Martin and Ostwalt,
    eds., *Screening the Sacred*, 55-63.
Patterson, Eric. "Every Which Way But Lucid: The Critique of Authority
    in Clint Eastwood's Police Movies." *Journal of Popular Film and
    Television*, 10:3 (1982), 92-104.
Penley, Constance and Sharon Willis, eds. *Male Trouble*. Minneapolis:
    University of Minnesota Press, 1993.
Polan, Dana. *Power and Paranoia: History, Narrative, and the American
    Cinema, 1940-1950*. New York: Columbia University Press, 1986.
Ray, Robert. *A Certain Tendency of the Hollywood Cinema, 1930—1980*.
    Princeton: Princeton University Press, 1985.
Ryan, Michael and Douglas Kellner. *Camera Politica: The Politics and
    Ideology of Contemporary Hollywood Film*. Bloomington: Indiana
    University Press, 1988.
Schatz, Thomas. *Hollywood Genres*. New York: Random House, 1981.
Schickel, Richard. *Clint Eastwood: A Biography*. New York: Knopf, 1996.
Smith, Paul. *Clint Eastwood: A Cultural Production*. Minneapolis:
    University of Minnesota Press, 1993.
Tasker, Yvonne. *Spectacular Bodies: Gender, Genre and the Action Cinema*.
    London: Routledge, 1993.

Tompkins, Jane. *West of Everything: The Inner Life of Westerns*. New York: Oxford University Press, 1992.

Warshow, Robert. *The Immediate Experience*. New York: Athenaeum, 1974 (1962).

Watson, Garry. "The Western: The Genre that Engenders a Nation." *CineAction* 46 (1998), 2-10.

Willis, Sharon. *High Contrast: Race and Gender in Contemporary Hollywood Film*. Durham, NC: Duke University Press, 1997.

Wills, Garry. *John Wayne's America*. New York: Touchstone, 1997.

Wood, Robin. *Hollywod from Vietnam to Reagan*. New York: Columbia University Press, 1986.

Wright, Will. *Sixguns and Society: A Structural Study of the Western*. Berkeley: University of California Press, 1975.

Yacowar, Maurice. "Re-Membering the Western: Eastwood's *Unforgiven*." *Queen's Quarterly*, 100:1 (Spring 1993), 247-257.

Zmijewsky, Boris and Lee Pfeiffer. *The Films of Clint Eastwood*. Secaucus, New Jersey: Citadel Press, 1982.